JACK NICHOLSON

JACK NICHOLSON

THE LIFE AND TIMES OF AN ACTOR ON THE EDGE

PETER THOMPSON

A Birch Lane Press Book
Published by Carol Publishing Group

A Birch Lane Press Book
Published by Carol Publishing Group
Birch Lane Press is a registered trademark of Carol Communications, Inc.

Editorial, sales and distribution, and rights and permissions inquiries should be addressed to Carol Publishing Group, 120 Enterprise Avenue, Secaucus, N.J. 07094.

In Canada: Canadian Manda Group, One Atlantic Avenue, Suite 105, Toronto, Ontario M6K 3E7

Carol Publishing Group books may be purchased in bulk at special discounts for sales promotion, fund-raising, or educational purposes. Special editions can be created to specifications. For details, contact Special Sales Department, Carol Publishing Group, 120 Enterprise Avenue, Secaucus, N.J. 07094.

MANUFACTURED IN THE UNITED STATES OF AMERICA
10 9 8 7 6 5 4 3 2 1

Library of Congress Cataloging-in-Publication Data

Thompson, Peter A.
Jack Nicholson : the life and times of an actor on the edge / Peter Thompson.
p. cm.
Includes bibliographical references and index.
ISBN 1-55972-420-X (hardcover)
1. Nicholson, Jack. 2. Motion picture actors and actresses—United States—Biography. I. Title.
PN2287.N5T56 1997
791.43'028'092—dc21
[B] 97-4094
CIP

CONTENTS

ACKNOWLEDGMENTS

My thanks go to my agents, Tom Wallace and Robert Ducas, in New York for their encouragement and professional guidance, and to my editor at Carol Publishing Group, Jim Ellison, for his dedication and expertise in getting this book into print.

JACK NICHOLSON

PROLOGUE

THE WEDDING DAY

RIGHT ON CUE, Jack Nicholson flashed the most famous smile in the world at the throng of photographers gathered outside 210 Palisades Avenue, Santa Monica. It was a glorious day for a wedding, and Jack's expression gave no hint that anything in his life was amiss.

For one thing, it wasn't *his* wedding, which meant he could play himself without any lasting consequences: goof around with his Hollywood buddies, drink a bit, smoke a good cigar, always remembering to keep his sunglasses firmly in place and to flash that smile at every opportune moment. "Jack's grin," said the actress Susan Anspach, mother of his son, Caleb, "is like Clark Gable's used to be—it comes from within."

Yet, as Susan and a number of other people had found to their cost, the outward glint of those naturally perfect teeth sometimes cloaked an inner smirk. Nicholson admitted as much when he said: "I've always been able to say the most horrible things to people's faces and have a smile on mine and not have it disrupt the proceedings." Former *Vogue* editor Diana Vreeland, a friend, had pronounced it "a killer smile," but regardless of motivation, that smile was about to be wiped clean off his face.

Saturday, April 27, 1996, had dawned sunny, and the temperature had passed 70 degrees before noon. Now, in the late afternoon, a cooling breeze drifted in from the Pacific. In a light gray suit, white shirt, and floral print tie, Nicholson arrived with Rebecca Broussard for the wedding of his "best buddy" Sean

Penn to the actress Robin Wright. He had spent the afternoon at the Forum, home of the Los Angeles Lakers, where he had watched his team square the NBA playoffs against the Houston Rockets at one game apiece.

Just five days after his fifty-ninth birthday, Nicholson's image among his millions of fans was that of an exuberant man overflowing with natural charm, a restless intellect, and an enduring sex appeal that seemed positively wicked. To this adoring multitude, his most vivid accomplishments were his fifty-plus motion pictures; even today, *Chinatown*, Roman Polanski's quintessential film noir starring Jack as the seedy private eye Jake Gittes, was showing at a theater just a few blocks away from the wedding. Ranging across the Hollywood spectrum from the biker sleaze of *Easy Rider* to the heart-tugging pathos of *Terms of Endearment* to the supercharged heroics of *Batman*, his movies crossed all barriers of age, race, and class. Dubbed into Portuguese, the Joker was just as mad and menacing in São Paulo as he was in St. Paul.

At his hilltop home up on fabled Mulholland Drive, two Oscar statuettes, half a dozen Golden Globe trophies, and the American Film Institute's highly coveted Life Achievement Award, plus a clutch of foreign honors, attested to his universal acclaim as a motion picture actor. There were also scores of people who were prepared to testify, hand on heart, that he was the most magnanimous, most lovable man in Hollywood. The director George Miller told me: "I've never met anyone quite like him. He's completely beloved within the industry. Only Tina Turner has as big a soul as him." The producer Robert Evans, who once memorably called him "the glittering vagrant," was eternally grateful to Jack for retrieving the Beverly Hills mansion he had lost in one of Hollywood's more bizarre power plays and returning it to him.

Yet, while Miller and Evans vouched for Jack's generosity, there were those who knew from firsthand experience that he was manipulative in his business dealings and that compassion wasn't high in his repertoire of virtues when his own money was at stake. Very few people ever saw Jack Nicholson, businessman, in action, a man who charged well above bank rates of interest on loans to friends and demanded collateral to secure them. Despite evidence to the contrary, he blithely described himself as a humanitarian working for the good of his fellow man in an often cynical world. But Polanski, Jack's friend as well as director, confirmed: "He can be the stingiest person in the world."

To his enemies, in fact, he was a figure of immense guile and cunning: talent with a twist, wit with a cutting edge, passion tinged with blazing anger. "To put it simply, he's a rager," one of his actor contemporaries told me. Susan Anspach, who had been on the receiving end of some of Jack's most violent tirades, said: "I can't believe a man who has been given so much love, adoration, and celebrity can go out of his way to hurt people." Nicholson was the first to acknowledge that there was a certain amount of antagonism toward him. "There are people, I know, who think of me as a flat-out asshole," he said, "but they shouldn't, because they don't know me." What virtually no one had heard was his candid admission to a relative: "If I hadn't been a movie star, I would've been a thief."

Surely he was joking? The person he said that to thought not. In his sixtieth year, Jack's own nickname for himself was Dr. Devil.

LIKE the bride and groom, Jack and Rebecca had broken up so often that some of the neighbors attracted by the commotion in this quiet little enclave were astonished to see them together again. Asked why Jack still saw Rebecca, Ali MacGraw told a friend, "She's the only woman who slaps him across the face in public." But such incidents were evidently forgotten as Rebecca, the mother of two of Jack's youngest children, clasped his arm and negotiated the curb in the briefest of miniskirts.

In common with the other eighty guests, Jack and Rebecca had received a verbal invitation to the nuptials only the previous week, but word had leaked out, and the media had swarmed down to Santa Monica to besiege the rambling gray-and-white home of Sean's friend the producer Art Linson. Reporters were rewarded with the arrival of one stretch limo after another bearing some of the biggest names in the Hollywood glitterati, among them Robert De Niro, Warren Beatty and his wife Annette Bening and the groom's collaborators in his latest film, *Dead Man Walking,* Tim Robbins and his real-life partner, Susan Sarandon. De Niro and Harry Dean Stanton, in particular, were long-serving members of Jack's inner circle, and they greeted each other with handshakes and warm hugs. Also present was the Sean Penn of an earlier age, Dennis Hopper, Billy the Kid himself from *Easy Rider*, the sixties classic that had made Jack a star. Sean and Robin were so fond of him that they had named their son, now three years old, Hopper in his honor. For good measure, the boy's middle name was Jack.

The celebrities entered Linson's property from the tree-lined street through a black iron gate set into a freshly trimmed hedge. They walked down a path to the back garden, where a vast tent had been tethered to the house in the shade of a hundred-year-old Moreton Bay fig tree. The wedding ceremony had been scheduled to start under the canvas at 4 P.M., but Penn kept his guests waiting for the arrival of Marlon Brando and his companion, the songwriter David Helsten. Half an hour dragged by, and there was no sign of them. "They'll be here," Jack assured Penn, rolling a flaming match around the tip of a Montecristo and blowing luxuriant smoke into the air. Secretly, though, he was a worried man. The scene he had left behind on Mulholland Drive before heading off to watch the basketball game that morning had been so volatile that anything could have happened up there.

Jack was still puffing away when, an hour late according to every Rolex in the place, Brando loomed into view, fat, balding, sweating, and very drunk—but minus the other missing guest. Violating protocol, the senior statesman of the Jack Pack, as this band of brothers was informally known, promptly fell asleep in a chair and started to snore. Penn shrugged, took Robin's arm, and gave the minister, Otis Young, the go-ahead to begin the service. "Not even the loud buzzing of a news helicopter could rouse the dozing don," one guest reported.

Since long before they had appeared together as frontier rivals in *The Missouri Breaks*, in 1976, Nicholson and Brando had been sharing a compound on the razor-backed spine of the Santa Monica Mountains. The actual postal address was Beverly Hills 90210, but the hijinks in the TV show of that name bore no resemblance to the real-life events that were taking place within its overgrown borders. It had been one helluva week for the two superstars and, in Marlon's case at least, the façade was beginning to crack.

The drama unfolding high above the great urban tracts of Los Angeles involved Nicholson, Brando, and the private estate's only other permanent resident, the former actress and nightclub queen Helena Kallianiotes. "Helena had been touting shares in a ranch-

and-spa resort with the help of a Colombian [whom I shall call Lorenzo]," said Frank Monte, a New York–based private eye. "He was a member of their inner circle who supplied drugs and girls for their parties. But Lorenzo had disappeared, and so had $6 million from Helena's bank account, including at least $500,000 of Brando's money. Brando and Nicholson hired me to extricate Helena from the swindle and to trace the cash. I was up on Mulholland Drive several times, and tempers were begining to fray."

The other absent guest, David Helsten, had invested $125,000 of his own money in the scheme and doubted that he would ever see it again. As Brando had wrestled his immense girth into his wedding outfit, an argument had broken out between Helena and David. "Helena wouldn't let David leave the compound," said the private eye. "He told me she had got drunk and started doing coke and was physically beating him up."

After he finally managed to escape from the compound, Helsten told me from his apartment in New York: "I was supposed to go to the wedding, but everything was happening up on Mulholland. Yeah, it was insane, it was insane."

IN KEEPING with Southern California's reputation for excess, the wedding wasn't the only headline-making activity taking place in Santa Monica that evening. Soon after 8 P.M., the Olympic torch was carried along Ocean Avenue on its overland journey to Atlanta. The runners bearing the flaming symbol of hope and unity passed within a few hundred yards of 210 Palisades. From my vantage point, it was difficult to tell amid the cheering crowds, the hovering helicopters, the police cars, and the exploding flashguns exactly where the Olympic marathon ended and the show business wedding of the year began. And above it all, in the darkening Pacific skies, loomed the specter of a scandal just waiting to break.

Happily for the bride, stunning in an off-the-shoulder gown with a pearl-trimmed satin bodice, things were proceeding more or less as she had planned. After a series of breakups and reconciliations, Robin Wright was having as conventional a wedding as the media circus would allow, and she was determined to enjoy it.

In an immaculate black tuxedo, the thirty-five-year-old groom beamed at the mother of his two children, and friends noted with relief that he was on his best behavior. At his wedding to

Madonna eleven years earlier, the heir presumptive to Jack's Mr. Hollywood crown had threatened to shoot a noisy news helicopter out of the sky. But today, after the vows had been taken without incident, he was able to proclaim to his thirty-year-old wife: "Aren't you proud? I didn't do anything wild or crazy."

As night fell, a bank of spotlights was switched on inside the tent and the guests began to unwind. Marlon still slumbered, his snores now a source of wisecracks. Dinner had been eaten, and after the retainers had cleared the plates away, it was time for the traditional speeches.

The first testimonial to the bride and groom came from the self-styled "reformed bachelor" Warren Beatty, whom Nicholson had once nicknamed the Pro. The two men had been notorious for their intense rivalry in seducing beautiful women, but that competition had ceased to matter since Beatty's defection to the ranks of married men. With two young children of his own, Nicholson wryly confessed: "We talk about changing diapers now." Addressing the newlyweds, Beatty said: "I truly believe in the institution of marriage. I don't have to tell you that I avoided it like the plague for years. But I can truly say that my wedding day was the happiest day of my life—and I know that yours will be, too."

It was during the toasts that Brando suddenly awoke from his siesta and, Godzilla-like, lurched to his feet. According to one of those present, he began to ramble incoherently before breaking into some decidedly off-key singing. Nicholson watched his friend with what appeared to be amusement. Privately, he was terrified of what Marlon might do in this state or, even more important, what he might blurt out to the assembly.

"Before Marlon was able to humiliate the bride and groom any further, Jack sprang into action," said the guest. "He took Brando by the arm and attempted to sit him down, smiling and saying, 'Thank you very much, Marlon, for those sentiments. I'm sure they were very touching.'

"That broke everyone up, but Marlon was not about to go quietly. As Jack eased him into his chair, Marlon ruffled his hair and undid his belt. He grabbed the top of Nicholson's pants and pulled them down. Jack finished proposing a toast with his pants down around his ankles. Fortunately, Warren Beatty and Tim Robbins quickly restrained Marlon so Jack could hitch up his pants."

Although Jack's smile had saved him once again from embarrassment, the Brando farce was proof that the hall-of-mirrors existence the two men shared was in danger of shattering, and that prospect worried Jack very much indeed. Lorenzo was out there somewhere, a loose cannon capable of blowing a big hole in the lives of all concerned.

Nicholson was in the kind of trouble that only visited playboys in later life when they started to believe their own publicity: that they were somehow special, untouchable, and possibly even omnipotent. Nicholson had raised that prospect himself in posing a conundrum to Blaine Novak, one of his moviemaking collaborators: "What's the difference between God and Jack Nicholson?" When Novak hesitated to reply, Jack supplied his own answer: "Jack Nicholson doesn't have to appease God." Allowing for even the grandiose standards of Hollywood, this sounded insanely egocentric.

In Jack's case, his apotheosis had given him permission to flout the rules of a society that had made him rich and powerful beyond his, or anyone else's, wildest dreams. In his inimitable style, he explained: "I've always felt that I'm a guy who's at odds with the establishment, but whom they'd love to have to dinner." His remarkable success had, of course, long since made him a valued member of that same plutocratic ruling class, and he wasn't too bashful to accept invitations to many of their black-tie functions. At the same time, his own private life proved one of the entertainment world's maxims, that the celebrity is a substitute for the hero, and substitutes are often pale imitations of the real thing. Nicholson was about to discover to his cost that there was a sting in the tail of the Big Wombassa, his term for the fame and fortune he had fought so tenaciously to achieve. Men like Lorenzo were reminders that he might just be vulnerable after all.

After forty years in movies, Jack was at his greatest visibility, prestige and privilege, even though his most recent film, *The Crossing Guard*, had been a box office disappointment. Ironically, he had taken the role as a favor to Sean Penn, its writer-director, even agreeing to play opposite his former lover Anjelica Huston for maximum dramatic effect. But Jack knew he was popular enough to survive this single setback, and he had since completed two new films that should restore his reputation as the greatest survivor in Tinseltown—*Blood and Wine* with Michael Caine, and

The Evening Star, the sequel to *Terms of Endearment*, with Shirley MacLaine.

George Miller, who directed Jack in *The Witches of Eastwick*, had no reservations whatever about his abiding appeal to the moviegoing public. "All his buddies, all the people around him—the Warren Beattys, the Robert Redfords—become more afraid as age erodes their beauty," he said. "Jack is the opposite. He might have fear about how he appears, but he uses that for the performance. He's got his own playful way of doing it."

With the passing of time, however, many Hollywood people put his "playfulness" down to the use of cocaine. In April 1972, he had expressed the opinion that the ego-boosting drug of the century "won't be fashionable for long." Exactly twenty-four years later, his drug consumption remained the subject of comment in the motion picture industry.

A Hollywood beauty said: "I was at a party with Dennis Hopper just before Christmas, and Jack spent half the time in the loo doing coke." Jack had then flown east to shoot *Blood and Wine* in Miami Beach, where one of the production team disclosed: "Jack was making no pretense. He was tooting in front of the crew on the set."

However, the drug-and-alcohol binges, the sex parties with leggy blondes (some of the most lurid tales appearing in the 1996 bestseller *You'll Never Make Love in This Town Again*), the bull sessions with his buddies, and even the $13-million-a-picture paychecks had lost their edge. The Big Wombassa might have propelled him to the top of his own starlit Olympus on Mulholland Drive, but it had also given free rein to the satanic side of his nature, complete with discernible Faustian overtones. After *The Two Jakes*, the star-crossed sequel to *Chinatown*, there was *Dr. Devil*, a possible biopic as intriguing as any Hollywood writer had ever dreamed up about L.A. life. *Chinatown* dealt with the city's water rights and *The Two Jakes* covered the exploitation of its oilfields; the subject matter of *Dr. Devil* was the pollution of the mind.

"Jack always had a mischievous relationship with life, and that's where his humor comes from," said Susan Anspach. "But the man who tickled the funnybone of the world is now behaving in a way that isn't mischief, it's mean. Everybody wants to see a little touch of evil, but not a humongous one. The mischief has turned malicious. Irish fun has turned cruel. It isn't funny anymore."

Tonight, Nicholson was preoccupied about the events unfolding up on Mulholland Drive. "He had good reason to be shit-scared," said Frank Monte. "The FBI has a big file on Lorenzo saying he is connected to the Gambino crime family—the Mafia."

As Jack Nicholson climbed into his limo for the thirty-minute run home, he was no longer smiling.

He knew he was in for a bumpy ride.

1

"TAKE NO PRISONERS"

At the Four Seasons Hotel in Beverly Hills, Jack Nicholson was holding court about his midlife image. "I guess I'm very hard to describe," he said, referring to the legions of journalists and authors who had wrestled with him in print. "They may say things about me that are great," he conceded, "they may say things that are great observations." But, he claimed, nobody had ever *got* him, and that was just as well, he admitted, because "I'd go crazy if somebody actually nailed me. I'd quit. Everybody would know who I am."

However, he was relaxed about that because, no matter what the writers, the critics, the TV pundits, or the armchair Freudians might think, he was convinced in his own mind that there was little likelihood of anyone cracking the Nicholson code. He would remain an enigma. Always. "Circuitous and well hidden" were the words he used to describe himself.

One promising clue to the puzzle was to be found in the name of his film production company, Proteus Films, Inc. Nicholson was raised in Neptune City, New Jersey, and his business was named after the elusive sea prophet in Greek mythology known as Proteus, a.k.a. the Old Man of the Sea, the keeper of Neptune's herd of seals. Whenever Proteus was captured, he would immediately change into another guise—a lion, a serpent, a leopard, a boar, even a tree—to avoid answering questions. Jack admitted he used the same avoiding tactics, slipping easily into any one of a dozen semiautobiographical film roles whenever he felt threatened. He was Jack the Nimble, Jack the Quick: the sum total of all his parts. "I like the disguise element of the theatrical profession," he said.

He had also given himself several nicknames to cover the protean facets of his personality, kicking off with the Great Seducer as a Hollywood wannabe in his twenties, changing to Johnny Thunder, Happy Jack, and the Jackser in his thirties and forties. In his fifties, he had finally graduated from the university of life as Dr. Devil, a title that implied some seniority in the hellraising movement and, incidentally, linked medicine with demonology.

George Miller, who was a qualified medical practitioner himself, was the only man who had actually ever directed Jack in the role of the Devil. "Only a good man can play the Devil," he told me, "and that's the thing about Jack: He definitely understands good and evil; he's aware of the difference."

Bob Rafelson was one of the survivors of the sixties new wave of filmmakers who also knew Jack's quirks extremely well. In the twenty-five years since he had directed Nicholson in *Five Easy Pieces*, they had made three other films, *The King of Marvin Gardens*, *The Postman Always Rings Twice*, and *Man Trouble*. When Rafelson read the script of *Blood and Wine*, he knew he had found the perfect vehicle for a new collaboration. Rafelson made no secret of his artistic delight in ferreting out Jack's idiosyncracies, getting them down in script form, and then recording the outcome on film.

"Very few of today's leading men have the type of complex character traits that Jack can bring to a role," he said. "Kevin Costner, Mel Gibson, and Tom Cruise are all fine actors, but they don't bring you an edge you can work with. I could never have made *Five Easy Pieces* without an actor as complicated and contradictory as Jack. He's a unique individual, and it's because he feels passionately about his freedom and the ability to enjoy life. You see it in his expression, which seduces everyone, even people who don't necessarily like him. Look at *Batman*; that film is an empty shell without Jack, and he deserves the $60 million he got for it. The trouble with Hollywood today is that there aren't enough personalities like Jack around."

There was an attraction of opposites between Nicholson and Michael Caine, the actor Rafelson had chosen as his costar in *Blood and Wine*. Caine had risen to fame as the aristocratic officer in *Zulu* in 1963 while Jack was appearing in *The Raven*, a camp sendup of horror flicks directed by Roger Corman, Hollywood's fabled Schlockmeister. As Jack struggled to make a living at the B-movie end of the market, Caine quickly showed that he was a major talent by playing a shopworn spy in *The Ipcress File* and a blond Cockney Adonis in *Alfie*.

The former Maurice Micklewhite had spent years as a small-time actor in Britain before he grabbed Hollywood's attention—and the big paychecks that reflected its admiration—at the age of thirty and settled down in Southern California as a genuine motion picture star. Caine was four years older than Nicholson and had a completely different acting style, so neither man had seen the other as a threat. The two stars had known each other in Hollywood for twenty-five years, and even though Caine had later resettled in Britain, there was a bond of friendship between them. Both had sprung from modest origins and made it to the top through their own endeavors: No one had ever given them anything. One thing they did not share in common was a credit in the same movie, and Bob Rafelson was about to change that.

"The way Bob saw it, Nicholson would play a Florida wine merchant who planned a heist, and Caine would be his partner in crime," said Florida-based publicist Carol Green. "The Jack character was married to Judy Davis, but he was having an affair with their young Cuban maid. He needed money to leave his wife, so he planned to steal a multimillion-dollar necklace from the mansion of one of his nouveau riche customers. The necklace was kept in a safe, and he enlisted Caine, a safecracker who had seen better times, to blow the safe."

The two stars had greeted Rafelson's approach with enthusiasm, but it had taken nine months of negotiations before the contract was signed. Nicholson lived according to the dictates of a very crowded schedule that had to be worked out well in advance; not the least of his many commitments was watching the Lakers in action. As he hated commercial airline flights, one of the things he insisted upon was a clause that he should fly only in private jets for the duration of the shoot, which, at a cost of $50,000 a trip, created budget problems for the production company.

Nicholson was demanding from the moment the cast assembled on location at Miami Beach in November 1995. "He made life very hard for some of the production people," my informant said. However, Kathleen Courtney, the film's production supervisor, refused to be drawn on the subject. "The level of difficulty with big stars is the same in that they demand a lot," she told me. "But the rapport between [Nicholson and Caine] was wonderful. Jack's acting is fantastic, and he was always good in front of the camera."

In fact, the two stars electrified the set. "They would crack each other up telling stories, and one night Jack did a Harvey Keitel impersonation that was so good it should have been filmed," said my informant. "But after they finished work each day, Jack would go out to play, and Michael would go home to his wife, Shakira."

Nicholson and Caine fell into an easygoing camaraderie with the tall, rangy Rafelson. Jack had addressed him as Curly ever since the sixties when his head had been covered with waves of jet black hair, and Curly it still was, even though the director's hair was now short, mainly straight, and a Brooks Brothers shade of gray.

The most important set in the film was the mansion where the jewel robbery was to take place. Rafelson's location scouts had found a residence in Miami Beach that was ideal for the purpose, "a marbled museum sort of place backing onto the water." There were even lion- and tigerskin rugs, as well as elephant tusks and other ivory pieces, among the kitsch furnishings. "Some of the carvings still had price tags attached to them," said my source. "It was absolutely perfect."

The house was owned by a multimillionaire businessman who agreed to rent it to the moviemakers more for his wife's sake than for the cash it would bring in. He was married to a striking Puerto Rican woman called Rachel, and she clearly loved the idea of having two of the most famous male stars in the world in her home.

"We couldn't afford to lose the mansion, so the important thing was to keep Rachel happy, and Jack was brilliant at it," said the insider. "He talked to her like he was a friendly neighbor chatting over the back fence. They flirted a bit, but it was nothing serious; she told him that her husband had more money than him or Michael Caine anyhow. Rachel had several Chihuahua dogs named after various fashion designers, and she really doted on them. One of them was called Ralph Lauren, and this dog had died and been buried in the garden. Rachel had been very fond of him, and she asked Jack to accompany her to his grave. So without a murmur Jack went with her to pay his respects to a dead Chihuahua called Ralph Lauren."

THIS little cameo was rich in irony. At the same time Jack was sweet-talking a woman into letting him use her house for the purposes of making a movie, he was trying to kick Susan Anspach out of her home in Santa Monica. As it was Nicholson himself who had once described Susan as "fucking unpredictable," he shouldn't have been too surprised when she didn't roll over and let him sell her house without so much as a whimper.

Since 1989, Nicholson, via the pensions offshoot of Proteus Films, had held a second trust deed on the two-story, four-bedroom residence set in well-tended gardens at 473 Sixteenth Street, Santa Monica. In August 1995, Proteus issued a foreclosure notice against Susan and threatened to sell the house to pay off a $650,000 debt (including $250,000 interest) that Nicholson claimed she owed him. The mother of his twenty-five-year-old son swallowed her pride and did something that, she said, was alien to her nature: She called in the lawyers.

In a lawsuit filed at Santa Monica courthouse on October 30, 1995, she sought damages for alleged fraud, breach of contract, and emotional distress against Nicholson, Proteus Films, Inc., Money and Purchase Pension Plan and Jack's business manager, Robert Colbert. "Nobody thought it would come to this, nobody wanted it to come to this," she told me. "But someone who's worth $200 million is kicking his family out of their home. My friends agree that I can't have worked my whole life to end up in poverty with my furniture on the street."

The script was worthy of Neil Simon. Susan's lodger at the time of the foreclosure was Tony Huston, the screenwriting son of John Huston, whom Jack had idolized, and brother of Anjelica, with whom Jack had spent seventeen stormy years of his life. As tall as his father, though minus the famous whiskers, Tony had rented Caleb's room on the ground floor of the house after Caleb moved to New York to further his career as a TV writer-producer. If Jack had got his way, Tony Huston would have found himself out on the street along with Susan, her furniture, her pet turtles, Cookie and Simon, and a green iguana called Lorca (named after the playwright Federico García Lorca).

Jack's unmarried daughter Jennifer Nicholson, the child of his only marriage—to actress Sandra Knight—lived in a $2.475 million house that he had bought for her directly opposite Susan's home. Jennifer shared the Spanish-style mansion with her newborn son, Sean. Asked if she had named the baby after Sean Penn, Jennifer had said: "No, it's French for John"—her father's real name. She had been devastated when the baby's father, a Honolulu-based surfer, had turned up on her doorstep just before the birth with a girlfriend at his side and announced: "We had an affair before you and it's restarted. I can't be a father to your child." Although Sandra Knight frequently flew to L.A. from her home in Hawaii to be with her daughter, grandfather Jack was rarely sighted at the house.

In yet another twist, thirty-three-year-old Jennifer had been a close friend of Rebecca Broussard before Rebecca had started the affair with Jack that had, thus far, produced two children, Lorraine and Raymond, and an agreed payment to the former waitress at Helena's nightclub of $1 million a year.

However, Nicholson had reached no similar arrangement with Susan Anspach, who had raised Caleb on her own earnings from motion pictures. As she had starring roles in such films as *Play It Again, Sam* with Woody Allen, *Running* with Michael Douglas, and *Blume in Love* with George Segal and Kris Kristofferson, money had never presented any real problem. Like many other strands in Jack's life, his relationship with Susan went back to the making of *Five Easy Pieces*, the 1970 movie that had established him as the most talented character actor of his generation. Twenty-five years later, the real-life sequel to *Five Easy Pieces* was about to be screened on TV channels across America.

At five feet, four inches tall, with blue eyes, curly blond hair cropped fashionably short, and a peaches-and-cream complexion, Susan cut an unlikely figure as the chauvinist stereotype of a feminist. "I first met Jack in the summer of 1969 through the audition process for *Five Easy Pieces*," she told me during the course of several long interviews at her home. "I already had a one-year-old daughter, whom I'd named Catherine after the heroine in my favorite book, Emily Brontë's *Wuthering Heights*.

"Jack and I were lovers during the shooting of the movie in the winter of 1969–70. He knew very well that I was planning to have a baby, but as it didn't seem to interest him, I left it at that. I got pregnant in December, and I couldn't make the New York premiere of *Five Easy Pieces* in September 1970 because I was about to give birth. Everyone involved in the movie suspected that Jack was the father."

Their son was born in Los Angeles six days after the film's release, and Susan named him Caleb after the younger son in John Steinbeck's *East of Eden*. At the time of his birth, Susan had been married for three months to the actor Mark Goddard, best known for his role as Don West in the TV series *Lost in Space*. She had given the Goddard surname to both Catherine and Caleb. It wasn't until 1984, when Caleb was thirteen, that Jack met the son whom he and Susan had been discussing for more than seven years.

"I didn't know that Jack harbored any grudge—as a matter of fact, there was on occasion very intimate contact with him," she said. "Every so often, Jack and I would get together, and it always seemed to me that we were okay. I would sometimes say, 'I'm sorry I took your son away. I hope you forgive me. I will always love you.' He seemed to find that all right. He never said, 'Watch out, because one day I'm going to punish you for all this.' He seemed quite all right with it.

"Certainly, I wouldn't have signed my house away to him if I'd thought there was anything wrong. I sent him birthday and Christmas presents every year, and he did the same for Caleb. Oh, he accepted Caleb in a million different ways. Jack said there was no need for him to have a blood test or tissue culture to confirm his paternity, but over the years he would say, 'I don't want to discuss Caleb publicly because I'm illegitimate. But you know I love him; I couldn't love him any more than I do already.' It was a sore point with me."

Susan's house had been built in brick, mortar, and fine timbers by the grandson of Henry Steinway, the pianomaker, in 1925 and featured an elegant wood-paneled music room where Arthur Rubenstein had once performed. "I bought it in 1979 for $420,000," she said. "I put $120,000 down, and I was paying $4,000 a month off on the mortgage. I had a nice life. I made a lot of movies and did a number of television films. I took care of the house, and in eleven years of living here I've put $650,000 into upkeep and renovations.

"In the mid-eighties, my agent said he had a hard time placing women over forty. It was a big shock. By then, I already knew things weren't happening the way they had been happening. I had been offered so many things over the years—I had choices of roles and had been supporting the family with really good money on my own. But then, boy, the pickings were slim. My work dried up, and I could no longer afford to keep up the mortgage payments. My house had been appraised for $1.475 million, and I knew that if I sold it I would make about a million dollars profit. I thought I had no choice because of my finances, but when the kids didn't want me to sell it, I spent sleepless nights wondering if it wasn't false pride not to ask Jack to help us; it seemed natural.

"So I called Jack in 1989 and asked for help. I knew how much home meant to him. He'd lived in the same house for as long as I'd known him. I remembered a friend telling me how he had helped Jack to buy all the land around it when Jack became frightened because developers were buying it and his view would be destroyed. I didn't know until much later that this friend had asked for a little spot off to the side, out of Jack's view, so he could build a house of his own. He saved Jack's home, but he never got that piece of land. 'Jack's marker ain't no good,' he told me, but I didn't know that back in 1989.

"If I had sold my house then, I would immediately have set up a trust fund for both of my children and bought myself a smaller home and got on with my life as a writer and drama teacher. A decision had to be made. Having been on my own at a young age, I knew I couldn't think clearly without the security of a roof over my head. This is the ridiculous part: When I swallowed my pride and went to Jack for help, I asked him to pay off the mortgage, which was then $390,000. The first ten years is all interest; the principal hardly changed.

"Jack said, 'I'm an empathetic (that was his word) and compassionate person,' and he offered to help. Since I was a little girl, I've written everything down, so I wrote all this stuff down. I said, 'Thank you very much, I really appreciate it.' I could have sold the house for $1.4 million in 1989 and walked away with a million dollars. Instead, I signed the second trust deed over to Proteus, as they suggested, and accepted two sums of $200,000 in increments over a six-year period.

"I'm embarrassed and ashamed that I ever got to a place where I needed to ask Jack for money. I'm ashamed that I signed those papers. I got home, and Jack was telling me it was fine and I didn't have to worry. I know I wasn't asking him to buy me a new Porsche, but I was still embarrassed. Even after I signed the first promissory note, our relationship seemed amicable to me. When Bob Colbert wanted me to sign, I went to Jack and said, 'This is bizarre. All I want you to do is pay off the first mortgage. I don't want to get into deeper debt. I've got a first [mortgage] already, I don't want a second.' He said, 'Don't worry about it. I'll never leave you stranded or abandon you.'"

And now, just a few days after spending a traditional Christmas at home with her children, the matter had reached the point of no return. Susan was going to court.

Sound bite from two TV reporters outside Room 104, Superior Court of the State of California, Santa Monica:

"I guess she was in the lounge eating popcorn while he was out getting famous."

"I guess."

At 1:35 P.M. on December 28, 1995, the temperature was 65 degrees on the Santa Monica seafront. The pale winter sunshine made it a good day for rollerblading through Palisades Park or tossing a line off the pier or just watching the seagulls divebomb the black rocks offshore.

Next to City Hall on Main Street, a freshly mown lawn ran up to the two-storied, cream stucco building that housed the Superior Court of the State of California, West District. A sign stuck to the glass courthouse door read NO SHIRT, NO SHOES, NO ENTRY. Hefting a TV camera up the courthouse steps, a blue-jeaned technician intoned: "No shirt, no shoes, no justice."

Inside Courtroom 104, the documents relating to Susan's seven causes of action against Jack Nicholson—Case No. SC 039121—were neatly stacked on a wooden table in front of the Great Seal of the State of California, which was flanked by the Stars and Stripes and the California state flag. On paper, the case might be about the title deeds to a nice house up on Sixteenth Street, but no number of depositions could ever do justice to the emotions heaving inside the protagonists. Bricks and mortar and mortgages were important only in the sense that they were symbols of a far bigger issue. For this case was really about an independent mother, a reluctant father, and a young man who was quietly making a name for himself in New York City.

Nicholson was still in Florida filming *Blood and Wine*, and with the Lakers on a roll of seven straight wins, he was in a bullish mood. Discussing the case with a relative two nights earlier, he had said: "Why should I pay Susan's rent just because I'm the father of her child? Well, Lawrence of Arabia is here, and I take no prisoners." When Susan heard about that, she replied: "It wasn't Lawrence of Arabia who said 'Take no prisoners.' It was Attila the Hun."

In their last conversation, Jack had forewarned Susan: "I'm not playing by other people's rules," and so it had proved. In the preceding weeks, lawyers from the firm of Mitchell, Silberberg, and Knupp had grilled her hour upon hour over four days about her relationship with Jack for depositions to be filed before the court. At one point, they had questioned her about Mark Goddard, suggesting that she and Mark had conspired long ago to bring this action against Jack, take him for millions, and then split the loot. Susan wept. The court-appointed stenographer stopped the interrogation and asked if she would like to take a break. She elected to carry on.

Nicholson and Colbert's legal team, five men in suits at a rate of $300 an hour each, were sitting in court when Susan walked in. In the legal documents piled up on the wooden table, they alleged that she had "embellished her complaint with a series of scandalous and entirely irrelevant allegations better suited to a supermarket checkout line than a court of law." But Judge Alan B. Haber, taking note of this submission, adjourned the case for twenty days to give Susan time to add even more substance to her charges.

Jack's legal team scurried past me so fast it looked as though they were late for a plane. The press contingent, all women, surrounded Susan on the well-cut lawn in a huddle of TV cameras and mikes. In beige skirt, white cheesecloth blouse, and new brown Caterpillar boots (a Christmas gift from Catherine), she stood beside her lawyer, civil rights defender Paul L. Hoffman, and smiled for the cameras.

Q Is this a show of vindictiveness on Jack's part?
A I hope not, but I'm afraid it is.

Q Why did you ask for financial assistance?

A I never wanted to ask Jack for anything so long as I had a career. When my career ended, I went to him and said, "Can you help us out?" And he did.

Q What do you really want?

A Peace. And I'd settle for a lot of love and joy between Caleb and Jack.

Q Do you think this case is fair?

A I really don't know what's fair anymore.

There was a grainy black-and-white photograph in the TV room at 473 Sixteenth Street of Susan and Jack taken on the set of *Five Easy Pieces*. On an adjoining wall were snapshots of Caleb as a baby, Caleb running as a schoolboy athlete at his school, St. Augustine-by-the-Sea, Caleb graduating from Georgetown, Caleb with his sister, Catherine.

At twenty-five, he had grown into an exact replica of his father at the same age: a fraction under five feet, ten inches tall and slimly built, with hazel eyes, brown hair, and long sideburns. But although he possessed many of Jack's physical characteristics, he had avoided a career in movies, preferring to work on a CNN business news program. Caleb kept in touch with his father but refused to discuss the situation between them. "Caleb is the reason Jack thinks Susan won't take this case all the way," said a friend. "He knows that she's protective of him and that he loves his privacy."

Susan freely admitted that the wrongdoing was not all on Jack's side. "In the last eighteen years I have often asked Jack for forgiveness for taking away his son," she said. "Jack clearly feels that I hurt him deeply. I robbed him of his son for seven years. I did, and I've apologized and acknowledged it straight to his face, hugging him and holding him and telling him that what I did was unacceptable. But to be punished for it in this way, a punishment that hurts not just me but the children as well, doesn't correspond to what I did as a young woman. I think what he was afraid of was he didn't know how to explain that I had his child and married someone else. He just never knew how to deal with it."

THIS combustible mixture simmered away until 1994, when it finally exploded. The eruption was triggered by a sequence of events that occurred in rapid succession during the early months of that year after it had been announced that Jack was to be honored with a Life Achievement Award by the American Film Institute.

These awards were normally reserved for veteran actors, actresses, and directors in the twilight of their careers—Bette Davis, Henry Fonda, and Alfred Hitchcock were previous recipients—but the powers-that-be had decided that Nicholson was worthy of elevation to this august peerage, even though he remained at the very top of his profession. They had not realized that they were stepping into a minefield.

Invitations to a huge party to be held in Beverly Hills on March 3, 1994, were duly sent out to Nicholson's relatives and members of his extended family, as well as to a huge cross-section of celebrities who had been connected with the many milestones in his film career. For reasons that were all too familiar to them, Susan and Caleb had not expected to be invited. But one of those who should have been high on the family list was Jack's half-sister, Pamela Liddicoat. Pamela was the daughter of Jack's mother, June, by her husband, Murray Hawley, and she greatly resented being excluded by her famous sibling. "Jack had extremely personal reasons for vetoing her invitation," said my source, "and she was very upset about it." Pamela, an alcoholic, started drinking heavily and was soon mixing with unsavory company in the bars near her home in Georgetown, in Northern California.

The nightmare had begun.

Less than a month before the ceremony was due to take place, Nicholson had lost his temper with the driver of a white Mercedes who, he believed, had cut him off. He had jumped out of his own car, attacked the other vehicle with a golf club and threatened the driver, Robert S. Blank. Blank later reported Jack's behavior to police.

Shortly afterward, Jack received the shocking news that Pamela had been shot to death during a sex-and-alcohol binge in Northern California. The tragedy was made all the more poignant because he knew that she had died holding a grudge against him for excluding her from his party. He was still reeling when he learned that he had been charged with assault and vandalism over the attack on Blank.

This was the backdrop to the star-studded night on which he turned up at the Beverly Hilton to receive one of Hollywood's highest accolades.

Nicholson was smuggled in through the hotel's back entrance to avoid a horde of newspeople who wanted to question him about the driving charges. At this stage, the media knew nothing about his connection with the murdered woman. Once inside the ballroom, however, he was among friends. Everyone in the audience, including Shirley MacLaine, Louise Fletcher, Cher, Kathleen Turner, Faye Dunaway, Warren Beatty, Robert Evans, and George Miller, donned sunglasses in lighthearted mimicry of the guest of honor. "I'm touched and I'm fortunate," Jack said, keeping his own shades firmly in place. In a reference to the driving charges, he added: "And I'm lucky to be at large."

His relatives at the gala occasion included his daughter Jennifer, her mother, Sandra Knight, and his aunt, Lorraine Smith, while Rebecca Broussard was also in the family group. The lights dimmed, and the audience was treated to a selection of Nicholson's work, ranging from his screen debut at the age of twenty-one in Roger Corman's *The Cry Baby Killer* to clippings from his latest, and still incomplete, film, *The Crossing Guard*, which unfortunately showed scenes of him in a rage and fighting mad.

Then the tributes flowed. One after the other, Beatty, Evans, Dustin Hoffman, Hector Babenco, Michael Keaton, Mike Nichols, and Danny De Vito paid homage to Jack. Shirley MacLaine said that he had been her acting hero ever since she had seen the famous "wheat toast scene" in *Five Easy Pieces*. Peter Fonda and Dennis Hopper recalled that they had cast him in *Easy Rider* for the simple reason that he was prepared to work for scale—then the princely sum of $392 per week. For their contribution, Art Garfunkel and Harry Dean Stanton serenaded him with a rendition of the Everly Brothers hit "Dream," while Bob Dylan and Joni Mitchell were among the guests who joined in the chorus. Even Kareem Abdul-Jabbar, the retired Lakers center, was there to remind everyone that Jack had a life outside of the motion picture industry.

"I've been to a few of those things," said George Miller, "and I've never experienced the level of straight-out love from the huge range of people who were there, the women, the men, the directors—everyone."

In his acceptance speech, Nicholson thanked them all for contributing not only to the success of the evening but also to the success of his career. And he praised Sandra and Rebecca for making him the father of Jennifer, Lorraine, and Raymond. Promising the audience, "You ain't seen nothing yet," he retired to the Monkey Bar, where his friend Alan Finkelstein had prepared a celebratory party.

The ceremony was recorded on film and shown on TV a couple of nights later. Knowing nothing about the trauma in Nicholson's life, Susan Anspach had picked up the phone. "I called Jack up that night," she said. "It was around midnight and I felt safe to call him at that hour because I knew he never got up until 11 A.M. He came to the phone. I said, 'This has to stop. This is really rude. If you don't want to invite me or Caleb, fine, but at least make a nice comment about your son.' His voice was slurred and slow: 'Don't you know it's really late? I don't know what all this hysteria is about. You call me at this hour with this shit. Call me in the morning and we'll talk about it.' He sounded the most stoned of any conversation I've ever had with him in all those years."

The following week, a new edition of *Vanity Fair* featuring a picture of Jack on the front cover in his role as half-man, half-beast in his new movie, *Wolf*, hit the newsstands. In Nancy Collins's interview, he talked fondly about Rebecca and his young family but, once again, omitted any mention of Caleb. Susan had had enough. Her response was to write a letter to the magazine asking that a correction should be made in their correction box. Instead, *Vanity Fair* printed the letter in its entirety: "There is a mistake in your recent article regarding Jack Nicholson. Jack's son Raymond is his younger son and youngest child. Our son, Caleb, is Jack's older son and second oldest child. I have asked Jack about this oversight, and his response to me is that he doesn't really want to talk about his children in interviews. Since Jack and Caleb have a very warm relationship, and because Jack loves Caleb, I'm sure he would want me to have you make this correction."

But Susan wasn't expecting the violent reaction she received after the letter reached *Vanity Fair*. "The first screaming phone call [from Jack] was the day of the Academy Awards in March 1994," she said. "*Vanity Fair* had called him and said they were going to publish my letter and he was really mad about it."

Her recollection of this conversation is as follows:

NICHOLSON: Because of you, I'm getting blackmailed.
ANSPACH: What do you mean?

Nicholson: Because of you, *Vanity Fair* is blackmailing me to go to their fucking Oscar party tonight or they're going to publish your letter.

Anspach: Jack, did you read that letter? There's nothing anybody could blackmail you with in it. There's nothing you should be nervous about.

Nicholson (his voice husky and cracking with emotion): I didn't read it, I'm not going to read it, I will never read that letter.

Susan said: "It was a benign little letter, but that's when things really changed. Jack has always said over the years, 'If you're my friend, you don't go to the press.' I have never in my life been screamed at, name-called and verbally abused like that. I just laughed. I kept thinking it was like April Fool and he would say, 'Just kidding!' I couldn't believe that he would turn like that. Since I wrote that letter, the way he's talked to me—the screaming, the rage against all women, using me as the main target—has been incredible."

In December 1995, Susan watched a video of *The Crossing Guard* in her TV room with the picture of her and Jack on the wall. "It was spooky," she said. "It looked like Jack just rolled out of bed and played himself."

The publicity line for *The Crossing Guard* neatly summed up the situation between them: *Some lives cross, others collide*. Susan said: "In one call, he said to me, 'If this house thing doesn't go away, I'm going to have to give it away or burn it down or shoot someone or something.' He can't have known when he said the words 'burn it down' that I had already been there, picturing how I was going to live without everything I had created, everything I had put my money into. To me, it was my spiritual death—that's what it felt like. To him, it was dumping his feelings.

"There seems to be a constant flow of connections to that *Vanity Fair* letter. This is a violent slap, a punch, really, and it's so disproportionate to what I did. He bought Jennifer's house for her in 1990, and that feels like it isn't just a slap at me, that feels like a slap at Caleb. You don't put your daughter in a $2.475 million house across the street and kick your son's mother out of the home she's holding onto for her son. You just don't do it. I have nothing against Jennifer; I think she's terrific. I love her. But it exaggerates the slap in the face somehow to have Jennifer right there. I really was heartbroken to go into my lawyer's office and sign the complaint against Jack and send it off to the court. Why is he doing this to me?

"You know, it's not just me. It's also Caleb. This is, as far as we know, his firstborn son. This is 'boy child equals dad.' This is Jack. I feel I am mom personified in his life and the target of any anger he had toward his mother or his grandmother or women in general. If he can spew all his rage at me, he will have conquered Mother. There's so much passion that I have to believe he's still in love with me, and I still deeply, deeply want the best for him, even though I've gone through torture in the last six years. I still feel a love for him, and I worry about him. When he says bad things about me to other people, I don't think about me, I worry about him.

"Jack has a concept of home—something that stays the same in a very transient culture. I know he does seem to think of himself as a victim, even in what he's doing to me; his emphasis is on what I did to him. I'd rather think he has no idea of how much this is making me suffer than to think he knows straight out that this is unbearable and he's doing it anyway. I'd rather think that.

"And this was an important part of why I'm not taking this lying down: When Caleb said, 'Mom, you can't sell the house, it's the family anchor,' it broke my heart to think of losing it. I won't keep quiet when Jack hurts our son."

Excerpt from a declaration made by Caleb Goddard in the case of Anspach vs. Nicholson concerning a phone conversation between himself and Jack Nicholson on December 27, 1995:

"I told Jack among other things that I hoped his anger and hurtfulness toward my mom would stop and that he would keep the promises he had made to her. Jack said that he was fighting the lawsuit for tax reasons, and that there is one other nonfinancial reason, but he could not tell me what it was in case I was forced to testify in court. He said he would tell me what this reason was after the lawsuit was resolved and that it would make everything clear.

"Jack told me that one of the reasons he was fighting was that he never liked my mom, and that his decision to go ahead with

the foreclosure and the lawsuit was a personal matter. In this conversation he called me his son, and we discussed the fact that this was the first time in my life that he had called me his son directly."

With filming of *Blood and Wine* continuing in Florida through January 1996, Jack plugged into the art deco funkiness of South Beach. One of the functions he attended was a party thrown by Island Records at the Marlin Hotel. Arriving after midnight, he retired to the library, where he drank bourbon and smoked a cigar while chatting to a group of young beauties. Then he got into his waiting limo with three of them and drove off for some late-night refreshment at his rented house near the beach.

Nor did he neglect his commitment to the Lakers. When Rafelson was taken ill and had to call off filming for two days, Jack flew to Chicago in a private jet to watch the Lakers in action against the Bulls. "This is like a great heavyweight fight," he said. "You don't know what's going to happen, but you don't want to miss it." The Bulls trounced the Lakers in a 99–84 cakewalk, and Nicholson returned to work on the movie. The round trip from Miami had stripped many thousands of dollars from the budget, and he was also spotted in his front row seat at two other Lakers games at the Forum in Los Angeles. When Rafelson wrapped filming in mid-February, Jack went to Houston for four days to shoot his scenes in *The Evening Star* with Shirley MacLaine. His arrival had been nicely timed to coincide with a couple of clashes between the Lakers and the Rockets.

When Jack makes his entrance in *The Evening Star*, Aurora Greenway, played by MacLaine, is fighting a losing battle to keep her grandchildren under control after the death of her daughter. Garrett Breedlove, retired astronaut and relentless playboy—Nicholson's Oscar-winning character from 1983—had drifted out of her life, but he returns at her moment of greatest need.

"Oh, Garrett!" she screams. "What are you doing in Texas?"

"Apollo reunion," mumbles Breedlove. "A bunch of old astronauts trying to fit into old space capsules—not a pretty sight."

The cast's respect for Nicholson was apparent when they all crowded round the monitors to watch playbacks of him and MacLaine doing their scenes. "He's so spontaneous he's incapable of doing a scene the same way twice," MacLaine said. "He's so brilliant that he stimulates you."

When *The Evening Star* premiered ten months later—on Christmas Day 1996—reviews panned it for being "fragmented" and "a pale copy" of the original.

Jack was onscreen for just four minutes, and the $13 million he was reputed to have been paid made this the most expensive cameo role in Hollywood history.

2

SUSPICIOUS BY NATURE

TWENTY YARDS SHORT of the statue of St. Monica on the Pacific seafront, a black Mercedes limousine slowed to a halt outside 100 Wilshire Boulevard. Jack Nicholson had seen the building rearing up on the horizon for twenty blocks or more as the vehicle cruised down the gentle Wilshire slopes toward the ocean. It was impossible to miss it. Twenty-one stories high and topped by a thirty-foot red-and-white communications mast, the curved glass tower was easily the tallest landmark in the city of Santa Monica. Standing in its shadow between two palm trees and set against a curtain of sea fog was the diminutive figure of the woman who had given the city its name.

Legend had it that St. Monica, the mother of St. Augustine, had converted her pagan husband to Christianity through the power of prayer just a year before his death, thus saving his soul from damnation. This added some intriguing symbolism to the tableau about another mother, father, and son that was about to be enacted inside the portals of 100 Wilshire Boulevard.

At 12:10 on the afternoon of March 1, 1996, the actor was late for his noon appointment with Susan Anspach's attorneys. Getting out of the car, he gave some instructions to the chauffeur and then gazed up at the circular white pillars that kept the acres of gleaming glass and white concrete erect. Dressed in an olive green sports jacket and light slacks, he walked past huge tubs of violet and white spring flowers and entered the black-glassed vestibule.

The lobby was adorned by a huge, wooden sculpture composed of multicolored wings. It was a striking piece of modern art, and Nicholson might have paused to study its futuristic motif had the circumstances been different. Stepping into one of the elevators, he was immediately caught in the glare of four overhead spotlights and his reflection bounced back at him from several angles. Wherever he looked, he saw images of himself: a full frontal view presented itself from the shining chromium double doors, his torso was bent around the tubular railings at the rear of the car, and if he glanced upward the top of his head was reflected in a metallic panel fixed to the ceiling between the spotlights. This was one time he really needed his sunglasses.

Nicholson had no wish to submit himself to questions, any questions, about his personal and business lives and had instructed his lawyers to delay this moment for as long as possible. The interrogation had been put off for three months while he made *Blood and Wine* and *The Evening Star*, his lawyers pleading that their client would be absent from California for much of December, January, and February owing to his acting commitments. However, his presence at several Lakers games in L.A. since the New Year had been noted, and Susan's lawyers had argued that if he could take time out to attend sports events, then he could devote a few hours to answering some of their questions.

After more wrangling, it had been agreed that Jack would be deposed in the conference room at Paul Hoffman's offices at 100 Wilshire. The venue had initially been opposed on the grounds that his very presence in the building would create such interest among the workforce that his safety could be threatened. Jack's lawyers "tried to have it at their own offices on West Olympic Boulevard for 'security reasons,'" said my source. "But that didn't work because O. J. Simpson was being deposed that day in the same building [in the civil action over the murders of Nicole Brown Simpson and Ron Goldman], and the press were crawling all over the place. Finally, they had to concede, but they didn't like it one little bit."

Nicholson emerged from the elevator on the tenth floor and entered Suite 1000. A secretary ushered him into the glassed-in conference room with a panoramic view of the Santa Monica coastline. The fog had lifted, and to the south the pier, the carousel, and the long stretch of sand to Venice Beach were clearly visible; northward were the Palisades and, further along the coast, Malibu. Nicholson sat down at the long wooden conference table. Susan was in Paul Hoffman's adjoining office when the secretary buzzed through: "Jack's here."

At 12:13, she and her lawyer walked into what would become a war room. Jack faced Susan across the table. His back was toward the ocean; she had the view. They had not seen each other for more than five years, and it was an awkward moment. Neither smiled. There was no sign of recognition, nothing in their brief eye contact to indicate that they had once shared the deepest of intimacies. "There was a lot of tension in the room," Hoffman told me later. "He clearly didn't want to be there."

NICHOLSON had been joined on one side of the table by three of his lawyers, Abraham "Abe" Somer, Russ Frackman, and Hayward Kaiser. Further down the table were Robert Colbert and his attorney, Jerome Mandel. Compared with the conventional Ivy League types in Jack's legal team, Somer stood out. His attitude indicated that he, not Jack, was in charge. Several times during the course of the afternoon he drew attention to himself, at one time addressing one of Susan's lawyers, the young and beautiful Lori Beckwith, demanding to know what she was doing there.

With Mick Jagger as his client at Mitchell, Silberberg and Knupp, Somer had been used to playing the big shot. In 1974, he had negotiated one of the most lucrative contracts in rock-'n'-roll history by signing the Rolling Stones to a multialbum deal with Atlantic Records. However, his position with the law firm had changed when he was forced to vacate his office and start working from home after a series of complaints about his behavior toward women. "His secretary used to come to me crying over sexual harassment," said a friend. "She was a former airline stewardess and he would lock the door to his office and chase her around the room."

Somer's interest in women had increased markedly after his dentist had performed some expensive cosmetic surgery on his mouth. "He used to be extremely homely with incredible buck teeth, but he had them fixed," said the friend. "His wife, Phyllis, was a beautiful woman, a cross between Grace Kelly and Michelle Pfeiffer. When she left him, she took off for Hawaii and even left her young daughter, Eve, behind with him in his mansion with an Olympic-size pool and two tennis courts in Doheny Estates. His second wife, Cindy, also left him, even though she was the mother of his two small children."

Somer had a record of sexual harassment complaints while he was at Mitchell, Silberberg and Knupp. In 1990, he and the firm were sued by a young law clerk for assault and battery. Somer "threaten[ed] physical contact in the form of lewd sexual contact, actually engaging in such improper contact and touching and physical abuse . . . without plaintiff's consent," the suit alleged. This case had been settled out of court, but it immediately emerged that a witness in a later case had claimed that Somer once disrobed in front of her and demanded sexual favors. That case, too, had been quietly settled. His position with the firm was now described as "counsel."

Somer had not appeared at the earlier court hearing, but his position in the hierarchy of Nicholson's legal team now became clear: His were the brains behind the defense; he was the main man. "Jack will do anything Abe tells him to do," said my legal source. "He's running the show."

And then there was Bob Colbert, Mr. C to Jack. One of his roles in Nicholson's outfit was that of court jester, but the normally jovial accountant was mute today. As the keeper of his master's secrets, he was in the unenviable position of knowing exactly how much the Anspach case and the other legal actions in Jack's life were costing in lawyers' fees and expenses, quite apart from the millions at stake in potential losses. Moreover, Colbert knew how highly Jack prized his free time, when he liked to play golf, read scripts, and hang out with his pal Alan Finkelstein. "I don't like having my leisure time interfered with," he had told an interviewer a short time earlier.

Colbert's years in service had made him adept at judging his boss's moods and anticipating his wishes, but this had also evoked an imitative effect. He had come to adopt so many of Nicholson's mannerisms that some acquaintances thought he impersonated his master to an unhealthy degree. He told one lawyer who questioned his authority to make decisions on Jack's behalf: "I am he and he is me."

Physically, the pair were unalike. Although only an inch shorter than his employer, Colbert was noticably fatter, with regulation paunch and well-rounded face. However, he was a man of considerable power in the Proteus empire and had earned a reputation for using that power with less than chivalrous intent. "He's the sort of guy who takes chicken soup to a sick woman and then tries to stick his hand up her shirt," said an actress who knows him well. Anjelica Huston described him as the Grabber or the Mauler.

Colbert's audacity toward women had increased to such an extent after his marriage to his wife, Nina, had ended in divorce that Jennifer Nicholson had been driven to comment on the impropriety of his hugs and kisses. Ironically, one of the objects of his desire had been Susan Anspach, who was obliged to meet him to discuss the money she was receiving from Nicholson to pay her mortgage on the Santa Monica house. Colbert had pursued her for dates, making his intentions clear in voice messages whispered onto her answering machine and in outspoken advances during their business meetings.

Hermine Harman, a friend of Susan's who is also a qualified psychologist, confirmed that Susan had found Colbert's behavior extremely upsetting. "I heard every time he made sexual innuendos and came on to her," she told me. "That was sexual harassment." In the end, Susan asked Paul Hoffman to accompany her whenever she went to Colbert's office.

Seated alongside Hoffman and his partner Gary Bostwick, Susan recognized the hallmarks of a vendetta when she saw Jack, Bob, and Abe lined up together for the first time. She realized then that taking away her house was not an end in itself, but rather a means to an end. The realization gave substance to a nagging fear she had held for some time that the forces ranged against her were motivated more by revenge than money: that these three men, each of whom she knew very well, were united in a conspiracy to punish her.

Susan had been introduced to Somer by Richard Perry, the record-producing ex-husband of Rebecca Broussard. "I have consistently felt that Abe has an ego thing with me and has been trying to get even with me by using Jack," Susan told me. "I dated Abe several times in the seventies and then said, in so many words, 'Goodbye, I'm not interested.' All three of them, Jack, Abe, and Bob Colbert, have a score to settle with me. They're all out to get me because, in one way or another, I rejected every single one of them."

With that chilling thought in her mind, Susan heard Nicholson take the oath while the court-appointed stenographer, Lagretta Reynolds, sat poised at the head of the table to record every word on her little machine. Hoffman posed the questions:

Q When was the first time that you learned that Ms. Anspach had had a child after the filming of *Five Easy Pieces*?

A I don't know the date.

Q What circumstances did you first learn it?

A At a party.

Q Do you recall whose party it was?

A Yes.

Q Whose?

A Burt Schneider [one of the team who made *Easy Rider* and *Five Easy Pieces*].

Q Was that here in Los Angeles?

A Yes.

Q Do you recall who told you that Susan Anspach had had a child?

A She did.

Q So Ms. Anspach was at this party?

A Yes.

Q Can you describe the circumstances in which you and she had the discussion about Caleb's birth?

A She was sitting on my lap at the party.

Q Do you recall anything about the conversation apart from that?

A Specifically, no—but I remember the gist of it, which is she said that she had something that she wanted to tell me, that she felt—I don't know—bad or wrong about that she hadn't ever told me before this, that she had a son, Caleb, and that she—I don't know if she said "believed" or simply stated that I was the father.

Q What was your reaction to that at that time?

A Suspicion.

Q Why was that?

A It's my nature.

Q What were your feelings toward Susan Anspach at the time of Burt Schneider's party? Did you have any feelings toward Susan Anspach as a person at the time?

A I had a suspicion enhanced, a vague antipathy.

Q What was that based on?

A My experience with her.

Q At the time you first agreed to make loans to Ms. Anspach, did you still have a mild antipathy toward her?

A Still have a mild antipathy toward her? Yeah.

Q Has there ever been a time when you have not had that mild antipathy since the filming of *Five Easy Pieces*?

A Well, the balance changes intermittently, but I'm always suspicious. And I have been given no reason not to be, I might add.

There were several adjournments during which Nicholson retired to the men's room. Telltale smoke lingered over the washbasins. He was behaving as he did at the Forum, where smoking was also prohibited. "I sneak into the men's room at halftime, like when I was in high school, and take my drags there," he said. A sports journalist recalls that Nicholson used to pop into the press darkroom at the stadium to take drugs until a security guard noted what was happening. The journalist says he was told to warn Jack that there would be trouble unless the practice ceased. He passed the message on, and Jack was never seen in the darkroom again.

After one such break in the deposition proceedings, Hoffman asked:

Q Why are you always suspicious of Susan?

A Because she doesn't always seem to follow good logical sense, and when I view this, I always ascribe motives to it.

Q In what ways has Susan not followed good logical sense to the extent that it's relevant to your assessment of her?

A I'm an illegitimate child. I don't think she protects her child vis-à-vis how she deals with the press. I believe she is mildly self-aggrandizing.

Q Are there any other ways in which Susan has not followed good logical sense that leads you to your conclusion?

A Well, she has a lot of complaints that are common in her profession, and those kinds of complaints make you suspicious if you are in the profession.

Q Would that include complaints that she is not working in part because of discrimination based on gender in the industry?

A Yes.

Q And you don't believe that's true?

A No, I don't believe that's true.

Q In the conversations or conversation that you had with Ms. Anspach around the time of the *Vanity Fair* letter, did you tell her that you were terrified by her, quote, fucking unpredictability, unquote?

A I'm not sure.

Q Do you deny saying that?

A No, it doesn't sound like me.

Q Did you call Ms. Anspach a miserable bitch in the conversation?

A I don't recall.

Q Do you deny that you called her that?

A No.

Q Did you state to Ms. Anspach in the conversation that women were all weak, frightened cunts?

A I don't think so.

Q Did you call her an unpredictable cunt?

A I'm not sure.

Q Did you call her a bitch?

A I'm not sure.

Q Did you call her an idiot?

A I don't know.

Q Did you call her a miserable, drunken bitch and indicate that she owed you money?

A When?

Q In this conversation in 1994 around the time of the *Vanity Fair* article.

A I don't recall.

Q Did you ever speak to Ms. Anspach when you were high on drugs?

A What?

Q Did you ever speak to Ms. Anspach when you were high on drugs?

Russ Frackman instructed his client not to answer the question.

After a different recess, Susan's lawyers nudged each other. There was white powder on Jack's nose and he took out a handkerchief to wipe it off his face. If that powder was a sign that Jack had been using cocaine, the drug did nothing to improve his composure. He took his sunglasses off, fiddled with them, and then put them back on again to shield his sensitive eyes from the combination of fluorescent and natural light. Sensing his master's discomfort, Colbert rose from his chair and purposefully closed the blinds, thus blotting out the daylight—and the view.

From Jack's answers, it was apparent that his memory was shot to pieces; his most common response to questions was "I don't recall." Several times he admitted he was unsure of dates and said he couldn't remember years. "He was like a wind-up toy that had run down; he had no energy," said one of those present. "Then he would go off like the Joker, and his lawyers had to shut him up. There were lots of interjections in his deposition."

One of the exhibits in the lawsuit was a transcript that Susan had made of a three-way telephone conversation she, Nicholson, and Colbert had about her financial difficulties in February 1995. It read:

ANSPACH: What if you lend Caleb the money to buy it [the house] back?

NICHOLSON: Run it by the lawyer. Run by something that works. I don't intend to just give you anything. I don't feel obligated to save Caleb's mom.

ANSPACH: Don't leave Caleb without a home. You don't leave Rebecca, Anjelica, Jennifer–

NICHOLSON: Let's call Caleb right now. Would you like that, huh? He told me when he talked to me that he wished to God he didn't have to do this. But, hell, maybe it's good for him. It puts him in touch with the tough side of life.

COLBERT (*interjecting*): We're not talking about you having to be out of there by tomorrow. It'll take six months to a year to sell it. For insurance purposes, you should be in the house.

NICHOLSON: We'll put it on the market. Sell it. Have that money and then *maybe* something else can be arranged. I'd like to help arrange something at the end, but because you are so difficult to help, you force people to find different ways of dealing with you. To help you costs me. Yes, we'll take care of you if you do mean in the spirit that I've tried to come halfway with you. There's a geometric progression on your fears. I do know you to be a person who, when you're not under pressure, I respect you. I don't want to see you come to misery. I don't think Caleb would respect me if I did do that. People do weird things when they're desperate. Why are you suing me for your shortcomings? Why don't you sue GM [General Motors]? Don't assume what I do for my family. I can't do for any of them, not Jennifer, none of them. I'm not Santa Claus. Deal with me honestly. Stay with me, I'll help you. The monster says, "After all, you're in debt to me already." You get me mad at Bob. I can't take it. You're fucking up my whole corporation.

ANSPACH (*laughs and then apologizes*): I can't imagine I'm that powerful.

NICHOLSON: I see you want to giggle on your little clitty.

ANSPACH: Jack, you're so negative. I have to talk to Paul [Hoffman].

NICHOLSON: Don't call and threaten to sue me. REMOVE THE SUIT! I got mad at Bob.

COLBERT: My lawyer says you're going to sue me, then I can't talk to you. I've sent your lawyer four or five letters, and within twenty-four hours after every letter from him I've responded to him.

NICHOLSON: Let me tell you three things: One: I have three cases like this. And what happens to me? They sue and I wind up settling and paying *my* lawyers and *their* lawyers. Two: It's an obvious inflammatory letter. Three: You need an actual plan. Don't put me in a situation that can do me harm. I can't afford to talk to anyone in life. You figure out a way to save this house related to ME! That was one way to do it. But your lawyers didn't find the variation that works AND NOW YOU'VE LOST YOUR HOME! (*he screams gleefully*) I have to risk everything that I own if you roll over the second [trust deed]. It will cost me $1.8 million to pay off the $625,000. It's illegal in the Proteus Plan. This never should have been put through Proteus in the first place. It's illegal in the Proteus Plan to roll over the second.

ANSPACH: They told me that "Jack doesn't want to support Susan, and besides, Caleb lives in New York," and that's why you don't want to help me.

NICHOLSON: I never said those things. Your lawyer is lying to you. You'll be suing me and I won't take it! Please don't do this—yapping about my business. It's just a misunderstanding. . . . The Proteus gift was an irregularity in my generosity. But now I've told you too much. I've placed a friend in jeopardy because I've given you information. There are some problems in my

> Proteus Plan. There! Another gift! I gave you the gun, but I don't want to give you the bullets. I trust no one. They're incapable of holding a decent relationship with a benefactor. They're all parasitic and dangerous enemies that benefit from my professional life, which is all that matters to me. I don't want to make you vulnerable to my truth—you might be subpoenaed one day.

Hoffman asked Nicholson to read the transcript and then asked him:

Q Did you ask Ms. Anspach the question, "Can I trust you not to discuss my life with others?"

A I don't know. It's a question I ask people. Usually, it's rhetorical. I know I can't trust them and I certainly know I can't trust Ms. Anspach. . . .

Q Did you say, "I see you want to giggle on your little clitty?"

A In life?

Q Did you ever say that to Ms. Anspach?

A I don't know if I used those exact words, no, but—

FRACKMAN: No, let him answer.

A But I—

FRACKMAN: I don't think I can stop you.

A That's okay. You can stop me. I don't need to do that kind of shit.

Q "I gave you the gun, but I don't want to give you the bullets." Do you recall making a statement like that?

A Well, I remember telling her I've learned through legal proceedings that it's better not to give [away] privileged information.

Q Was there a particular piece of information you did not wish to share with Ms. Anspach because she might be subpoenaed?

A There may have been lots of things. Practically the totality of my life that I wouldn't want Ms. Anspach in a position to testify about.

Q Have you discussed your feelings toward Ms. Anspach with anyone other than your lawyers?

A In my life?

Q Yes.

A Yes.

Q Did you have such discussions with Michael Douglas?

A I believe I probably have had some discussion.

Q Why, in light of your antipathy toward Ms. Anspach, did you agree to provide her with any financial assistance for her home?

A Mild antipathy. . . .

Q Mild antipathy. I stand corrected. Why, in light of your antipathy toward Ms. Anspach did you agree to provide her with any financial assistance for her home?

A I'm a humanitarian.

Q When you say you're a humanitarian, what exactly do you mean by that term?

A It means I believe in being good and charitable to my fellow man and if possible fulfill a need.

Q And that is the only reason?

A That—and fear of the cynicism with which humanitarian acts are viewed.

Q Have you ever had any conversation with Burt Schneider about your relationship with Caleb or Susan Anspach?

A I don't recall. I haven't spoken to him in seven years or so.

Q How about Warren Beatty?

A I don't recall, but he would fall under [the category of] a person that's familiar with my household and may have heard my ranting.

The session finished at 5:30 P.M. Jack snapped his sunglasses back into position. When he left the conference room, he ignored the building's strict fire regulations again and lit up a Marlboro in the hallway while waiting for the elevator.

Later, Susan Anspach told me: "It's painfully obvious that Jack wants to crush me. I never did, and still don't, understand his wrath. He said that I was pretentious on the set of *Five Easy Pieces* because I mentioned I'd worked on the New York stage with Robert Duvall, Jon Voight, and Dustin Hoffman. How was I to know he had wanted Dusty's part in *The Graduate*? Yet, during Jack's evidence, Gary Bostwick remarked, 'This kind of hatred has a sensuousness that can only come from love.' "

Abe Somer had a quiet word with Paul Hoffman: "Jack said to tell you that he was angry before, but now he's really furious."

Hoffman told me in an interview that Nicholson's attitude during the hearing had been "fairly hostile." "His lawyers certainly tried to avoid having his deposition taken, and they instructed him not to answer a great many questions that we thought were relevant," he said. "The way the case has been portrayed by Nicholson's side has been that this is just a regular business transaction. There was a promissory note, there was a deed of trust, there was a loan. It might as well have been the Bank of Nicholson and if you don't pay the loan this is what happens to you.

"Our understanding of the facts—and the facts as they certainly appear—is that this was not anything like that. There is a relationship between Susan and Caleb and Jack that's a profound one, and there are a lot of unresolved issues on a personal level between all of them. The financial transactions that are at the middle of this controversy arise in the context of family relationship; of Jack agreeing to assist the family, which includes Caleb and Susan, in maintaining their family home and in making, according to Susan's allegations, a variety of promises that we contend in the lawsuit are legally enforceable against Nicholson; that he just can't make promises and then decide not to go along with them."

The psychologist Hermine Harman said: "There are these three men—Bob, Abe Somer, and Jack—who've been rejected or emasculated by this woman and they're just out to get her. I totally think it's a vendetta. There's no other reason why Jack would buy his daughter a house directly across the street and not even buy Susan's house, put it in Caleb's name, and let Susan live there. Susan could have been a built-in grandma right there for Jennifer's baby, but Jennifer has to side with Jack against Susan and can't let herself be involved, whereas they were all very close for a while. It's painful for Jennifer; she could use the help, and it's right there—right across the street.

"Susan dropped off a plant and a card for Mother's Day, and Jennifer didn't even call to say thank you. She has to be with Jack; that's where her bread is buttered; she has to side with the money, and it's disgusting. Jack has already paid out $300,000 to his lawyers [in this case], and you know it's a vendetta if he's going to spend more money on legal fees fighting it than paying it. He's got to win, no matter what the cost. He has everyone around him who yes-es him and kisses his ass. Empathy does not exist for this man."

Commenting on the situation between Jack and Caleb, Dr. Paul Fleiss, father of "the Hollywood madam," Heidi Fleiss, told me: "I've known Caleb since he was born; I was his pediatrician. I thought they had an understanding that Jack would kind of help out, but he has failed to meet his obligations. The court case will probably make these relationship problems worse. There'll be a lot of angry words spoken, and I think Caleb is the one who stands to suffer. Jack is a totally recognizable character, and he's a celebrity wherever he goes, so it makes it very difficult for him."

SUSAN wasn't leaving anything to chance for the next court appearance when the judge would consider a motion for dismissal filed by Jack's lawyers. Eleven days after Nicholson had given his deposition—at 11 A.M. on Tuesday, March 12, to be precise—she phoned Edna, a ninety-six-year-old Las Vegas psychic, for a consultation about the likely outcome. "Some things won't go smoothly," the old lady told her. "But you will win today."

The first positive sign that things might be brightening up was that a heavy downpour stopped as Susan drove into the parking lot at the back of the courthouse. Once again, Case No. SC 039121 was on the list of Judge Alan B. Haber, who was also the judge in the latest pretrial phase of the O. J. Simpson civil case. "You really put me to work on this case," His Honor, a gray-bearded, black-robed figure in gold-rimmed glasses, told Paul Hoffman and one of Jack's lawyers, Hayward Kaiser.

Kaiser argued that the arrangement between his client and Anspach was purely economic. "Unfortunately for Anspach, the law is straightforward," he said. "When you borrow money, eventually you will have to pay it back."

Hoffman responded: "In our view, this is not an economic case, it is more a family case. We can prove fairly easily that Miss Anspach's son is Mr. Nicholson's. One of the points that distinguishes this case is that there were promises to Miss Anspach from Mr. Colbert and Mr. Nicholson. Given these relationships, a jury should decide whether these promises were reliable or not."

Susan alleged in her complaint that the defendants, in the guise of helping her and Caleb to keep their family home, tricked her into signing "loan" documents that gave them the power to prevent her from speaking to the press about Nicholson's relationship to Caleb and enabled Colbert to sexually harass her and Nicholson to humiliate and degrade her.

Hoffman submitted: "While promising that the 'loan' agreements were for Nicholson's tax purposes only, the defendants trapped the plaintiff on a financial treadmill that has given them the power to crush her. The defendants now claim that the 'loans' were run-of-the-mill business transactions carried out by defendant Nicholson's pension fund, defendant Proteus, for its ordinary investment purposes. Instead, these loans were merely the instrumentalities of a fraudulent conspiracy by the defendants against the plaintiff. In the context of this demurrer, this court must accept the plaintiff's factual allegations and reject the defendants' attempts to portray these events as an ordinary business dispute. It will be up to a jury to determine which version of reality is true."

Referring to Susan's breach of contract claim, Hoffman said: "Susan Anspach was justified in relying on the defendants' promise because of their confidential relationship. Had she been dealing with strangers or a bank, she would not have agreed to sign 'loan' documents that differed from the defendants' promise so that Nicholson could gain tax advantages. It is not unreasonable as a matter of law for the plaintiff to accept promises from the father of her child, a wealthy movie star, and his longtime business manager, that they would give her the money to save the family home of Nicholson's son Caleb and that she could pay Nicholson back if and when her career rebounded.

"The defendants conspired to control and humiliate the plaintiff, acquiring financial power over her by exploiting her faith in them, which then enabled the defendants to subject her to a pattern of humiliation, sexual harassment by defendant Colbert, control over her ability to speak publicly about defendant Nicholson's fatherhood of Caleb, vulgar and belittling tirades by defendant Nicholson, and ultimately to crush her by taking the family home."

Judge Haber commented: "The allegations do not paint a very nice picture of the defendants, to put it mildly." Dismissing the claims of fraud and emotional distress from the suit, he ordered that the breach of contract allegation should be tried before a jury and a trial date was later set for March 1997. Nicholson was now faced with the type of publicity that movie stars dread and viewers of Court TV can only dream about. But Susan was quite clear about her motives. Back home on Sixteenth Street, she said: "I look around here and I just don't accept that all this is going to be gone.

"That's why I'm suing him—not to get his money, but to save my home."

3

MULHOLLAND MADNESS

WHENEVER JACK NICHOLSON needed advice on a personal matter, he turned to his friend Alan Finkelstein. A quiet-spoken man with a drooping mustache, Finkelstein played the hip sidekick to Nicholson's Quixote. As Nicholson's collaborator in many exploits, including the opening of the Monkey Bar restaurant in West Hollywood, he had carved a unique role in the Jack Pack. "He's a partner in my whole life," said Finkelstein. "He's a partner in everything I do." One of my informants put it differently: "Alan is Jack's right-hand man, even though he's seriously addled. The others—Somer and Colbert—are just bean counters."

The problem that Jack outlined to Finkelstein in April 1996 would have made an excellent pitch for a movie to any producer in search of a script. Nicholson's friend Helena Kallianiotes planned to open a ranch-and-spa resort on some land she had bought north of Los Angeles. "The idea was that wealthy male members would be able to fly in by helicopter and enjoy the kind of pleasures usually associated with Hugh Hefner in the heyday of the Playboy empire," said a friend. To finance the enterprise, Helena had become involved in a share-selling venture with the Colombian Lorenzo, who was a close friend and, it appeared, an accomplished confidence trickster. Lorenzo had later vanished from his usual haunts in Los Angeles at the same time as $6 million of investors' money had disappeared from Helena's bank account. There was a very good chance that she would be targeted for questioning if an official investigation was held into the sting.

Jack had promised to sort out the problem before that could happen.

The story had a familiar ring to Finkelstein. Whenever Helena was in trouble, she turned to Jack for help, invoking the old-pals act and playing on his sympathies. "Jack's got a real problem with Helena Kallianiotes, but he still feels responsible for her," said the friend. "He wants her out of his life, but she knows a great deal about him, perhaps too much for comfort."

Jack had met Helena when she was working as a belly dancer at a Greek nightclub in the early sixties. She played poker with him and his cronies, and after encountering problems in her marriage, she had moved into a spare bedroom on Mulholland Drive. Later, Jack had allowed her to take over the second of his two homes up there, and she had acted as estate manager and chatelaine from then on.

Finkelstein suggested they should call in a professional investigator and recommended Frank Monte, a tough Australian who ran a detective agency out of a suite in Rockefeller Center on Fifth Avenue in New York City. Finkelstein had met Monte when he had opened a branch of his detective agency in Los Angeles a few years earlier and had visited the Monkey Bar with Monte's girlfriend Justine Ski, a twenty-five-year-old blond Australian model. Finkelstein told Nicholson that as a young man Monte had worked as an industrial spy and bodyguard for Aristotle Onassis and later had assisted the Sheik of Dubai in a little matter of guns, mercenaries, and a band of dissident Arabs. No less an eminence than the Rockefeller family had hired him to find out what had happened to the family's missing heir, the anthropologist Michael Rockefeller, who had disappeared in the swamps of Western New Guinea (now Irian Java). Monte had returned from an expedition to the area with the skulls of three unidentified white men who had been eaten by cannibal tribesmen. The Rockefellers took possession of the skulls and paid him $250,000 for his trouble.

Nicholson lapped up the story and asked Finkelstein to approach the investigator. Here was Jake Gittes with more than a touch of Indiana Jones. Finkelstein made a phone call to check that Monte was available, and they met at the Four Seasons Hotel in New York on the evening of Tuesday, April 16, 1996. Over drinks, Finkelstein told Monte about Helena Kallianiotes and Lorenzo and asked the private eye if he could find out how much money was in Lorenzo's bank accounts. He also asked him to check out "the probability of the man being a confidence trickster."

"Lorenzo was Jack and Marlon's Colombian drug connection, and he had scammed them over shares in the ranch-and-spa resort," said Monte. "He had got $6 million for air, for nothing, and they wanted the money traced. The original thing was to look after Jack's interests. Get into this woman's [Helena's] head, figure out what's going on, and save Jack from any embarrassment. Then Brando got involved and hired me on at $5,000 a day because he wanted me to go after the Colombian. He hired me to be the heavy. Between them, Nicholson and Brando promised me the world, and I got incredible results for them."

Monte realized it was a great chance. He had recently completed a screenplay called *The Private Eye* and was trying to raise funds to turn it into a motion picture. Working for two of the heaviest hitters in the movie business could only help to get his project off the ground. He assured Finkelstein that initially he would give him some of his time in New York free of charge. "Otherwise, I told him I charged $125 per hour, $150 when out of town, plus expenses and disbursements to my information brokers." Finkelstein agreed to the arrangement. "Whatever you want, Jack will pay," he said, and returned to the West Coast.

Monte began contacting his sources on Wednesday, and, he said, "the matter escalated, and Finkelstein faxed me and verbally engaged me with more requests, searches, and inquiries. On Friday, April 19, Finkelstein said to me from Los Angeles with Helena in the background, 'Marlon Brando said if you do this for Helena he will do a day on your movie.' I questioned whether he was joking. He said no, he was serious. He asked me to send him my script immediately. I did so.

"On Monday, April 22, we continued with searches and reported the results of these inquiries to Finkelstein. I faxed relevant information to him as it came in by hand, mail, and fax from my contacts. Helena became involved with discussions and started issuing directions to me on the telephone. At 6:30 P.M. New York time that day, Marlon Brando telephoned me at my offices and had a half-hour conversation with me about the situation and its ramifications. I have his Bell Pacific bill to prove that the call was made, and two witnesses who were with him at the time have since confirmed it to me.

"He also rang me a second time for forty minutes—that's on his phone bill as well—and we talked about the movie. We also discussed how to protect him and Jack Nicholson from any fallout should this matter reach the press or if Helena was found to have acted inappropriately. I promised I could handle that situation, given my obvious expertise with the press and media."

Brando wanted Monte to find Lorenzo's present whereabouts and check whether the missing money was in his accounts at Merrill Lynch and the Bank of America or whether it had been moved out of the country to other banks. He also wanted to know whether Lorenzo had a criminal record, either in the United States or some other country, and whether he owned any cars, boats, or properties anywhere in the world.

"Over the next two days we investigated telephone numbers, addresses, and bogus leads," said Monte. "I found secret accounts that Lorenzo had opened in Luxembourg and Zurich, and I found some of the money that he had salted away in San Francisco and Georgia as well as Bogotá. At 5 P.M. New York time, I received a call from Mr. Abe Somer, who requested an update and expressed [concern that] his own client's interest be served foremost.

"Helena then requested me to go to Los Angeles to attend to the assignment firsthand. I told Finkelstein I no longer had a necessity to do so, but he agreed with Helena that I should attend to the matter personally. I informed him that my expenses were mounting up as this was now a full-time job." According to Monte, Finkelstein wasn't worried about the expense. "Jack is good for it," he said. "As soon as you land, you can have whatever you need in cash." Monte left New York on Thursday morning, April 25, and "immediately upon landing went to 12830 Mulholland Drive, Beverly Hills, California 90210."

AT THIS point, the road was very narrow with the shoulders dropping away on both sides into the canyons below. Just after the asphalt snaked into one of its many hairpin bends, there was a strip of macadam about thirty feet wide with three big white mailboxes inscribed with the numbers 12830, 12850, and 12900: respectively Helena Kallianiotes, Jack Nicholson, and Marlon Brando. The boxes were stationed under the branches of a large pepper tree to the right of a huge iron security gate, painted black and hung between white brick pillars topped with two-foot-high spikes. To the left, there was an intercom system with the same numbers imprinted on three buzzers. A video camera monitored the mailboxes, the buzzers, and any new arrivals to the premises. The gate itself was made of sharpened vertical spikes eight feet high and topped with coils of razor wire. This fortification was set into a chainlink fence, which was partly obscured by a dense thicket of trees, hedges, and rosebushes that provided perfect cover not only for the occupants of the estate but for any intruder who might try to break in—and several had.

At 2 P.M. on April 25, Frank Monte pulled his rented white Lincoln sedan onto the macadam and announced his presence to the intercom marked 12830. When the gates automatically swung open, he drove in and accelerated up the hill for several hundred feet before the driveway split into a Y, the right fork leading to Nicholson's and Helena's homes and the left to Brando's place hidden behind a wall of bamboo on slightly higher ground. Monte drove to the right.

The spring rains had brought out lush growths of wildflowers in the heavily timbered grounds, and the greenery cloaked the view until he got out of the car. Then he saw three mountains covered with chaparral, scrub oak, and eucalyptus, plunge down through rocky gorges to the floor of the valley below.

Monte's first thought as a professional was about the appalling lack of security protecting the property. "You know, Jack has Picassos and Matisses in that house, and anyone could walk in, take him hostage, rip him off and drive out again with absolutely no problem," he said. "There's no bodyguard. You could short that gate with two wires. The security camera hardly works and it's only on in the kitchen and the gym, and Helena works it with a button. A woman did get in one night, and she had a gun, but Helena spotted her and called the police. Nicholson and Brando together are worth $600 million, and they've got no security."

Monte discovered when he got to Helena's house that Finkelstein did not have a check ready to give him as he had promised. They were arguing about this in front of Helena and a couple of Nicholson's secretaries when Monte saw Nicholson come out of his house and start putting his golf bag into his Mercedes. Despite protests from the entourage, the investigator ambled toward him, and as he did so, the star looked up and grinned.

"So you're the PI?" he said.

"I want you to know that you're my favorite actor," Monte replied.

"Is that right? I guess you're too busy for a game of golf, huh?"

"When I was taking all those lessons, I never thought you'd ask me to play golf with you."

"Yeah? Well, I was a PI once, y'know."

"Yeah, *Chinatown* went real well."

"No, I was a real PI."

"Where was that?"

"I was working for a guy in San Diego."

"Yeah? I never knew that."

Nicholson sized the bigger man up. "Do you carry? You got a piece?"

Several of Jack's employees were anxiously watching this exchange. One of the secretaries came over and reminded him of the time. He nodded, shook Monte's hand, and said, "Well, thanks for the great job you're doing."

"Jack, I'm going to do you a favor if you don't mind. I'm going to give you a terrorist's-eye view of how somebody could attack this place and take you out in five minutes.

"Impossible. Only you could do that, buddy." He poked the detective in his stomach. "But you're too old now."

In fact, Monte was eight years younger than Jack, who had celebrated his fifty-ninth birthday three days earlier.

"Believe me," said Monte, "three men could take your art collection and kidnap you at the same time."

"Nobody would do that to me."

"I'll do the report anyway."

"Okay," said Jack, climbing into his car. "We'll have a drink later and talk about it."

With that, Nicholson drove off to his golf game as though he hadn't a care in the world. "Jack thinks he doesn't need security because everybody adores him," said a friend. Soon afterward, Monte drove down the winding mountain road into the heart of Beverly Hills and registered at the Peninsula Hotel, where he set up a work station with two of his L.A.-based operatives, a former member of the FBI and an attractive blond woman. It wasn't until 1 A.M., "after lengthy entreaties," that he received a check for $5,000 drawn on Finkelstein's personal account at the Marathon National Bank in Beverly Hills.

In the morning, Monte contacted several Los Angeles law firms on behalf of his famous clients and instructed the firm of Manatt, Phelps, and Phillips to call Helena about the case with a view to representing her interests in any legal action. He had, he said, received some news from Washington that had made even his seasoned eyebrows shoot up. "I got information that Lorenzo was on the FBI red flag list," he said, "and is reported to be involved with the Gambino crime family. Whether he was a supplier of drugs or a financial middleman I had yet to learn.

"I also discovered that Lorenzo had defrauded Helena Kallianiotes after she got all these other people involved. Two of them were David Helsten, who was staying with Marlon, and Laura Alvarez, a former Vanderbilt wife who had been taking care of Jack—she had been his lover on and off for many years, including the times he was with Anjelica Huston and Rebecca Broussard.

"David had been ripped off for $125,000, Laura for $300,000, Laura's sister for $100,000, and it goes on and on. There's a couple of little old ladies, and there's Marlon Brando in there for half to three-quarters of a million. Helena had lost $800,000—she said Lorenzo had forged her signature at the bank—and she was furious.

"Everybody thought the project was safe because Jack and Marlon had put their money in. Lorenzo was a scam artist who had been involved with these people for a long time. He had been in their circle, getting them women and cocaine, and throwing parties. He disappeared the week before I started my investigation, and according to one of my investigators he was later spotted at the Cannes Film Festival."

There was ample proof that Lorenzo was an intimate acquaintance not only of Helena but also of David Helsten, Laura Alvarez, and Anjelica Huston. He was present at a party to celebrate Helena's birthday on March 24, 1994. Photographs taken that night showed guests including Anjelica, her husband, Robert Graham, and David Helsten enjoying themselves while Harry Dean Stanton played the guitar. And there, presenting Helena with a piece of jewelry in one picture, was Lorenzo. Other photographs taken on different occasions showed him helping Helena with the dishes in her kitchen, dining with Helena and Laura Alvarez at a restaurant, and in a group photograph with Helena, Anjelica Huston, and Robert Graham. Lorenzo had plenty of cash to spend on gifts and nights out. One of the documents that Monte had secured was from a Swiss branch of the Banca Commerciale Italiana in Loewen Strasse, Zurich, where Lorenzo was Customer No. 01 222068. A statement made out in his name and dated January 4, 1996, showed a balance in that account of 1,769,354 Swiss francs.

David Helsten confirmed to me that he was a close friend of Marlon Brando and Jack Nicholson and that he had been a victim of the fraud. "We were all embezzled by a friend whom everyone knows in Hollywood and whom I've known for years," he said. "I was taken for a great deal of money, and I was thinking, well, I wasn't really done right by at that moment. Jack, Marlon and Helena were thinking about themselves and how they were going to weather the storm, so to speak. There is a storm, and it's continuing as far as this case goes."

Born in Northern California, Helsten had spent long periods in Europe after making a fortune from his designs for various models of the Swatch watch. He had lived at Brando's house for several years. Talking about events at the compound, he said: "Amazing things become normal, even though anyone else would think it was crazy. But to me it was 'that's Marlon, that's Jack, that's what happens,' and we deal with it each day. Helena was famous in her club [the now defunct Helena's nightclub] for protecting the biggest stars in the world, and I learned from her. She's really my closest friend; she's like family to me. Through her, I met everyone in Hollywood. I knew some of them from her club anyway. I met so many famous people, it's just normal: You're having a dinner and you're sitting next to John Travolta. You're in a circle of people who are famous, and it just becomes an everyday occurrence."

Helsten was speaking to me from his apartment in New York after things had got out of hand on Mulholland Drive and he had decided that his wisest course of action was to leave Los Angeles altogether. Frank Monte said: "The trouble began on the day of Sean Penn's wedding, when Helena started physically bashing David. She was behaving like a real bitch. I arrived there the next day to drive Marlon to the law office of Barry Rothman in Century City to sort out the mess. Rothman was the original lawyer for the boy in the Michael Jackson case, and I'd dealt with him on several cases before.

"When we got back to Mulholland Drive that evening, it became apparent to me that Helena was furious about the missing money. I got David and Laura out of the compound and took them to the Peninsula [Hotel] at 1 o'clock in the morning. Both escaped from the compound that night—they had been more or less prisoners there—and we talked until dawn about Marlon Brando and Jack Nicholson."

Monte had been paid only $5,000 for his services thus far, and by his reckoning he was already owed $24,500. What's more, he had been told by a French friend of Brando's that the sum of $200,000 had been earmarked for the inquiry.

"Jack's lawyer, Abe Somer, rang me up at the Peninsula and said, 'Okay, you bribed all these people to get this information [about the bank accounts]. Okay, but we want receipts.' I said, 'Receipts? For bribing some cop in Bogotá?'

"He said, 'Why not? That's the way we do business.'

"I said, 'You're full of shit and you know it.'

"He said, 'Don't talk to me like that. I'm Mr. Nicholson's lawyer.'

"I said, 'Get off my phone. I don't deal with lawyers.'

"Then I was dealing with Bob Colbert, his business manager, who said to me, 'Don't worry. I'll fix it all up. I'm a businessman. I'll pay everything.' But when I rang him up at home, he said, 'You'll have to talk to Jack.'

"They treat private eyes like shit and then expect them to have morals. Once I found the money, it didn't matter anymore.

"So I went back up there to Jack's house, but I was told he was away for the day. Since then, David has told me he was actually at home; he didn't go anywhere. He had the shits about something, and he was there all the time. I had a couple of my guys staking out the place all night because I knew Jack's Mercedes and I wanted to know where he was on that Sunday night and early Monday morning. I was going to follow him and ask him for my money. The thing is, he didn't fuck me; Alan did and all these other people around him. I think he half doesn't know what's going on. I don't think he's a bad guy at all."

All was quiet when I went up to Mulholland Drive. A sleepy haze drifted in from the ocean, and no one was in the mood to talk about Lorenzo. When I did eventually discuss the case with Helena on the telephone, she admitted that money was missing from her account and claimed that Lorenzo was implicated in its removal. "He's very clever," she said. "I'm taking legal action to get people's money back, but I can't say any more about it."

WHILE these shenanigans were taking place, the foreclosure notice was being enforced on 473 Sixteenth Street, Santa Monica. Susan had opened her front door one morning to find a notice of sale pinned to the woodwork. It informed her that the house would be sold at public auction on the steps of the town hall at Cerritos, a town an hour's drive from L.A., where the trust deeds were held, at 11:30 A.M. on Tuesday, April 30.

Appraisers acting for Proteus had made a tour of the property to value its worth. Bob Colbert had arrived with them to look after Jack's interests, only to be turned away at the front door by Lori Beckwith, one of Susan's lawyers. The appraisers poked around in every room. In Susan's study, they saw a letter that Caleb had written to her after he moved to New York. It was pinned to the wall, and one of them read it. It said, "Dear Mom, I miss your singing around the house." One of the appraisers said to Susan, "You sure are a great mom." She managed to see them off the premises before she broke down in tears.

Anyone who knew Susan, Catherine, and Caleb vouched for the fact that they were a tremendous threesome. "Susan always provided them with a loving environment," said Dr. Paul Fleiss. "It's a very loving family."

Caleb had taken a week's vacation from his job in New York and flown to L.A. to lend his support. Oblivious to the revelry taking place at Sean Penn's wedding just a few blocks away, Susan and Caleb had driven off in a battered red Toyota to spend that Saturday evening at a Dodgers baseball game. She had totaled the family Volvo two days after filing the lawsuit against Jack. "I was beside myself," she said. "All these photographers were following me. I turned around to look at one and ran right into a pole."

The following day, Caleb posed with his mother for some "farewell" pictures shot by photographer Alan Markfield, a long-standing family friend. The garden was in full bloom, with birds of paradise, orange hibiscus, flaming scarlet bottlebrush, and purple bougainvillea adding a tropical touch to the setting. In the backyard, the loquat tree was heavy with clusters of ripe, yellow fruit. The low murmur of a passing jet mingled with birdsong, and only the occasional explosion of Markfield's flash equipment in various parts of the house disturbed the tranquility.

Caleb walked out into the garden, where the turtles, Cookie and Simon, were lazing in a sun-drenched pool near the garage.

He paced out a few steps on the lawn between the garage and a huge hedge. "I buried a time capsule here about ten years ago," he told me. "It had some *Sports Illustrated* magazines, one with Pete Rose on the cover, and some money and a few other odds and ends." He was wondering whether he should get a shovel and dig up his buried treasure or leave it for the new owners. He didn't have to say it; this place was his home, his emotional anchor.

Susan had just one last trump card in her hand to save the house. In desperation, she played it. The following day—just twenty-four hours before the auction was due to take place—she instructed her lawyers to enter Chapter 11 as a prelude to bankruptcy. All her assets were immediately frozen and the house was automatically withdrawn from sale. "Jack's lawyers have worked so hard to kill my case against him that it must have cost him $500,000 by now," said Susan. "So he won't make a damn cent out of the house even if he gets it—he's lost it all in legal fees. What a sad waste!" She admitted that the reprieve was the best thing that had happened to her since the legal battle had started.

Instead of going to watch her home being sold at auction to complete strangers on Tuesday, Susan, Caleb, and I went to the movies. The film we saw was called *A Family Thing,* starring Robert Duvall. "My very first role out of college I played Bobby Duvall's stepdaughter in *A View From the Bridge,*" said Susan. "I learned as much from acting with Bobby as I ever did." As Duvall's name popped onto the screen, Caleb slung his bare legs over the vacant seat in front and sat back to enjoy the film. Had things been different, he might have spent the day up on Mulholland Drive with his father, watching the Lakers go down to the Rockets in the third game of the NBA playoffs on his wall-sized TV screen.

And had Jack been a spectator in his own life, he would have realized that he had lost something far more important than a basketball game.

4

A FAMILY THING

THE PLOT OF *A Family Thing* hinges on the fact that the Southern redneck played by Robert Duvall has a black mother. He has always believed that the white woman who had raised him as her son was his natural mother. The unsettling truth that his real mother was a servant girl who had worked in his father's home and died giving birth to him comes to confront him in later life.

Chewing bubble gum in the fourteenth row of the AMC theater on the Third Street Promenade in Santa Monica, Caleb Goddard could identify with the feeling of what it was like to be told you were someone's else's child. The same thing had happened to him when he had been old enough to grasp the meaning of such a happening in his own life but too young to appreciate that it would lead to complications. Later still, he learned that this was one situation he shared in common with the man who was his real father, Jack Nicholson. Caleb loved and respected Mark Goddard, the man he had grown up calling Dad, but he also had great empathy for his natural father, whom he addressed as Jack. Like the cinematic Duvall's *Family Thing* character, both father and son had been the innocent victims of a deception regarding the true state of affairs surrounding their births.

Caleb was just four years old when Jack discovered the truth about his own parentage. "I'd say it was a pretty dramatic event, but it wasn't what I'd call traumatizing," Nicholson explained. "By the time I found out who my mother was I was pretty psychologically formed." He had never wavered in his love for his

Jack played Barbra Streisand's brother in *On a Clear Day You Can See Forever,* but most of his performance hit the cutting room floor (Kobal Collection)

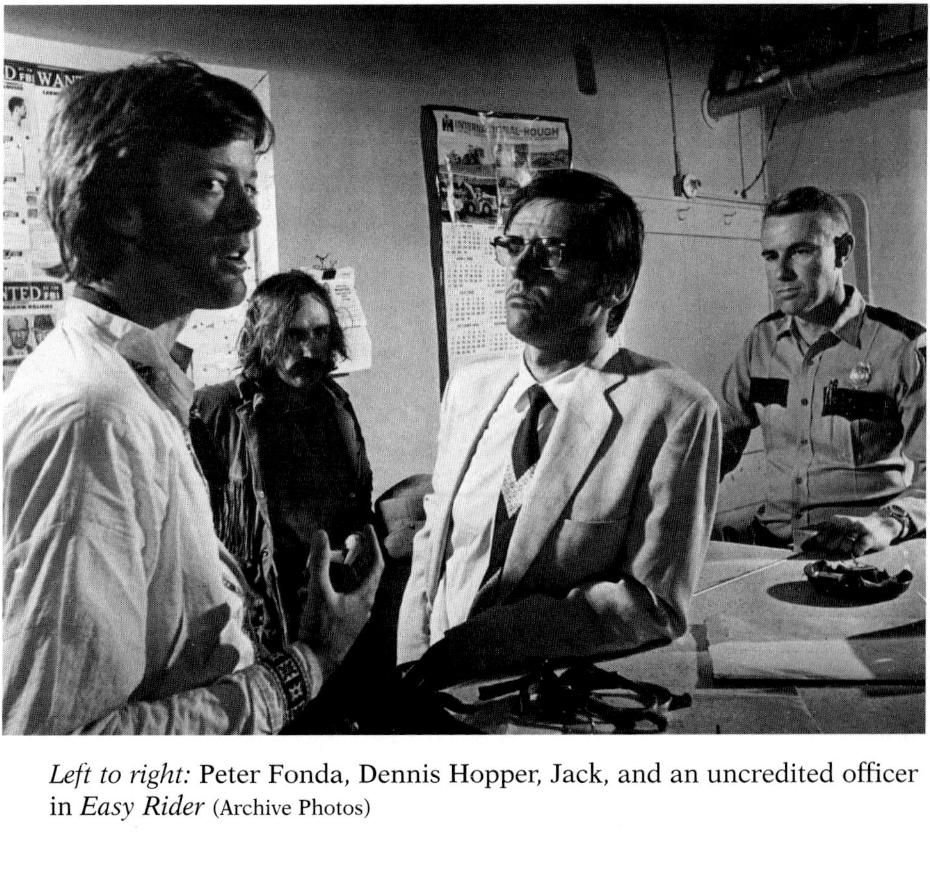

Left to right: Peter Fonda, Dennis Hopper, Jack, and an uncredited officer in *Easy Rider* (Archive Photos)

Jack, Peggy Lipton, and Lou Adler at a party for Sen. George McGovern during the 1972 presidential campaign (Archive Photos)

Michelle Phillips and Jack (Archive Photos)

Jack imprints his footprints, handprints, and autograph in the cement in front of the Chinese Theatre
(Archive Photos)

Jack poses with his daughter Jennifer at the footprints ceremonies at the Chinese Theatre
(Archive Photos)

Susan Anspach, mother of Jack's son Caleb, shown here starring in *Blume in Love* (Archive Photos)

The Sixteenth Street house in Santa Monica that Jack claimed from Susan Anspach (Author's collection)

Louise Fletcher as Nurse Ratched, and Jack in his Oscar-winning performance as Randle Patrick McMurphy in *One Flew Over the Cuckoo's Nest*
(Archive Photos)

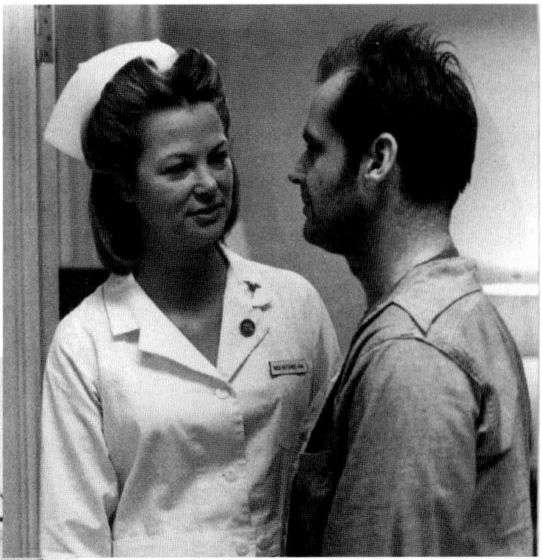

One Flew Over the Cuckoo's Nest
(Archive Photos)

Jack after receiving the Oscar for *One Flew Over the Cuckoo's Nest*
(Archive Photos)

Left to right: Jack, Anjelica Huston, Diahnne Abbot (De Niro's then-wife), and Robert De Niro at the New York Film Critics awards in 1977
(Archive Photos)

The Shining (Archive Photos)

Orson Welles and Jack at the Hollywood Foreign Press Association tribute to Welles in 1981 (Archive Photos)

Jack and Shirley MacLaine with their Oscars for *Terms of Endearment,* hers for Best Actress and his for Best Supporting Actor (Archive Photos)

Jack and Anjelica Huston in happy times (Daily Mirror)

mother-figure, the indomitable Ethel May Nicholson, or Mud, as he called her—short for Mudder or Mother—and he was impressed by the way she had kept her secret to the grave: that he was not her son. Jack's illegitimacy was the reason he gave for taking so long to acknowledge his paternity of Caleb. If nothing else came out of the case of Anspach vs. Nicholson, it had officially established their son's true birthright.

And what a legacy it is. Nicholson insists that everything he does onscreen is in some way autobiographical, but delvers into what makes him tick find contradictions and confusion at almost every turn. In fact, when his colorful personal life is added into the equation, the line between reality and fiction becomes very blurred indeed.

The very starting point of his story, his birthdate of April 22, 1937, provides instant clues to the mystique and the aura. He was born on the cusp, a Taurus caught in the influence of Aries, which makes him bullish and a bit of a ram. Under the Chinese system of horoscopes, he is an ox, which also rings true: "as stubborn as. . . ."

All of this provides an image of a person who has lived his entire life with feelings of a split personality, to such a degree that Nicholson was moved to study "cusp people" in his own search for explanations. According to the encyclopedic *Secret Language of Birthdays*, "the greatest challenge for April 22 people is to control power urges," and as this group includes Lenin the Russian revolutionary and Robert Oppenheimer, father of the atomic bomb, there may be some truth in that. Never one to occupy the pyschiatrist's couch for long, Jack preferred practical explorations of the mind, even to experimentation with LSD. As students of the star signs will verify, the cuspate divisions help to explain his ability to carve the characters he plays into different personality fragments to give them added depth. He is also one of the few major screen actors able to alter his identity from part to part; one Jack Nicholson performance is usually vastly different from the next, while retaining the kind of personal stamp that often attracts the criticism, "Oh, it's just Jack Nicholson playing himself again."

Opposing traits were already evident in his makeup during his last year at school, when he was voted both class optimist and class pessimist, though at that time he had yet to appreciate the complexities of character on which he would draw for his screen creations. His divided nature led him also to the study of existentialism, whose definition seems to sum up what Nicholson has become: "a free agent answerable to no one in a deterministic and seemingly meaningless universe."

Predetermined astrological influences may have provided the outline. Existentialism may have given him some guidelines. Life itself added the boldest brush strokes, and when finally Jack Nicholson in person confronts the world it is as a man of unquestionable charm, intelligence, and capacity for friendship, yet who possesses an indefinable menace.

And who said that when he agreed to play the Devil in *The Witches of Eastwick* it was because he had been practicing for the role all his life?

He did!

HIS identity was ambiguous even from conception. June, the elder of his two "sisters," was his mother—only he did not know that until his other "sister," Lorraine, reluctantly confirmed it for him in 1974. "I am an illegitimate child," he said. "I never knew my father. I didn't learn the truth until I was thirty-seven years old."

Jack appeared philosophical on being informed of this startling revelation and always spoke warmly of the Nicholson women. "I was raised in a very positive environment, and I couldn't have been loved more," he said. "Mud, June, and Lorraine gave me everything they had. I have no sense of feeling betrayed because they kept that secret from me; that was the way society worked in those days. A fourteen-year-old girl just didn't have a baby. How could I ever feel let down? They were my only family and wanted only the best for me."

But according to his friend Peter Fonda, the deception wounded him more than he would show and gave him a "real deep hurt inside; there's no way of resolving it, ever."

The boy Jack—it was John in those days—was born into an uncertain and rather gloomy world. Hitler was on the march and his bombers, summoned up by Franco, were in the process of wiping out the Basques' spiritual and cultural home of Guernica. The exiled Leon Trotsky was calling for the overthrow of Stalin, then engaged in his most murderous purges. A new king was about to be crowned in England, the previous one having abdicated for an American divorcee. Nazi Germany itself suffered a massive blow to its pride when the zeppelin *Hindenburg* crashed in a ball of flames just a few miles from Nicholson's hometown, Neptune, New Jersey, soon after he was born.

The arrival of this bonny, bawling boy had caused considerable consternation. A baby born out of wedlock was a great sin then and a huge embarrassment to the family. Jack appreciated that thirty or forty years later he might never have been born. There was a chance that he would have become just another abortion statistic.

Although Ethel May Nicholson was not a broad-shouldered woman physically, she carried the family—and occasionally her husband, when he was too drunk to stand without support. Hard times confronted her, and she doggedly fought back to make sure her young family never suffered. She was from strong and wealthy Dutch Protestant stock, a religious family from Pennsylvania who virtually cut her off when she fell in love with and married a handsome Roman Catholic, a rakish window dresser and part-time signpainter of Irish descent named John Joseph Nicholson. He was initially a good provider and noted for his smart clothes in the post-Depression days. He won the local Easter parade a couple of times as the best-dressed man, which, in the threadbare thirties, must have put him in the mold of exhibitionist. All through Prohibition, John J. never took a drop of alcohol. Then, Mud told Jack when he was old enough to understand, "he got drunk on apricot brandy after the firehouse baseball game one year and never stopped drinking. Never, never, never."

His liking for convivial company, found only in the male-dominated bars of New Jersey, eventually forced them into a difficult matrimonial situation from which he occasionally evacuated himself to go off on a drifting reconnaissance of the world outside. But no matter where he strayed or how drunk he was, he never betrayed the secret of Jack's birth or the name of Jack's real father.

The two daughters of the marriage had proceeded through childhood and into their adolescence just like a thousand and one other girls in the community. In those days, it *was* a community, and most people knew their near neighbors well. Ethel May was well known and well liked, which certainly helped when she was forced to support the family singlehanded by opening a beauty shop in her own home. Everyone came to her for advice, as if she did not have enough problems of her own to solve. Daughter June, born on November 5, 1918, had inherited some of her father's wanderlust and had a yearning for show business.

A onetime Italian singer with the grandiose name of Donald Furcillo-Rose came out of the woodwork in October 1980 to claim that he and June had been lovers and that he was Jack's father. He put her age at sixteen when she became pregnant. Donald's real surname was Furcillo—he had added the hyphenated Rose for professional reasons—and he claimed that June's age was one reason he had remained silent at the time: Ethel May, who had hoped June would become a Hollywood star, had indeed threatened him with prosecution.

The other reason for Furcillo's reluctance to speak out was that he was already married and had a son, Donnie Jr., although this marriage was in the process of being dissolved. "June wanted to marry, but her mother wouldn't allow it," he said. "So we eloped and married under her stage name [of Nilson]." Jack already knew the family secret by the time Furcillo came forward, and in the absence of a marriage certificate, his version of events remained a matter of speculation. Jack has always declined to accept Donald Furcillo as his father or even to acknowledge the possibility.

In the spring of 1937, June went to Bellevue Hospital in Manhattan to have the baby and then returned quietly to the family home. As the birth was unregistered, there is no birth certificate to confirm the time or the place of Jack's arrival. Ethel May finally gave a sworn statement in 1954 to enable him to get a driver's licence after he had turned seventeen. This document gives his place of birth as Neptune, and that is the birthplace that has gone into many almanacs and reference books. When I asked his agent, Sandy Bresler, for some biographical details, all he would say was "Born in Neptune, New Jersey. . . ."

In concert with Lorraine, Ethel May, and John Joseph, June resolutely began the charade that had already been planned: that the child had been born to her mother and father. If Donald Furcillo was the father, he was no longer around to become involved in his son's upbringing, and even June, masquerading as the sister, left home four years later to become an Earl Carroll showgirl in Miami. Lorraine stayed in New Jersey and married a local boy, George Smith, to whom she remained devoted for the rest of his life. He died in 1986.

At some point, though Jack has never discussed this publicly, he appears to have suspected that all might not be as seen in the Nicholson household. He developed what psychologists might describe as a reluctance to address members of his family by their given names or titles. Mother became Mud; Father became Jack; Lorraine was Rain; and her husband, George, the man who became the father-figure in his life, was nicknamed Shorty. This continued into adulthood, where he had a habit of creating nicknames for his closest friends: Anjelica became Tootie; Beatty was the Pro, Bob Rafelson was Curly; Robert Colbert was Mr. C; and John McEnroe was Johnniemac. Even more telling is the story that, as a small boy, Jack once burst out about June: "Don't let her fool you. She's really my mother." But if he did in fact possess this knowledge in childhood, he buried it so deeply in his psyche that he forgot about it altogether.

John Nicholson wafted in and out of their lives, and Jack's recollections of the man he imagined was his father are tinged with a certain sorrow that he was a chronic alcoholic; Jack remembers scenes on the home front and cooling his heels outside one bar or another with a fizzy drink while his "father" stood inside demolishing neat brandies. But there were some happy moments as well. "I remember the first outing I ever went on alone with him was up to the Polo Grounds," Jack told the *Los Angeles Times*. "I saw Mel Ott hit a home run. I saw Bill Nicholson, my namesake, park one. It was the Giants and the Cubs." But then John J. would be off again on his lonely travels. Jack remembers him as a melancholy figure. Even schoolfriends in Neptune recall that John Nicholson's drinking caused the family some worry. Salesman George Anderson, Jack's classmate in high school, can recall Jack's telling him, "I saw my father yesterday," as if it were an event to be noted. "The poor old guy, I feel sorry for him because he can't help it." When he died in 1958, Jack—by then impoverished and attempting to gain a foothold in an acting career in California—did not fly east for the funeral.

There weren't many secrets in that neighborhood, and it is a wonder that Mud's own was kept for so long. Mrs. Nicholson did rather well in her beautician's business, and when Jack was five they moved from the less salubrious surroundings of Sixth Avenue in Neptune to Fifth Avenue in Neptune City, which was, as Jack recognized years later, a slightly classier address. In fact, he has continually made a point of recording that he was not a boy from the wrong side of the tracks, as some tried to indicate, but that his mother-grandmother made sure they were well provided for. They were never rich, but neither were they poor.

He was still surrounded by women, of course, mostly ones receiving Mud's beauty treatments. That his early life was dominated by female presence rather than male may help to explain his future attitude to women, for which flocks of emerging feminists, and a few of his friends, would berate him. In part, that may be explained by his own view of women formed from those days in Neptune: They should be independent, taking their strength from the inner self and not relying on men, except for moral support—"Mud was like that, a tiny little elephant carrying everyone on her back."

JACK was a fairly typical boy of his neighborhood, well liked by his friends and with the hazel eyes and facial features that remained pretty much unaltered through youth and early life, except for a tendency toward baby fat. No harm was done by the apparent lack of male influence. The heavy hand of a resident father would probably not have stopped him being suspended from school three times, once for smoking, once for swearing, and once for self-confessed vandalism (breaking a rival basketball team's scoreboard because they played dirty; he took a part-time job to pay for the damage). Nicholson recognized later that Mud had given him his head. He appreciated the responsibility and did not do anything too foolish; irresponsibility came later when he was well outside of any parental influence.

Stubbornness was an early characteristic and he would call a halt to any admonishment from Mud. He would storm off upstairs, banging his feet on the steps as he went, groaning, "For cripes sakes." According to Lorraine, he sometimes threw tantrums that rocked the house "like an earthquake." Later he was sorry, and much later he was appreciative. In one of his rare public reflective moments, he looked back on the three women in his early life, Mud, Lorraine, and June, with gratitude because they gave him a good start, independence, and the belief that he could always take care of himself, come what may.

Shorty was also a good guide and mentor for a growing lad, as good a father as any man could want. He was a man of simple tastes who had a down-to-earth view of life that he passed on in an almost unconscious way with an innate goodness that is found among those local pillars of the community who never stray far from their birthplace. True, he was an All-State football player, which gave him some excitement and fun, but he always stayed in Neptune with Lorraine and with Mud.

Jack progressed; school was no problem. He had a relaxed attitude toward learning. He later told Caleb that he got *C*'s in examinations and couldn't see any advantage in slaving over schoolbooks. When he eventually became an overnight star after fourteen years of hard labor in Hollywood, the seekers of his past came knocking on the doors of his teachers and former friends. They usually disappointed everyone by recalling that he was remarkable for his unremarkableness, just another kid on the block; not a hero, not a superstar at sports, not especially remembered for outstanding feats of school bravado. He did, however, make a lasting impression on one dancing partner, who recalled that he had escorted her to the prom and behaved like a perfect gentleman: "He didn't even try to kiss me good night."

A former teacher, Virginia Doyle, who was discovered in retirement in Sherwood Forest, Toronto, remembered him as a clowning, cunning boy who was good enough to get high marks without apparently doing a lick of work. She thought him a most responsible and sensitive young man and then reflected that all his fooling around probably masked his unhappiness and disappointment over his "father." The jollity was a cover for hidden sadness.

An echo: Once in fourth grade, he was sent to stand in the corner, next to the blackboard; while there, he powdered his face with white chalk, and when he turned around he was a clown, beaming a smile at the class . . . the Joker in Batman.

Jack's assessment of his schooldays was covered in his own biographical notes as having "deportment problems," which he later explained in more explicit terms as "fucking up, not in line or as with adolescents nowadays, making a big show that they don't give a fuck, that's bad deportment."

Harry Morris, Jack's principal teacher in his senior year at Manasquan High School, also remembered his clowning and had a vivid memory of him as always being late for history class, which followed gym period. He was, said Harry, always interested in entertaining fellow students, a good dancer, and always involved in after-school events.

Jack disagreed. He only joined the drama group because the best chicks were in plays; he didn't especially like dancing in his mid-teens because he had become too fat; sports interested him, and he was fanatical about basketball. He was never good enough to make the team, but he was always there on the sidelines cheering and managing. He joined the air cadet corps in high school and just after his fifteenth birthday became a part-time lifeguard at the beach—Mr. Cool, with mirrored sunglasses and zinc oxide on the nose. Cool was the thing. The DA and Tony Curtis haircuts were making their debut. The bebop era was just fading, Presley had not quite arrived, and the advance guard of popular fifties music that the kids in Neptune listened to were Johnnie Ray, Ray Charles, and Chuck Berry. Somewhere off in the distance, the sound of Bill Haley was heard. The rock-'n'-roll years were just beginning.

That was the hometown boy.

He arrived at his final year at high school with enough good grades to go to college if he wanted. His old classmate Gil Kenny, who later became a local police chief, said no one thought Jack would set the world alight. "He was a clown, he wasn't serious about anything." He was offered a Du Pont chemical engineering scholarship to Delaware University and might have become a captain of industry somewhere in middle America, balding, bloated, and with a houseful of his own children. However, the prospect of pursuing a largely uneventful career in that worthy but slightly boring structure of management in a giant U.S. conglomerate never appealed to him. "I wasn't filled with a burning desire to make something of myself," he said. After graduation, he hung around Jersey for a year, made money at the racetrack and worked as a lifeguard during the summer. Then he took a certain route leading to another kind of life and ended up famous.

Fame? "So what can I tell you?" said Shorty to the umpteenth magazine interviewer who came to call, looking for the definitive analysis in the search for Jack Nicholson once he had become a star. "You know, he was just a fine kid. Loved his mother. Loved peanut butter and jelly sandwiches. To be honest, I'm getting pretty goddamned tired of talking about Jack. What more is there to say?"

There was plenty, not about the past but what was to come. To get there, there was a quantum leap to be taken, the proverbial turning point in a young man's life when fate takes a hand. It was then that June, whom he still believed to be his sister, reappeared as a catalyst in what would ultimately prove to be the most important decision in his life.

IN THE seventeen years since his birth, June had stopped being a dancer in Miami, become the straight lady to entertainer Pinky Lee for a time, and, during the war, done her bit for the American effort in the control tower at Willow Run airfield in Michigan. Through this work, she met and married Murray "Bob" Hawley, a dashing test pilot who was the son of a wealthy Boston surgeon. They had two children—Murray Jr. and Pamela—and lived in some style in Michigan, with vacations on Long Island, where Jack spent many weeks lapping up the upper-class luxury.

The marriage ended because of her husband's drinking and womanizing so June came back to Mud's house at Neptune with her two children and returned to work as a dance instructor at Arthur Murray's dance center in New York. In the early fifties, she decided to branch out on her own and drove with her two children across America to Los Angeles, where she became a secretary in an aircraft factory and later a fashion buyer at J. C. Penney's.

Jack went west for a holiday in the summer of 1954 and stayed at June's Inglewood apartment with his half-brother, Murray, and half-sister, Pamela, who knew him as Uncle Jack. It was quite coincidental that June, by her search for a new life in California, drew Jack toward what would be the hub of his existence, and at first it was touch and go whether he would stay or go back to Neptune. James Dean had just arrived in Hollywood for his first major role, having been brought from New York by the famed director Elia Kazan to star in *East of Eden*. If Jack had strolled down Sunset Strip, he would have caught sight of Dean at Googie's or one of the other coffee joints where the moody star would meet with Natalie Wood and Dennis Hopper. The Strip at the westerly end of Sunset Boulevard and closest to the film industry was the avenue for poseurs, where every young hopeful—and plenty not so young—hung out to be discovered in one of the dozens of coffee bars that eventually gave way to rock-'n'-roll clubs and then the strip joints of the sixties and seventies. Dean, an early influence on anyone of Jack's age, had little more than a year left of his life and was in regular attendance. That was also the year that Marlon Brando made it very big indeed in another Kazan film, *On the Waterfront*. They were both notorious for racing up and down the Strip on their motorbikes or in flashy sports cars. Warren Beatty was flitting in and out of Los Angeles, visiting his sister, Shirley MacLaine. But this was a world that Nicholson had no thoughts about and no prospect of joining.

In fact, Los Angeles scared him a little, and for the first six months he rarely ventured far from the house alone. When he did go out, he was sharp enough at the pool halls to hustle a few dollars, which he then invested on the horses at Hollywood Park. He bought his first car, a 1947 Studebaker, from his winnings. In his late teens, there were still signs of baby fat, and his rounded face sat under an unruly head of brown hair trimmed to the current style, though not especially trendy. He could be lost in a crowd as just another boy on the block, unassuming and unspecial. His upbringing among women, though, served him well in mixed company. "When I was a young guy, women didn't frighten me," he said. "I was pretty self-confident."

He made the decision—and June did not try to dissuade him—that he would not go on to college. He'd had enough of learning. A self-styled lazy student and with no wealth in the family to support higher education, he saw no point in continuing. Emerging in his mind was the thought that he might become a writer. In the meantime, he earned his keep with a part-time job in a toy store. Nothing more exciting than that appeared on the horizon in his first six months in California, and he was already talking to June about going back to Mud and Neptune.

Then out of the blue he got a job as a mail boy in the MGM studios at Culver City at $30 a week, twice as much as he was paid in the toy store. He was attached to the office dealing with Tom and Jerry, the MGM cartoon characters, who were at their peak and needed an assistant to handle their fan letters.

Well, it was a start. More than that, it gave him the opportunity of lying on the grass at lunchtime, trying to catch sight of Lana Turner's legs.

5

DESPERATION

WHEN JACK NICHOLSON flunked his first Hollywood screen test, he was dismissed with backhanded praise. "You're such an unusual person we don't know exactly how we could use you," a studio executive told him. "But when we need you, we'll need you badly." Instead of rejection, this turned out to be more of a prophecy; it was the mid-fifties, and Hollywood didn't need Jack Nicholson because it hadn't got around to making Jack Nicholson movies yet. But when the new wave of filmmaking came crashing onto West Coast shores a decade later, Jack and his "unusual" persona would find themselves at the crest of the huge roller that would wash away the old Hollywood.

The screen test had taken place at MGM, where Jack saw all the famous movie stars who populated that most famous of studios. To his friends, he name-dropped a few—like Grace Kelly, with whom he fell in love from afar before she ran off to marry her prince. It was Hollywood's most glamorous studio. Louis B. Mayer used to boast that there were more stars in MGM than in heaven, and nowhere had they shone more brightly. Garbo, Garland, Gardner, Garson, and Gable were there—and that was just the *g*'s; but Mayer wasn't what he used to be and had been ousted from MGM by the time Nicholson arrived as a messenger boy in the animation department.

The turmoil that surrounded Mayer's departure epitomized the convulsions of change that were sweeping through the film capital, eventually spawning an underground of new, raw, and raucous talent of which Nicholson was to be part. A new Hollywood was being born, but no one realized it at the time. New arrivals on the street scene were to be the stars of tomorrow, and the mink-lined coffins that were the grand old studios were about to disappear forever.

The money men, the purveyors of soft drinks, the bankers, the lawyers, the agents, and the wheeler-dealers were taking over; the stars themselves, those in a strong enough position to negotiate new financial benefits, were demanding a bigger slice of the cake. As Harry Cohn, head of Columbia, said shortly before a heart attack killed him in 1958, "The lunatics have taken over the asylum." There were many in the Screen Actors Guild who would have agreed with him. Under the old system, hundreds of young actors and actresses at least found regular employment under contract—which meant they were paid whether they worked or not—whereas in 1990 the figures from the guild showed that at any one time as many as 85 percent of its Los Angeles membership was unemployed. For better or for worse, the studio system, created by the moguls three decades earlier and dubbed by its detractors "the slave trade," was on the verge of collapse, though, as Elizabeth Taylor put it so succinctly, "the death rattle seemed never ending."

By the mid-fifties, many of MGM's greatest stars were drifting away, either voluntarily or forced out, as the accountants hacked away at costs. It was not a fun place anymore, and doors were already slamming shut to the hundreds of young hopefuls hanging around outside the studio gates about the time Nicholson began his search for work. What emerged was a far more open industry, less secure for the multitude perhaps, but one that would provide top stars with multimillion-dollar paychecks, which they apparently felt disinclined to share with lesser-known mortals in their trade.

Nicholson almost crept under the wire before the studio system was finally extinguished at MGM. As mail boy, he had picked up the habit of addressing everyone, no matter who, on a first-name basis. Why not? Everyone else did. And when he saw producer Joe Pasternak, the renowned MGM starmaker, approaching him in the corridor one day, Nicholson spoke up: "Hiya, Joe! What about giving me a film test?"

Pasternak was sufficiently impressed to agree. Many other actors had kick-started their careers through similar bravado.

Pasternak arranged for him to be tested. In earlier days, even that formality might not have been necessary for a contract. Nicholson dreamed for a day or two. Then Pasternak's office called him and told him he had failed the test. Joe advised him to join a local theater group to get some acting experience now that the studio training scheme had been abolished.

Other things were happening in Hollywood that affected Nicholson's outlook, both on the film business and on life itself. He had become interested in the culture of the place as he ventured out and made new friends, youngsters in the industry who talked nothing else but films and stars. There was much talk in the coffee shops about the new film James Dean was working on, called *Rebel Without a Cause*; Brando was stunning everyone with his performance in *On the Waterfront*. Talk was intense among the Young Turks, as Jack later called them, and the young actors and actresses roaming Sunset Strip were no different from the youth of America in that they were also a disoriented bunch in search of idols; Clift, Brando, and Dean were providing them with a whole new repertoire of sayings, postures, stances, and gestures.

These were exotic, impoverished days for Nicholson and, above all, big experiences for the boy from Neptune. By now he had left the protective custody of his sister-mother and was sharing an apartment with one of a group of friends with whom he remained close when he became well known. It is one of his strengths that he displays and expects loyalty from a friendship, and those who were still in his life in 1996 had judiciously respected that *diktat* from the start. Several of them went to the Players Ring, an acting class run by Jeff Corey. Luana Anders, who was a bicycle messenger at MGM, urged him to join, and when he turned up in the spring of 1956, he found that other aspirants such as James Coburn, Sally Kellerman, Robert Towne, Carole Eastman, and Roger Corman had exactly the same dream of making movies. Corey was not especially impressed by Nicholson's acting. He said it lacked poetry. Nicholson responded that perhaps Corey hadn't seen the poetry he was showing him.

They were gathering on the Strip in coffee houses like the Unicorn, Mac's, Pupi's, and the Renaissance. When they had no work, which was often, they'd spend all afternoon sitting over one coffee or one Coke, trying to write plays. Other new faces were arriving. Steve McQueen had followed Dean west from New York after three years of casting-call lineups. Paul Newman had just secured his first major film role, with Pier Angeli in *The Silver Chalice*, which was so bad that when it was shown on television in the sixties, he took out newspaper advertisements apologizing to viewers.

By comparison, Dennis Hopper, a mere passing acquaintance of Nicholson's then, had made it big at nineteen, appearing with Dean in *Rebel Without a Cause* and *Giant*. The less fortunate among them, like Nicholson, Robert Towne, and Monte Hellman, got together and literally built their own theater, stealing timber from building sites for their scenery, ripping a toilet from a gas station, and acquiring lighting and sound systems by similar means.

The acting bug had caught him, and he was as determined as anyone to make it. "It was a time of freshness and discovery of what acting was all about," he said. "It was about meeting new people and being inspired by other people's work, or watching an actor or actress who could hardly talk come into a class and then six months later suddenly do a brilliant scene. That was part of the early days."

Friends were important if for nothing else than moral support and sharing food and money. The guys shared their women, too. Jack reckoned he was known among his male friends of that era as the Great Seducer—his own words—but Robert Towne did not quite remember it that way. There were plenty of girls around in Hollywood, but no Hollywood girl wanted relationships with nobodies, and that's what they still were. They worked occasionally and acted and wrote their plays and read Jack Kerouac like Dean had done a couple of years earlier. When someone in the group got a job and became temporarily flush, there would be a red wine party.

One day in 1958 it was Nicholson's turn—an acting job at last, and not just any part, but the lead in a new film. True, it was in one of the cheap, filmed-in-a-fortnight type of movies for which producer Roger Corman was to earn the dubious title of master of exploitation movies; other nicknames like Schlockmeister and King of the Bs also stuck. But it was a start for Nicholson, and a good one.

Corman, a young independent producer, did not know it at the time, but he was about to make a significant contribution to the new Hollywood through the personalities he hired to act in, write, or direct his low-budget films—or to do all three. Peter Fonda,

Peter Bogdanovich, Francis Ford Coppola, Steven Spielberg, Bob Rafelson, Martin Scorsese, and Robert De Niro were among the many who found a toehold in Hollywood by working with him. Nicholson, while rejecting Corman as his "mentor," gladly acknowledges the start and the subsequent ten years' work that he gave him.

Corman was not consciously in the business of developing talent. His job was to produce inexpensive movies for American International Pictures. He never paid more than the basic union rate, but he made available to the newcomers all the equipment and facilities required to make films. They used it and prospered. So did he. The cult value of his early work was purely accidental. A lot of his films were unpretentious junk, but they made money. Nicholson and the others came along for the ride.

The Cry Baby Killer, the film for which Nicholson was chosen as the lead, was typical of the late fifties genre and one of dozens that rode in on the back of *Rebel Without a Cause,* exploiting the cause and increasing the violence. While parents and local burgomasters were complaining about Elvis's pelvic thrusts, the jiving in the aisles at Bill Haley concerts, the sexual implications of Chuck Berry's hip movements, and increasing violence in the American classroom as depicted more responsibly in *The Blackboard Jungle,* the Corman film went straight for sensationalism with advertising that read "from Teen Rebel to Mad Dog Killer." The link with Dean's *Rebel* was deliberate, so that *Killer* could be seen almost as a sequel. Nicholson believed he had arrived: "I said to myself, 'This is it. I'm meant to be an actor.' It was a thrilling feeling."

The movie, however, attracted such critiques as "vapid" and "mob voyeurism." It was so down-market that many theater chains refused to take it. It was filmed in eleven days and cost $7,000 to make. There would be many more to come when Roger Corman got into his stride in the early sixties, turning out back-to-back movies, using the same set and actors, in two weeks or less, with self-imposed budgets of under $30,000. *Cry Baby Killer* did not bring Nicholson any new offers, and he did not work again in films for nine months. He returned to the bosom of his friends, somewhat dejected but still determined.

Martin Landau, a friend of James Dean's when they were both in New York and again when they came to Hollywood, was running acting classes between jobs. Like Dean, Landau had studied the Method approach to acting devised by Stanislavski and modified for the Actors Studio by Lee Strasberg. With Brando and Dean mumbling their way through the currently most talked about pictures, the Method was very much in vogue, passionately discussed and used among the younger actors. Many more established figures were none too sure about it, possibly because the exercises might involve exposing one's private parts, displaying secret and personal habits, and using expletives in the bewildering search for one's inner self.

Nicholson's exercises, devised by Strasberg and taught by Landau, were rather less shocking. He had to sing "Three Blind Mice." "I sang that song in Marty's class for two years. It's an exercise Lee Strasberg invented, the song exercise, for what he called 'the diagnosis of the instrument.' I guarantee I can tell what kind of actor a person is if I hear them do 'Three Blind Mice.'" It was one of many Method exercises taught to help the actor to reach inside the self, unleashing personal emotions in an effort to heighten realism. Over the next few years, Nicholson went from one teacher to another in his quest for knowledge. Eventually, he rejected the Method and developed his own style and approach, which, he insisted, had no set parameters such as those required if the Method was followed to the letter.

In between acting class and all-night parties at the homes of one or other of the inmates, Nicholson slotted in some compulsory Air National Guard service as a fireman, attached to an air-crash firefighting crew. Some have suggested that this was a draft dodge on his part. He, in turn, said it was not; he merely regarded compulsory military service as a waste of time. Back to acting, he found occasional work in television drama, but nothing substantial came along, nor would it for some time to come.

LONG after Jack Nicholson had gone platinum and was in a position to appreciate his altered status, he talked about those early days in Hollywood. "As a struggling actor, you are in a certain kind of desperation," he said. "That's the real danger period for an actor, when you have to consider that there are many other ways in life you could make it. I was basically willing to risk my twenties on acting. It was a big risk. I risked my life."

Jack was on the fringes of Hollywood, appearing almost entirely in low-cost, quickly made horror films and teenage exploitation pictures, mostly with Roger Corman. "We follow the current of the river," Corman explained, "but try to find a new tributary." These new tributaries gave Nicholson the chance to practice some of the underhand humor that eventually became part of his art. With the old B-movie system virtually gone, there was no other place for mediocre talent to apply, and that was how he would be brutally classed. There is no better early example of his ability for natural, laid-back humor than *The Little Shop of Horrors*, in which he plays Wilbur Force—they all had names like that in Corman films—who was the masochistic patient of a sadistic dentist.

"This is going to hurt you more than it's going to hurt me," says the dentist in true written-in-ten-minutes dialogue.

Wilbur replies, "No novocaine. It dulls the senses." The dentist begins his drilling, then pauses for a moment, and Wilbur screams out: "Oh my God, don't stop now."

At the end of the session, he thanks the dentist and says: "I can truly say I've never enjoyed myself so much."

Corman's *Little Shop of Horrors* became a cult classic largely through its star—not Nicholson, but a plant that thrived on human flesh. It devoured human bodies, of which the sadistic dentist was one. Reviewers who took it all too seriously said Corman's movie and Nicholson's part in it were bad filmmaking, bad acting, bad taste, and quite undeserving of consideration. But soon college students came to grips with *Little Shop of Horrors* as a topic for campus debate, and they decided that Corman wasn't trying to hide the fact that it was a cheaply made film, nor was he trying to pass it off as serious moviemaking. It was all intended as a subtle joke.

When Jack saw the movie at the American Film Institute in 1994, he opined: "*Little Shop* looks like a parody. At least in that movie we were intentionally trying to be funny. You know, back in those days, it took three days to make a half-hour television show. Roger Corman wanted to prove that he could film a full-length feature in just two days. So he shot most of *Little Shop of Horrors* in two days. I did all those movies because they were the only work I could get."

The next few films in which Nicholson appeared had none of *Little Shop*'s subtleties. *Too Soon for Love* was, like *Cry Baby Killer*, blatant sensationalism of the still current topic of youth rebellion and teenage violence, yet another sequel to *Rebel Without a Cause* with Jack playing a secondary role in a gang of second-rate, cut-price actors who had clearly been chosen to look like the originals in the Dean film. Two other roles secured in that year, 1960, held better promise but in the end brought him no further progress in his career. The first gave him his debut in a major studio production; for United Artists, he played one more Dean-like character in *Studs Lonigan,* adapted from a successful trilogy of novels by James T. Farrell. Like a number of similar literary projects around in Hollywood at a time when mainstream studios were trying to discover what to do next after the demise of musical and religious epics, it was not a success. *Studs Lonigan* dropped through the floor into a bottomless pit, never to reemerge even for a moment's campus debate.

Tail between legs, Nicholson returned to the Corman factory for another in the psychotic youth genre, *The Wild Ride,* with a cast of three and running a mere sixty-three minutes. Served up as B fodder, it at least provided him with a salary, albeit on rock bottom union rates of around $300 for a full working week, which assured him a place barely above the poverty line.

Financial security became something of an issue at the beginning of the new decade. At the time, he was sharing a house with two friends, writer-to-be Don Devlin and producer-in-waiting Harry Gittes, on Fountain Avenue, a few streets from Sunset Boulevard. It was, in his own description, the wildest house in Hollywood for a time until he moved out to set up housekeeping with actress Sandra Knight, a slender, auburn-haired girl of striking appearance whom he met in Martin Landau's acting class.

Sandra joined the Nicholson crowd in the B-movie circle and was to become a model of the women in Nicholson's future long-term relationships. She was an actress who, like the rest of them, had high hopes. But she was not in the flighty, dumb-blonde mold. She was intelligent, quietly responsible, and capable of holding her own in the group's endless meaning-of-life conversations. Slightly dominant, she admirably fulfilled the mother-substitute role that Nicholson seemed to require a woman to play for stability—as opposed to the more sexually desirable women who figured in his life with frequency.

Jack was smitten not so much by Sandra's looks as by her whole demeanor. Those who were around at the time must have thought he had understated his feelings when he said later, "It was no big-deal act for me. I got married not thinking about it one way or the other; I just loved the girl."

Days of wine and roses and wild, wild parties with Devlin, Gittes, and fellow night owl Harry Dean Stanton became temporarily less important to him after his wedding in 1962. For a couple of years, he settled into the life of a happily married man with Sandra, who was seemingly intent on becoming the loving, homemaking wife. A year later, she produced his only legitimate child, a daughter whom they christened Jennifer, which Nicholson immediately shortened to Jenny. In between minor television roles in series like *Divorce Court,* Jack took to practicing scriptwriting while waiting for work. Nothing came along, and a couple of lean years were in store. Sandra had virtually given up her career to devote herself to the task of keeping house and raising a family, though in that respect the relationship did not mature as she had hoped. The studious intensity of learning a craft together, the long and fanciful discussions about the philosophies of life, and the unorthodoxy of their nightlife did not easily transfer to a happy family home. They grew apart.

Some blamed Jack for wanting to continue the way he had before marriage, which, of course, meant occasional flings with the abundance of available women. It was also in this period of the early sixties that he experimented with LSD. He and Sandra consulted a psychiatrist who recommended treatment with the mind-expanding acid. "The therapist didn't really understand LSD. He had never taken it himself," said Jack. "He gave it to Sandra first, in conjunction with a five-hour therapeutic session, but he gave her the maximum dosage. At one point, she looked at me and saw a demon, a totally demonic figure. For whatever reason, either because it's true about me or because of her own grasping at something, it was pretty bad."

Jack himself spent four hours with the same therapist who administered the drug to him, and he remained under its hallucinatory influence for a further five hours at home. He was blindfolded for part of the time, which had the effect of making him "look inside of himself," and he admitted that he was not ready for the experience and some of the discoveries he made. At one point, he was screaming at the top of his voice; he also relived his own birth, met his fears of homosexuality, and had the most terrifying fright "that my prick was going to be cut off." He said it was all highly graphic visually, especially the part when he was inside his mother's womb. When he got out, he had the feeling he wasn't wanted and that as an infant he was a problem to his family—a feeling he expressed publicly long before he became aware that his sister was really his mother.

Nicholson said he found the trip "enlightening," but the experience terrified Sandra, who turned to religion and became fixed to what he called a firm, mystical path. God was not a subject he could handle with any real heart, nor compete with. Her religious leanings and slightly Presbyterian view of life did not match Jack's own. "I'm not an athiest," he said, "but I'm not really a believer, either." He had, however, opened the doors of perception and was vastly intrigued by the landscape.

Toward the end of the marriage, Jack was trying many things in his efforts to bolster his career, writing furiously and looking hard for the elusive break. The marriage had been good, he said, for two or three years, and then they drifted toward the rocks until they agreed on only one thing, their incompatibility. A mirror image of the way their marriage had developed was captured in that typically frightening Nicholson scene in *The Shining*, in 1980. He recalled: "I was under the pressure of being a family man with a daughter, and one day I accepted a job to act in a movie in the daytime and was writing another movie at night, and I'm in the back in my little corner, and my beloved wife Sandra walked in on what was, unbeknownst to her, this maniac, writing furious and tired. I told Stanley Kubrick [his director for *The Shining*] about it, and we wrote it into the scene. I remember being at my desk and telling her, 'Even if you don't hear me typing, it doesn't mean I'm not writing.' "

His behavior became so bizarrre that Sandra felt compelled to ask him to leave the house. The formal separation was dated April 1, 1967, and the following year they had a "good divorce—nonviolent and nontumultuous. . . . We had come to a real separating of the ways, and it was obvious there was only one thing to do, and we did it very simply."

Sandra moved away, eventually to Hawaii and a new married life, taking Jennifer with her. Jack agreed that she should have custody of the child, and an amicable arrangement was made over visiting rights. He continued to see Jennifer on a regular basis over the years, and she came to enjoy her excursions to visit him at work on film sets.

In 1962, Jack was surely wondering what it would take to get bigger, more important film roles. His next was a Roger Corman western, *The Broken Land*, but it did not light any new fires and died a quiet death. Even so, Jack was not ungrateful to Corman: "He was giving me work when no one else would, and without him I would not have survived."

Corman returned to horror, and Nicholson went with him. Some years earlier, Corman had inspired the onset of his cult following with idiosyncratic adaptations of Edgar Allan Poe classics like *The Tomb of Ligeia*, *The Masque of the Red Death*, and *The Pit and the Pendulum*. Now, he came back to the theme with a script loosely based on a Poe poem, *The Raven*; in fact, the connection was so loose that no one could discover what it was. There were a number of horror stars looking for work who would not want the earth in salaries, and he assembled a notable team of players that included Vincent Price, Boris Karloff, and Peter Lorre. Corman added Nicholson and a couple of attractive females to the cast, and the result was another Corman classic, a comic-strip horror tale, silly in conception but wittily funny. With those arch-weirdos speaking their lines with magnificent mock-seriousness, poor Jack looked sadly dull.

An echo: "There was a radio show called Lights Out," *Nicholson said, recalling childhood nights in New Jersey. "There was an episode about a woman who threw a chicken heart out the window, and the ground started thumping. Of course, unbeknownst to me, the show stole from Edgar Allan Poe, who created the genre."*

Corman called "It's a wrap" on Friday evening and realized that he still had almost forty-eight hours' usage left on the warehouse and sets he had rented for *The Raven*. That left two days available for filming before the sets had to be taken down and returned to the owners. He had a brainstorm, to start another picture over the weekend. He asked Karloff, who was on the payroll for another three days, if he would do it. Yes. He cast Nicholson in the lead role. All he needed was a female. What about Sandra Knight? (She and Jack were still married at the time.) Jack called Sandra and asked if she would appear in a Corman film that weekend. Yes.

"What is the play to be called?" Karloff asked his producer. "And where is the script?"

There was no script. Nor even a title.

Overnight, Corman wrote the start of a screenplay for a piece of nonsense set during the French Revolution and entitled *The Terror*. The cast and crew went to work hurriedly the next morning to shoot what they could on the sets before they were torn down—mostly the scenes involving Karloff, because his were the only words Corman had written.

Corman directed most of the picture, but then turned it over to his assistants. Francis Ford Coppola, then an AIP assistant producer, directed some scenes, and Monte Hellman did some more. On the last day of shooting, Nicholson chirped up: "Look, everybody else in town has shot part of this picture. I want to shoot the final sections." He did, and they all edited it together a week later. The film was a mess, naturally, but Jack, Coppola, and Hellman all had their first try at directing—and in the same film.

All of this racketing around with has-beens and yet-to-bes, filming on rented sets in disused warehouses, ought to have been doomed to failure, even laughed off the screen. Often it was. It was chaotic, certainly, but Corman's pictures always made money, and that was the way everyone was judged. Of his first eighty films, only two went into the red. Yet the chances of failure in the legitimate side of the business were even greater, as Nicholson discovered with a new role that, on the surface, seemed a godsend—to appear in *Ensign Pulver*, the much-discussed sequel to *Mister Roberts*. The original film, with Henry Fonda, James Cagney, and Jack Lemmon, based on Thomas Heggen's novel of the same name, was applauded worldwide. Lemmon won an Oscar for his magnificent portrayal of the coward who becomes a hero. Warner Brothers producer Joshua Logan and Heggen wrote the script for the sequel, and Jack Lemmon was asked to return but adamantly—and wisely—refused. The rest of the cast looked strong, with Robert Walker Jr., Walter Matthau, Burl Ives, Larry Hagman, Tommy Sands, and, albeit in a minor role, Jack Nicholson. It flopped, badly.

Universal pans from the critics gave the film fans, who were already vanishing in droves from the theaters by the mid-sixties, further encouragement to stay away. Heads rolled at Warners.

Nicholson was left smarting and wondering why he had ever strayed from the safe haven of Corman's minibudgets and rented sets.

Although Nicholson's part in *Ensign Pulver* was small, being attached to such a poor movie depressed him intensely. It was also a bad time personally. It was while filming *Ensign Pulver* in the summer of 1963 that he received news that his "sister" June, who had been diagnosed with cancer, had died. She was just 44.

IT WAS a time for reflection in 1964, when the film was released. He was coming up to his twenty-seventh birthday, and his face had already acquired some of the lived-in looks that became one of his trademarks later in his career. He was not what might be described—in comparison with his contemporaries Robert Redford or Warren Beatty—devastatingly handsome or outwardly charismatic. His appearance and demeanor were fairly average and he was not a head-turner for female fans. He kept his hair fairly short and neatly trimmed across his forehead to hide the evidence of recession. He had filled out, too, with broad shoulders and strong though not overly muscular arms. In other words, he was still developing the looks that would eventually make him a character actor.

Nicholson's interest in writing was reawakened by his scriptwriting assistance on *The Terror*. His next project was a screenplay in which he was encouraged by Roger Corman, who thought it was a good idea because, though he personally felt Nicholson showed great potential as an actor, others around him did not always agree. Nicholson teamed up with his friend Don Devlin to write the script for *Thunder Island*, a thriller shot with a tiny budget in the Caribbean. The topical plot was about a corrupt dictator who had been exiled from his Latin American country. Once more, the critics placed his work where it honestly belonged, in the basement of B movies. His next two films, *Back Door to Hell* and *Flight to Fury*, both directed by Monte Hellman, were relegated to the same place. Still, they provided employment; the second also gave Jack a further chance to hone his writing talents, since he both acted in it and wrote the screenplay. The collaboration between Nicholson and Hellman was to continue for two more pictures.

Hellman recalls that they were both toying with the idea of a western and talked to Corman about financing. He naturally said, "Well, if you are doing one western you might as well do two." They agreed and he agreed; so, with an advance check from Corman's company deposited in their bank, they formed Proteus Films, rented an office, bought a couple of typewriters, and began work. Nicholson had an idea already; among other friends who were asked to submit outlines for a screenplay was Carole Eastman, who wrote under the pen name of Adrien Joyce. None of their ideas was really in tune with what Corman had suggested—as Jack described it, "plenty of tomahawk numbers and a lot of ketchup." These were the mainstays of western movies then, especially in the face of competition from such popular television series as *Bonanza, Rawhide,* and *Bronco.*

Nicholson's own idea was to write the first existentialist cowboy story, which would make it a complete departure from the current genre; he was surely right in his assumption that Corman might not see the potential, if such existed. The title was *Ride in the Whirlwind.* Carole Eastman had already written her screenplay, *The Shooting,* on the inspiration of a Jack London story. Its plot was slightly more complicated than *Whirlwind*'s, but it had similar undertones of mythical melancholia.

They collected their actors and actresses, a film crew of twelve, and their livestock and moved off to the Utah desert to begin filming the two movies. Nicholson had an acting role in both.

Eight weeks later, they returned with their films in the can. Hellman began the cut, with Nicholson by his side. Eventually, the finished products were ready for viewing by Roger Corman.

"Interesting," said Corman, as he sat back in his chair and banged his feet down on the row of seats in front of him. "You've done something with a western that I've never seen before. You've made the characters intelligent, and life isn't like that. There's no beginning and there's no end. Audiences won't like that." Raising his voice, he shouted, "There are no Indians. Where are the Indians?"

Hellman cautiously inquired, "Does this mean you don't like them?"

"Oh, sure. They're different. I like them for being different," said Corman. "But who is going to buy them? Tell me that. They just aren't commercial enough. No theater booker in the land is going to take them."

That prediction proved entirely correct. No one did want the films, not in America at least. Nicholson and Hellman had tampered with the popular view of western history and had taken it to deeper levels, failing totally to appreciate that mass audiences enjoyed westerns purely because they provided escapism. Moviegoers did not want arty, philosophical essays. Three, then four months went by, until only two routes for selling the films remained unexplored. One solution was to cut their losses and sell to television. The other was to try Europe, which Nicholson decided he would do. He arrived in Nice full of hope and indeed managed to secure a showing for both at the Cannes Film Festival. Almost immediately a French company made an offer for the European rights. Nicholson accepted and flew back to Los Angeles in better spirits. Bad news followed in his wake; the French company went bankrupt before it could pay out the check.

So even moderate fame still eluded him, and he remained unknown outside a small Hollywood clique. He was now approaching thirty, and he wanted desperately to get an audition for the new movie they were all talking about, in which the star was to be a young man playing opposite an older woman. It was called *The Graduate* and, said Nicholson, they were "auditioning everyone I was having lunch with." He was put up for the role himself but wasn't called back to do an audition.

Dustin Hoffman was unknown in Hollywood, although he had impressed director Mike Nichols with his performances on the New York stage. Also thirty but looking much younger, he was running favorite. The night it was announced in *Variety* that Hoffman had been given the role, Nicholson swore violently and went out and got drunk.

6

EASY DOES IT

JACK NICHOLSON was seriously considering giving up acting altogether shortly before *Easy Rider*—the movie he refers to today as "my Rosebud"—came into his life. "I was a relatively unsuccessful actor who wanted to direct," he admitted. In 1968, he was approaching thirty-two, and the elusive big break at rainbow's end seemed no nearer. True, the word "star" could be loosely applied to him on the basis that he had "starred" in more than a dozen films. The reality was that he could walk into any bar or restaurant anywhere in the world and no one would give him a second glance.

His talisman appeared in the headlights of a large Harley-Davidson when the biker movies roared toward filmgoers of the mid-sixties along with all the other fads of the emergent, decadent age. Suddenly, Hell's Angels were hip, and Nicholson, though never a Hell's Angel or a Ken Kesey/Hunter S. Thompson follower, trailed along in the slipstream until he found his Rosebud through a twist of fate that was truly amazing. When he later declared, "I got lucky with *Easy Rider*—that movie just came out of the blue in an odd way," he neglected to mention that he had been standing in the right place for a very long time.

Before *Easy Rider* made him an overnight star, he had appeared in close to twenty films, written six, coproduced three, and edited or assistant-edited five. Numerically, it was an impressive record, but it did not bear much scrutiny. Nicholson's contribution to the film industry had been almost entirely tied to

Roger Corman's own eccentric career. There wasn't a lot to be proud of in a mixed bunch of movies that were largely exploitation of current trends.

In the end, the sixties counterculture had burst to the surface with surprisingly little resistance. The Beatles had taken America by storm in 1964 and swept Elvis off his pedestal with their mop-tops and pleasing harmonics. Beatniks, bomb banners, and campus peace groups gave way to smile-on-your-brother hippies as the flower children of the postwar baby boom came out to play. Psychedelia burst onto the scene with Sgt Pepper, painted VWs, and Dr. Timothy Leary extolling the virtues of LSD and eating strange mushrooms. The revolution was here at last, and social commentators spoke with alarm about the march of freedom.

In the middle of this explosion of pop culture, Nicholson had become a free agent again. He had parted from his wife in 1967 and moved in with his actor friend Harry Dean Stanton in Laurel Canyon. The Great Seducer was on the loose and quietly and anonymously returned to a more vigorous social exchange. Money was still short and days were long but parties were frequent and red wine was cheap. Thrill-seeking impulses led Jack and his friends to transitory adventures with drugs and women, and it was this period of his life he referred to when he said he had never been in an orgy of more than three people, although he tried ineffectively to promote it a time or two. His parties certainly looked like orgies. "I guess you could call them orgies in the strictest definition," he admitted. "There were a lot of rooms in my house and people could take their private little trips. I don't know what they were doing and I guess that could be called an orgy. But it wasn't where everybody's naked and fucking one another all over the place. I've never been into that scene."

He was writing and acting, but he was still dogged by the need to continue working in cheap, exploitative films in between making do-it-yourself repairs on his beloved VW Karmann-Ghia out on Stanton's front lawn—like a massive brake job to save $50.

Several studios were making biker movies after Roger Corman's runaway success in 1966 with *The Wild Angels*, starring Peter Fonda, Nancy Sinatra, and Bruce Dern. Corman brushed off accusations that it was total exploitation, which it was, of the California motorcyle gangs, full of disgusting gang bangs, orgies, sadism, and drugs. But *The Wild Angels*, which was made on a shoestring budget, had grossed $8 million in no time at all, and other producers began to take notice. (Jack did not appear in the film; Corman had used him as a production assistant.)

Nicholson's initial contributions to the biker craze, *Hell's Angels on Wheels* and *Rebel Rousers*, were insignificant and forgettable. In the first, a critic said, his acting consisted more or less of variations on a grin. Warren Beatty, on the other hand, was making $450,000 a picture and was shooting *Bonnie and Clyde* with Gene Hackman and Faye Dunaway, which turned him into a multimillionaire overnight because he also prised some percentage points from the backers. Steve McQueen had starred in such epics as *The Magnificent Seven*; Robert Redford and Paul Newman were about to start *Butch Cassidy and the Sundance Kid*; Dustin Hoffman was on the verge of international fame and $200,000 a picture after *The Graduate*.

Yet when Nicholson crossed the street again to the legitimacy of a major studio to join an all-star cast for 20th Century–Fox's *The St. Valentine's Day Massacre*, he had only a minuscule role as one of the gunmen, with one line to speak. Asked what he was rubbing onto the bullets he was loading into his tommy gun, he says: "It's garlic . . . if the bullets don't kill ya, ya die of blood poisoning." Roger Corman, for once, had landed a big-budget contract with a major studio and wanted Jack to share his momentary joy of being able to spend it. Bruce Dern said Corman did him and Nicholson a favor by getting them a part, because they both needed the money at the time; Corman arranged it so that their shooting schedules would require them to be available for the first and last weeks of the four-week stint, thus under union rules guaranteeing them a salary check for the full four weeks.

Nicholson got nothing out of it except a few good paydays and suffered occasional touches of melancholia about his work; he was getting "old," yet nothing substantial was in sight. He was his own harshest critic. He kept telling himself that he was as good as anyone around, "but unless someone else says that about you, there's no way of believing in it totally."

While working on the two biker films and his one line in *The St. Valentine's Day Massacre*, Nicholson was also writing another screenplay, *The Trip*, for Corman. Once again, the Schlockmeister was ahead of the field in latching onto the latest craze sweeping through the youth movement; this time, dropping acid. *The Trip* was to be the world's first LSD film, costarring Peter Fonda and Dennis Hopper. Nicholson wrote a part in it for himself, but Corman refused to cast him; Bruce Dern played the role instead. Dern said Jack was "very pissed off" about being passed over.

On reflection, Nicholson remembers this as a difficult time; not only was he facing the task of writing a film about a new subject on which there was very little written research material, he was going through his divorce. "Most of the trauma I was going through at the time is written into that film," he admitted. But there was more: Because of the subject matter, Nicholson could draw on his own experiences of tripping on LSD to describe hallucinations and create visual effects. It was also familiar ground for Fonda and Hopper, who were already good friends. They came to Corman's office and established what would become a long, though intermittent, friendship between them and Nicholson.

The central character in *The Trip*, Fonda's part, is a writer of television commercials who cannnot stand the effect his job is having on his wife, Sally (played by Susan Strasberg), and their marriage. He begins to experiment with LSD in an attempt to obtain more understanding of his problems. In the beginning, the experience is serene and peaceful with lots of idyllic scenes and brilliant colors, but it ends with him being confronted by the nightmare of attending his own funeral. These elements were inspired by Nicholson's own trips during the breakup with Sandra.

Fonda thought the screenplay was brilliant. He took it home with him that night and sat reading the words. His wife, Susan, suddenly noticed he was crying.

"What's the matter, baby?" she asked.

"This script. . . . it's so beautiful, you have no idea. Listen to this." Fonda read a page to her. Though she had never joined him in his LSD excursions, from her husband's descriptions of expanded-mind experiences and images she understood the intensity of his feelings. He said, "I don't believe it. I don't believe that I'm really going to have the chance to be in this movie. This is going to be the greatest film ever made in America."

That statement was a bit of an exaggeration, but it demonstrated just how strongly Peter Fonda felt about the Nicholson screenplay. Dennis Hopper was equally ecstatic. So was Bruce

Dern. "The original script was just sensational," he said. "He injected into it some really way-out visual ideas that no one had ever tried before."

Fonda finished reading and drove to Nicholson's house. They were not yet close friends, more acquaintances. Nicholson was surprised to receive the visit and more surprised when Fonda told him, "Listen. That is the greatest script I have ever read. I think Fellini wrote it."

"Are you serious?" Nicholson replied. "You really understand it?"

"I understand every single word," said Fonda. "It's right on the nose."

However, Corman, who was both producer and director of *The Trip*, was unsure. He wanted certain scenes spelled out, and he could not understand some of the subtleties. Fonda, Hopper, and Nicholson all knew what they meant, and they knew that most of the youthful audience would also grasp their meaning. Corman remained unconvinced, especially about how the multicolored fantasy scenes were to be portrayed. He made changes.

Fonda exploded: "Now it's going to be just a predictable film with a beginning, a middle, and an end. The ending's a copout." When *The Trip* duly lived up to his worst expectations, Fonda made his feelings known by blaming the producers. As he cleared off to lick his wounds in Canada, he spoke of his displeasure: "By trusting AIP [Corman's parent company] to make a beautiful flick, I put my balls on the table, and they got lopped right off."

IN THE months Nicholson had spent writing and filming *The Trip*, flower power had reached its peak and the Haight-Ashbury district of San Francisco had become the Mecca of hippiedom. Naturally enough, this provided AIP with the backdrop for another psychedelic outing, called *Psych-Out*, directed by Richard Rush. The cast again included Susan Strasberg and Bruce Dern, with the addition of Dean Stockwell and Henry Jaglom, and this time there was a role for Nicholson.

The central character is a seventeen-year-old runaway from New York City who ends up in California trying to locate her brother. There, she is befriended by Nicholson, playing a rock 'n' roller who rescues her from the world of LSD. The script gave the producers the chance to create some enticingly colorful kaleidoscopes, largely through the camera work of Laszlo Kovacs; otherwise, there was little in the film about which Nicholson, Dern, or Strasberg would admit to being proud.

It was notable in one respect, in that it saw the development of Jack's romance with the stunningly attractive former model Mimi Machu, who appeared in *Psych-Out* well down the list of credits under the pseudonym of I. J. Jefferson. He had met her previously when she was given a similarly small part in *Hell's Angels on Wheels*, and now they were both unattached and deeply attracted to one another.

An invigoratingly stormy relationship was in the making, and if Nicholson had been gossip column fodder at the time, the writers would have had a field day. Mimi was tall, dark-haired, and strong-willed, characteristics that were largely repeated in all of Jack's long-term partners. She was a little like Sandra Knight in looks and, in some respects, temperament. She was also slightly taller than Nicholson. His friends viewed the affair with interest as it gathered a fair head of steam.

Mimi's sexuality captivated the Great Seducer. Jack, they said, was in love again. As the relationship progressed, it was apparent that Mimi had the upper hand.

Creatively, Nicholson took a step nearer transferring his energies to the other side of the camera with his next project, which was so outlandishly eccentric that it disappeared almost immediately without a trace. The film was called *Head*. He wrote it (and appeared in it briefly as himself) for Raybert Productions, a combination of two dynamic young filmmakers, Bob Rafelson, director, and Bert Schneider, producer.

Head says a lot about the times and includes snatches of Nicholson's wit, such as a line delivered by Peter Tork: "Nobody ever lends money to a man with a sense of humor." It was dreamed up for the Monkees, a totally plastic rock group created from nothing as NBC's teenybop answer to the Beatles. Conceived as a loose parody of the Beatles' films *A Hard Day's Night* and *Help!*, Nicholson's offering, in his first working partnership with Rafelson, was more than that. Between relentless, disjointed images of everything from cowboys and Indians to Vietnam clips, with cameo appearances by Frank Zappa, Sonny Liston, and the star of a former age, Victor Mature, playing a giant called the Big Victor, he managed to write the featured group's obituary.

Rafelson, whose later acclaimed directoral skills were—like Nicholson's acting—still largely undiscovered, had an interest in the Monkees. He and James Frawley had been their virtual creators for the television network and the group had seen some excrutiatingly successful years. By 1968, the Monkees had all but swung from their last branch; their infantile antics were making even the perpetrators sick.

Still, they might have had a few more years left in them, so it was rather courageous of them to accept Nicholson's script. It virtually put them out of business. In one scene Mickey Dolenz calls out to Rafelson, who also appears as himself, "I don't want to do this anymore. It stinks, Bob. I'm through with it." Which he was; they all were. They themselves had been exploited for the purposes of exploitation, and although they had made a stab at the psychedelic scene, it hadn't really come off. In *Head,* Nicholson had kindly provided them with a suicide note, for which Mike Nesmith was eternally grateful. Not many reviewers really saw the point he was trying to make. Renata Adler sat down at her typewriter at the *New York Times* and scolded Nicholson for a "dreadfully written script."

Nicholson was naturally defensive and protective of his own work: "I saw it a thousand and one times, and I loved it. It was the best rock-'n'-roll picture ever made because it was anti-rock-'n'-roll. It had no form, no structure, and believe me, that's a difficult, unique thing to achieve in movies." His assessment was vindicated nearly thirty years later when *Head* was rediscovered, dusted off, and shown on television as a superb example of anarchic pop art.

UNDERSTANDABLY, the myths surrounding the origins of *Easy Rider* are as intriguing as the movie itself. Bert Schneider, the film's eventual producer, told me: "I wish I had $500 for every mistake. I'd be able to retire all over again." According to one popular version of the story, the moment that would finally lead to Nicholson's recognition as an actor came in Peter Fonda's Toronto hotel room in a light haze of vodka late one night in September 1967. The idea for another film came to him like a flash of lightning, and he was so excited that he picked up the telephone and called Dennis Hopper in Los Angeles.

"Wow, I'm glad you called, man," said Hopper, who thought his friend had telephoned to patch up a quarrel they'd had before Fonda left for Canada.

"Fuck that," said Fonda. "Listen to this, man." He outlined his idea for a movie plot, which was basically the story of two California friends who decide to make a once-and-for-all fortune by selling a consignment of cocaine and then set off across the country for marijuana-cum-motorbike adventures.

"Whaddaya think?" asked Fonda. "We'll take the two leading roles."

"Wow, man, that's great. Jesus, that's great, man."

"I'm going to produce this movie, and I want you to direct it," said Fonda. "Will you do it?"

"Gee whiz, man. Are you kidding me? Wow, babe. Jesus that's great. Of course, I'll fucking do it. Wow!!!"

Romantic though it is, that story makes no mention of John Gilmore, a young screenwriter who claimed he told Dennis Hopper about a script he had written called *Out-Takes*. "It was about two guys who make a big score selling cocaine and who take off cross-country on their motorcycles looking for their version of paradise, only to get blown away at the end by a guy with a shotgun," Gilmore said. "Dennis called me to say he wouldn't use my biker script and that they were going to develop an idea that Peter had suggested. All I would have gotten for it was a few hundred dollars and story credit, but I would have been happy with that."

Meanwhile, Hopper and Fonda had turned Peter's idea into a twelve-page outline with the help of Terry Southern, the gifted screenwriter behind *Dr. Strangelove* and *Candy*, who came up with the title *Easy Rider*. Hopper suggested adding another character—"fairly representative, somewhat alienated and ultimately sympathetic"—and thus Southern crafted the role of "the third man," Hanson the alcoholic lawyer. The partners showed the outline to Nicholson and Rafelson, who were in the process of shooting *Head* on the Columbia lot. Rafelson referred it to Bert Schneider while Fonda and Hopper waited in an outer office. Nicholson chipped in with the observation that his biker pictures had all grossed respectable money and made very handsome profits from a low outlay.

"How much will it take to make it?" Schneider asked Hopper and Fonda.

"Half a mill, maximum," said Fonda, but he was ready to negotiate because he desperately wanted to make the picture.

"Okay. I'll give you $375,000. Go and do your picture and come back and show us," said Schneider, who also offered to take the idea to the New York headquarters of Columbia Pictures with a view to arranging distribution of the film. Corman's AIP had already turned *Easy Rider* down because, although they liked the idea of another biker film, the odds were against Hopper's bringing in the picture without problems. Their reaction was pretty typical of Hollywood: What's Dennis the Menace up to now?

There were other imponderables. The partners were talking about having most of the roles, aside from the three main characters (to be portrayed by Hopper, Fonda, and Rip Torn) and a few bit parts, played by real people, not actors. Whoever heard of putting real people into a film?

At quite an early stage, there were reports of trouble from the location work in New Orleans. Torn had finally rejected the pleadings of Fonda and Hopper and pulled out of the project. He wanted $4,500 for the job once he had seen what it entailed, whereas everyone else was getting only a few hundred dollars because of the limited budget.

There were rows between him and Dennis, who could become exceedingly tired and emotional and was already shooting in New Orleans without a script. Schneider seriously considered firing Hopper; the pressure of moving a production team of twenty-three people from state to state, writing the script on the run, and persuading innocent citizens who just happened to be passing at the time to appear in the movie was a heavy burden for all.

Hopper would probably agree that he and the movie were saved by Nicholson, who was sent down by Schneider as a troubleshooter in the role of executive producer. When Rip Torn departed, Schneider offered the role of George Hanson to Nicholson. Hopper objected on the grounds that he lacked a Southern accent, but Schneider overruled him. Mercifully for all, Jack got the part.

"I'd been sent along to watch over the production, primarily because it was an unorthodox production and had some problems already," Nicholson said. "They had gone down to film Mardi Gras live before they even finished the script—had some problems down there between the partners. It was logical for the company to want me just to be there. Then, when they asked, I said, 'Yeah, I can play this part easy.' "

Nicholson brought instant stability to the production by introducing some of the rigid controls he had learned from the Corman modus operandi. He was also responsible for bringing in Laszlo Kovacs, the cinematographer whose filming of the American landscape brought untold dimensions to the movie. Later, he joined in the selection of another of the film's major plus points—the magnificent music performed by Steppenwolf, the Byrds, the Jimi Hendrix Experience, the Electric Prunes, Electric Flag, the Band, Fraternity of Man, and Little Eva.

The themes of *Easy Rider* are free love and excessive drug use in American society, as perceived by Hopper in 1968, with some moralistic undertones about the consequences of such a lifestyle, though only if you are actually looking for them. Otherwise, any tendency toward moralizing is overshadowed by the film's exciting, humorous, tragic, and horrifically violent elements.

The two central characters—Wyatt, nicknamed Captain America (Fonda), and Billy, known as Billy the Kid (Hopper)—embark on a drug deal, selling cocaine in California, to provide the cash to purchase a pair of customized Harley-Davidsons for a journey across America to the Mardi Gras in New Orleans. It is the ultimate biker-drug-sex film, and it owed a lot to Kerouac. Wyatt and Billy saw all America and its split personality; the American Dream and American small-mindedness were typified by their confrontations with a hopeless band of hippies at one extreme and a team of redneck bigots at the other. As Hopper said, "Don't be scared. Go try and change America, but if you're gonna wear a badge, whether it's long hair or black skin, you'd better learn to protect yourself."

After shooting the New Orleans scenes, the caravan moved back to California, then on to Arizona, New Mexico, and Texas before returning to Louisiana. Then they stopped for two months to write and prepare the remainder of the film before taking to the road again.

As he watched Hopper work, Nicholson came to the conclusion that he was working with a genius, flawed perhaps, but a man whose artistry was, and still is, quite awesome. Hopper's direction of *Easy Rider* had much to do with his own appreciation of historical art and his painting skills. The script itself was trendy and repetitive, rather naive, but tuned directly to the youth of the moment.

Nicholson's character enters the scheme of things when Captain America and Billy are jailed by a police chief who regards them as undesirables. In an adjoining cell is George Hanson, a once-well-intentioned liberal who is now equally at odds with the heartland of American society. He awakes from a bender, slow and bleary, and introduces a sardonic charm that jolts the film to a sudden halt and makes Jack a star, instantly.

Hanson decides to join the outlaws after springing them from jail and they continue their pilgrimage on the two bikes. That night, Wyatt and Billy introduce Hanson to marijuana while the three of them are sitting around the campfire discussing the problems of the world. This scene is the most memorable and supposedly dramatic in the picture, the one containing the monologue, on what was wrong with American society, that made Nicholson famous. Filming started well, but Hopper, who was acting, directing, and smoking the props, could not get the take he required. In order to get those few minutes of screen imagery in the can, the three actors finally inhaled 105 real joints of excellent-quality Mexican grass.

The trio became close friends off the set. Fonda was a committed monogamist, but Hopper and Nicholson often went off into the night. On one such escapade they shared a memorable LSD experience. When Nicholson described it later, it was always with the preface that his previous uses of acid had been clinically supervised to avoid bad trips; thus he had "come to terms with things that you perceive would be otherwise impossible—things that help you understand yourself . . . plus if used properly it can mean quite a lot of kicks."

On this particular day, after shooting at Taos, they dropped some acid and took off with two other friends to visit the nearby tomb of D. H. Lawrence. They began hallucinating as they lay at the foot of the grave. Later, as dusk fell, they got sentimental about each other and began to cry. Jack said, "We're geniuses. You know that? Isn't it great to be a genius?" Dennis agreed that it was.

Somehow, a beautiful young woman appeared—this was no imagined vision—and she took them to some hot springs, where they all ended up naked. Dennis eventually went off with her on his own, leaving Nicholson to return alone to their hotel, where he acted out some kind of ritual guarding of their rooms, ready to forewarn of the Indian attack he was expecting at any moment. Still under the drug's influence at dawn, Nicholson found himself atop a forty-foot tree—he had no memory of climbing it—and looking down on a vast meadow, flecked with patterns of multicolored light and rocks that turned into horses, which all filled him with "tremendous emotions."

The first cut of the film ran to more than ten hours. Schneider hired Henry Jaglom to do the final editing, and after ten weeks' hard labor he presented the definitive version of *Easy Rider* to its creators. A print was flown to the Cannes Film Festival for its first major screening. Nicholson was in the auditorium that night when, during his very first scene, the audience came to life and an electrifying buzz ripped around the theater. "I'm one of the few people who was actually present at the moment I became a star," he said. "I mean, I could actually sense it in the audience. It was great."

FEW people in America had paid much attention to *Easy Rider*, but industry insiders who saw preview screenings began to spread the word that Fonda and Hopper had produced a very good film. After its release on July 14, 1969, the establishment magazines began by deprecating the film's free-and-easy attitude to drugs and sex, and especially to violence. It promoted the use of marijuana, they said, although it started with an antidrug message.

The underground and radical publications more readily saw some of the intentions of the screenplay and the overall concept summed up in the movie's slogan: *A man went looking for America and couldn't find it anywhere.* In fact, *Easy Rider* was rather slow to catch on, but when it finally caught the attention of the counterculture, even the establishment newspapers and magazines began to offer up praise.

Hollywood did not care much for it. It was one of those pictures that went totally against the grain of everything that the movie industry believed it stood for. To say that it stood for anything at all was self-delusion; the truth was, the Tinseltown establishment types were just jealous they hadn't thought of it first and made all that money. That was the key—the box office was the final arbiter of success or failure. *Easy Rider* took in $45 million worldwide for an outlay of less than $400,000, and there are few comparable profit-to-cost examples in the history of Hollywood.

For once, when Hopper said "Wow!" it was an understatement.

Nicholson especially won some excellent notices, although Fonda felt that Dennis Hopper's performance had been the best of the three. Reviewers reported glowingly that "an actor named Jack Nicholson . . . is magnificent" and "gave a brilliantly witty performance." The *New York Times* demonstrated how little impact he had made on the movie world until then with the observation that the lawyer Hanson was "played by Jack Nicholson, whose sharp, regular features may be vaguely familiar to kids who go and watch drive-in movies." Rex Reed made the point that Jack's performance would appeal to the average male filmgoer: "There was something so touching about his alcoholic Southern aristocracy, searching for a philosophical grass-roots identity with the new hip and the cool in his faded fifties Ole Miss football jersey, that made them want to revel in their own squareness. There's a nice-guy squareness about Jack Nicholson, too."

The very fact that Nicholson was nominated by the Motion Picture Academy for Best Supporting Actor spoke for itself—even though he lost the vote to Gig Young for his role in *They Shoot Horses, Don't They?*

Curiously, success as an actor placed Jack in a quandary. The day *Easy Rider* opened in America, he had bumped into Richard Rush, director of *Hell's Angels on Wheels* and *Psych-Out*. "What am I going to do, Dick?" he asked bemusedly. "Here I was happily on my way to becoming a writer and a director and this thing just happened—this accident, really.

"Should I become a big movie star or walk away now?"

7

"WE'RE GONNA BE RICH!"

JACK DECIDED to stick to the star trail. Although he was famous, he was far from being rich and famous. Bert Schneider made sure that he received a percentage, albeit a tiny one, of the money that rolled in from *Easy Rider,* but he had plenty of time to adjust to fame before he needed to worry about the complications of how to manage a fortune. He did not know it then, but the chance to be both rich and famous in the style of Beatty, Newman, Redford, and Hoffman was just a few key strokes away.

Bob Rafelson had been toiling with Carole Eastman on the script for a new film, and as it neared completion they began to see it as the perfect way to capitalize on the success of *Easy Rider*. The title of this little opus was *Five Easy Pieces* after a book of elementary exercises for budding pianists. Fortunately, Jack was already contracted to make another film for Rafelson and Schneider, who had taken on a third partner, Steve Blauner, to form a new production company called BBS (Bob, Bert, and Steve). Its aim was to produce intelligent low-budget pictures—the thinking man's Roger Corman movies, someone said. Working for BBS meant that, although Jack wouldn't receive a huge paycheck, he would be making a movie that he really wanted to do.

He desperately needed to be the lead in a film suited to his talents after a disastrous piece of miscasting in *On a Clear Day You Can See Forever* as Barbra Streisand's brother. Vincente Minnelli, a director of the old school, had been looking for a touch of modernity to attract a young audience to his film about psychiatry and reincarnation, and he had a lot of money to spend. Minnelli had seen Nicholson as the hippie rocker in *Psych-Out* and decided to write an additional part into his movie especially for him. He would be a sitar-playing, transcendental character, though with short hair. "Whoever heard of a hippie with short hair?" scoffed Nicholson. He also had a singing part—he had to belt out "Don't Blame Me"—which was eventually left on the cutting room floor, along with about twenty minutes of his spoken dialogue. So much of his part was cut that there seemed hardly any point in leaving him in at all. Rex Reed said that he was "wasted so criminally that he should have stayed in bed," but he appreciated the money while he was waiting for *Five Easy Pieces* to roll off the typewriter.

Rafelson, Schneider, and Blauner had plowed part of the very substantial returns from *Easy Rider* into improved new quarters, which included a fifty-seat private theater. Producers, writers, editors, and directors were to be found walking around the corridors in bell-bottoms, puffing on joints and calling each other "babe" and "doll." The mood of the place, and an indication of what they were about, could be instantly gleaned from the huge posters around the walls in the reception room of blowups of the 1968 French student riots.

More than that, BBS was populated with Jack's pals. "Bob and Carole are among my friends whom I have very familial feelings for; it's like we grew up together," said Nicholson. When he read the script of *Five Easy Pieces*, he immediately saw the possibilities—and the challenge—that the role of Bobby Dupea presented for him. In retrospect, it seems that all his previous acting experience had been aimed toward this one particular target: to be himself in a character role that would dominate a major motion picture. The title was designed to echo with *Easy Rider* (though there were no other connections apart from Nicholson himself and the thematic stance), and although it was devoid of drugs, the sexual content more than compensated for that.

Carole—to Jack, she was Speed—had written the script especially for him, with nuances that would mean something to him and no one else, nuances that could only come from a friendship and working relationship spanning fifteen years. He said proudly to one of the other actors, "They're building this film around me," and he was excited at the prospect.

The biographical elements were there to be discovered, slightly falsified certainly, but nevertheless recognizable. For instance, the famous scene in which Bobby clears a table in a roadside diner because he can't get an order of plain wheat toast was based on an incident in Pupi's pastry shop when he was a struggling actor in Hollywood. For those who did not notice the similarities, Nicholson made a point of mentioning them in interviews; it made good copy and helped with the film's publicity.

Filming began on locations around Bakersfield, California, and Eugene, Oregon, before the cast and crew headed further north across the Canadian border in the winter of 1969/70. Jack brought an explosive sensitivity to the role of Bobby Dupea, a promising musician who rejects a career as a concert pianist to become an oil-rigger; a rebel who, like Nicholson himself, could have had a college scholarship but went to Hollywood instead, who had the chance of a life of comfort and stability but chose a different route. Jack described Bobby as "an extraordinary person posing as a common man." It was another road movie with a Kerouac-style character, depicting a man who had "auspicious beginnings"—a line Jack wrote himself—searching for fulfillment and running into the harsh realities of life.

There were other similarities. Dupea was to be portrayed in many ways as a selfish loner walking out on his family; refusing to tell the girl he lived with that he loved her or to play the role of a caring son. Dupea did not want to be tied down by anything or anyone—which seemed to be Nicholson's own philosophy—and he wanted, above all, to keep on the move. Deep down, however, he actually seemed to be yearning for the stability that steady and better-paid work would bring. Near the end of the film, Dupea's liberation is being challenged because his girlfriend, Rayette, is pregnant, and he is looking for the quickest possible exit. He is psychologically incapable of sticking to stable relationships, and he breaks down in front of his father and admits to disappointment with his life.

Karen Black, who played the abused and frequently tearful Rayette, fell in love with Nicholson, although their friendship remained platonic. She was, however, able to describe the scenario that would be repeated in most of his most spectacular films, where he personally fell in love with his costar. "I was going with someone and he was going with someone, so we never made it," she said. "I think working with someone like Jack, an actor of that quality, turns you on. A lot of leading ladies end up marrying their leading men simply because they imagine that guy as their husband while they are working with him. The next thing you know they are getting married. So we had gotten to be friends, and it stayed like that."

THE "someone" Jack was "going with," as Karen Black put it, was still Mimi Machu. Their relationship had survived all predictions, but it did not prevent an entanglement with another of his co-stars, Susan Anspach, whom Rafelson had originally considered for Rayette. Susan had told the director: "I could never play Rayette as cute and sympathetic. I would have to show a lot more rage and pain. As I don't want to argue with you on the set about it, I'll pass on this one." Rafelson called Susan back to say that this was precisely the kind of strength he wanted in the character of the more liberated classical pianist, Catherine Van Oost, and he offered her that part instead.

Susan, who had just celebrated her twenty-fourth birthday on November 23 and was already the mother of a one-year-old daughter, Catherine, had been the female lead in the Broadway love-rock musical *Hair* and had starred with Dustin Hoffman, Robert Duvall, Rip Torn, Al Pacino, and John Voight on the New York stage. She had given birth to Catherine in Los Angeles after deciding that making films in Hollywood would be more conducive to motherhood than the constant night work and intense concentration attached to acting on the stage. She made it plain to Nicholson and the others in the cast that she did not consider marriage a necessary formality for having children. Hence Nicholson's later description of her as "an avant-garde feminist."

However, he knew nothing about the forces in Susan's life that had converted her to this radical outlook. Susan's grandfather John Joseph Kehoe—ironically, he had the same Christian names as Jack—was a wealthy New York stockbroker who lived in a mansion in Flushing, had other homes in Poughkeepsie and Florida, and enjoyed evenings in the Stork Club drinking with his pal Sherman Billingsley. When his daughter married Renald Anspach, a factory worker, Kehoe disapproved of the match so strongly that he cut them off without a cent.

"I lived with my parents and younger brother Robert in a cramped apartment in Queens," Susan told me. "Our apartment was the kind of place where the landlord could legally turn off the heat at 9:30 at night; my mom cried because it was so dark you couldn't keep a plant there. As a little girl, I used to send for the rosebush catalogue and look at the pictures for hours. As a little kid at Christmas, people would ask what I wanted, and I'd say, 'I'll draw it,' and I'd draw a house. It was always like a magical dream to have a house; to own a house was a big, big symbol.

"I was out on my own at fifteen, so when I was at college I was the first one there in September, I was there at Thanksgiving and often through Christmas. I had no home, I never had the security of a roof over my head. As I got older I didn't care, because I just wanted to act and do my work. I had a nightclub act when I was nineteen years old in which I deliberately put together all these songs with lines about women, like 'Mean to me, why must you be mean to me?' What else did women have except to feel sorry for themselves? The women's movement was about everybody being independent and fair, and that is still my belief. Women had been giving men a hard time because they had no position in the world. They were unfulfilled, themselves."

Nicholson had no time for women's lib. His own image of womanhood was firmly rooted in the uncertain though vital independence that women like Mud, June, and Lorraine carved out in Neptune, New Jersey—uncertain in that times were tough and the future offered no guarantees. "Sometimes I think all women are bitches," he said in one published interview. "Other times I have to admit I can't figure women very much. But sometimes I can't understand myself very well, either." He was still at the figuring stage when he met Susan Anspach during auditions for *Five Easy Pieces* in Los Angeles in the summer of 1969. She was a cool, poised blonde with great dancer's legs and an excellent singing voice.

Nicholson was questioned about the encounter twenty-six years later in his deposition in the case of Anspach vs. Nicholson. Paul Hoffman asked him:

Q Did you meet her before filming began?

A I don't think I did other than maybe a couple of days before. I don't remember actually.

Q And the filming was in Vancouver. Do you recall that?

A Some of the filming was in Vancouver.

Q Where else was it?

A Oregon, up the shore. I think we shot some in Los Angeles. We shot some on the freeway. I can't remember where we shot. I think a bowling alley in California was another main location.

Q Do you recall whether you and Susan Anspach were on the set together at all these different places?

A I might. I could probably run it through my mind. My memory is that she only worked in the scenes, I guess, in the second part of the picture where the family home was, which was shot on that island up in British Columbia.

Q Do you recall how long the filming took place up in British Columbia?

A No.

Q Do you recall at some time during the filming of *Five Easy Pieces* you had a romantic affair with Susan?

A Yes.

Q Did you have a sexual relationship with Susan Anspach?

A Yes.

The relationship that would alter both their lives had started in what was the Dupea family house in the movie—in reality, a forty-two-bedroom seaside mansion on Vancouver Island—after a minor incident triggered a reaction that was pure Nicholson. It was wintertime, and the young actors were passing a cup of hot vegetable soup around their huddled circle during a break in filming. When Jack handed the cup to Susan, he had left a tiny piece of carrot sticking to the edge. Instead of turning the cup around to a clean spot, Susan licked the carrot off with her tongue and drank from the same place.

Nicholson was ecstatic. "You're not an intellectual," he shouted. "You're a sensualist. A fucking sensualist, like me!" The embraces that followed soon afterward found an immediate echo in scenes that Rafelson shot for the movie. Bobby gets Catherine Van Oost into his sights, breaks down her resistance, and starts an affair with her, even though she is engaged to his brother. One exchange between them after Catherine hears Bobby playing the piano showed that sparks would fly:

CATHERINE: Look, you played. I was honestly moved—then you made me feel embarrassed about responding to you. It wasn't necessary.

Bobby: Yeah, it was. Look what happened. I faked a little Chopin—you faked a big response.

Nicholson was asked about the off-set affair in his deposition:

Q How often did you have sex with her during the filming, approximately?
A I don't remember.
Q Did you discuss whether she was using birth control during the filming?
A I don't remember.
Q Do you recall if she told you that she wasn't?
A No.

Nicholson was too engrossed in the movie they were making to pay much attention to matters of procreation. "He would come back from seeing the dailies and he'd be so happy," said Susan. "He'd never say, 'Ansie, we did such beautiful acting, people are going to love this.' He'd never say, 'They shot this so incredibly, the lighting was just great, we all look so beautiful . . . you should see it.' He'd never say that. He'd come back from the dailies and say, 'Ansie, you should see this film—we are gonna be rich. *We're gonna be rich!*' "

He used huge amounts of cocaine. "Bob Rafelson did thirty-nine takes of a bedroom scene between me and Jack," said Susan. "Jack had one toot [of cocaine] every six takes. He frequently left the set to snort cocaine."

The process of shooting the film's ending was typical of the uncertainty that had been evident throughout filming. Jack wanted Bobby to walk off down the street on his own, emphasizing his aloneness. Carole's original script had him dying in a car crash and Rayette weeping at the loss. Rafelson wanted something more prosaic. As they couldn't agree, they filmed three different versions of the ending. Jack, as he always did, deferred to Rafelson's judgment.

The one that the director chose perfectly fitted the Nicholson credo. Driving back to the oil field with Rayette, Bobby pulls into a gas station, goes to the men's room, and looks in the mirror. This is his defining moment: Can he face the prospect of being a father to Rayette's child, or is personal freedom the only imperative? The film ends with Rayette getting out of the car to find out what is delaying Bobby. Unseen by her, he has hitched a lift in a lumber truck and at that very moment is riding off up the highway to God knows where—shivering, for he has abandoned even his jacket in the restroom.

Filming had just wrapped on *Five Easy Pieces* when Mud died of cancer in a New Jersey hospital at the age of seventy-four. Nicholson had visited her several times and found her semiconscious and incoherent. Even if she had wished to tell him the secret of his birth, she was too ill to do so. "I felt the grief, the loss," he said after attending her funeral in Neptune. "There was no hidden grievance between us." Mud had slipped away knowing vaguely that Jack was going to be a star, but she didn't live to see *Five Easy Pieces* establish him beyond doubt as the most effective actor of his kind in America. His performance was immediately rewarded with a second nomination for an Oscar; he did not win, but the inclusion of a relative unknown for the second consecutive year was unheard of in Hollywood.

Critical acclaim also had a pleasant ring to it, with phrases extolling his virtues such as "one of the few gifted movie actors we have" and "a superb performance." *Time* magazine still regarded him as a bit of an upstart, stating that his attempts at humor made him look like a third Smothers Brother and that his laconic manner appeared to be a handy substitute for acting. His audiences were clearly defined, perhaps more so than any other actor's around; they appeared to be generally under thirty, long-haired, with bearded males in the majority, and "intelligent" females, usually blond. They were quite different from the followers of the more conventional actors like Newman and Redford.

Soon after *Five Easy Pieces*, Nicholson's personal life fell into disarray when Mimi found out that there were other women. Nicholson also had the added problem of a huge work schedule, and Mimi was being viewed as the girlfriend of a very successful actor—when time allowed. So Mimi walked out, and suddenly he faced a kind of emotional turmoil he had never before experienced. Now it was his turn to be hurt.

Whereas his parting from Sandra Knight had been "sensibly negotiated," this time he was left with what was, for him, an odd feeling of being "dumped on." "I had been with her for three years, in love," he said. "After she left I couldn't even hear her name mentioned without breaking out in a cold sweat." It preyed on his mind for a time, and eventually he had to work out a kind of therapy to get rid of the obsession. At thirty-three, he was like a lovesick teenager, which was a strange state for a man who had had so much experience with women.

Susan Anspach gave birth to his son, Caleb James, on September 26, 1970. "Jack tried to see me, but I had married someone else and my husband couldn't accept Jack," she said. "I was supposed to meet him in a nearby restaurant on one occasion to talk to him about my pregnancy, but my husband wouldn't let me go. I can still picture Jack sitting there waiting for me. It had tragic proportions."

Susan's husband, Mark Goddard, became the devoted and willing father of her two children. "The Goddards" formed a tight-knit family group who were admired wherever they went. "Mark was so drop-dead good-looking that women used to just stare at him whenever he walked into a restaurant," said Susan. "We were never separated, even when I was making my movies. When Catherine was five and Caleb was three and a half, we did twelve cities in fourteen days. It was crazy.

"I took the family up to San Francisco to make *Play It Again, Sam* with Woody Allen and to Venice when I did *Blume in Love* with George Segal. Someone asked me, 'Are you taking the kids to Venice?' and before I could answer, the director Paul Mazursky, said, 'Of course she is! They're her security blanket.' They came to Kenya to make *The Last Giraffe*. They would go on safari while I was working. We traveled all over the world on publicity tours for the openings: There was Cannes, and there was London. The word 'tribe' isn't p.c., and I do respect that, but I called it my tribal method of child rearing."

Dr. Paul Fleiss told me: "It's very obvious if you've seen Susan with her children that they meant more to her than anything else, even though she had a major career. They had a very stable home for a long time with Mark Goddard; he was the father-figure in their lives, and Caleb was very close to Mark."

For much of 1970, Nicholson was working on *Drive, He Said*, from which he hoped to emerge as a recognized director. The basic story is the conflict between two college students: Hector, the basketball star who starts out with no political convictions, and Gabriel, a radical anti–Vietnam War activist. The interaction of the two students' lives is played against a backdrop of explicit sex and some fairly violent antiwar protest. Hector is having an affair with a professor's wife, whose demands begin to affect his basketball.

Gabriel, meanwhile, receives his draft papers and starts to take large quantities of drugs to make himself medically unfit for service, until he verges on insanity. In this state, he attacks the professor's wife and tries to rape her. Apart from the political overtones, Nicholson knew he was breaking new ground with one specific scene in which he showed full frontal nudity and a fairly complete filming of the sex act itself, still unheard of in the movies.

When he screened it privately for the director of the Cannes Film Festival, he was delighted with the reaction and was duly invited to exhibit *Drive, He Said* at the next festival in May 1971. He flew to Europe nervous and not knowing what to expect. The lights went down, and he sat at the back, trying to gauge the reaction of a packed audience. Word had already gone around about the sex sequence, and recent attempts at peace in Vietnam and Nixon's pledge to end the war generated interest in the political content.

As the film ended and the lights went up, Nicholson got a surprising reaction. First there was cheering, then jeering. Blows were exchanged between members of the audience somewhere at the front, and the whole scene developed into a riot, with people not wishing to get involved in a fight scrambling for the exit. Nicholson said that the level and violence of the response at Cannes surprised him, then flattered him. When he had thought seriously about the reaction, it left him puzzled because he did not see the film as being particularly controversial. It was only later, when he saw that the comment seemed to center around the sexual scene, that he realized the riot would hurt the picture. He reflected, "It was a disaster, this movie, and I knew then it was going to set me back."

THINGS brightened up when Michelle Phillips—the beautiful one among the "California Dreamin'" folk rockers, the Mamas and the Papas—came into his life. She had been married to another member of the group, John Phillips, and they had been involved in a bitter fight over the custody of their child. Michelle had then been married briefly to Dennis Hopper, but her passion for him had begun to cool between the engagement and the wedding. Eight days after their nuptials, she flew to Nashville to perform with Leonard Cohen and telephoned Hopper to say, "I'm not coming back."

Soon afterward, she was seen in various L.A. nightspots with Nicholson, who had been a friend for years. She was depressed, he offered her support, and their friendship developed into a love affair. Hopper received a call from Nicholson to say that he and Michelle were together. "Best of luck, man," said Dennis. "It's over between her and me anyhow."

Nicholson went house-hunting in Beverly Hills. He chose a split-level stucco and wood house in a sloping compound off Mulholland Drive at the top of Hollywood's highest hill. In 1996, he had lived there twenty-six years, spurning all efforts and offers to settle him elsewhere in the movie capital. "This is the dead center of L.A.," he said, "the actual center like if you were at Fifty-fifth and Fifth Avenue in New York."

The eight-room villa was carved into a cliff overlooking not merely Beverly Hills but huge sections of greater Los Angeles. There were breathtaking views of Coldwater Canyon below and the skyscrapers of downtown L.A. clustered together in the smoggy distance. On a clear day, there was a longer view stretching as far as the Pacific at Santa Monica, and from one vantage point there was a spectacular nighttime vision of a hundred-mile carpet of lights in the San Fernando Valley. Schneider loaned him some of the down payment as an advance against his future earnings from his small stake in *Easy Rider*. "I bought it before I could afford it," Jack admitted.

One of the other two houses in the private canyon was occupied by Marlon Brando, with whom Jack shared an entrance and driveway. "The guy on the hill," as he called Brando, had always fascinated him, and he looked forward to the chance of getting to know him.

Nicholson installed his ornamental collection of pigs and began his art collection and, of course, his library. Reading was and is one of his absorbing pleasures, and on the bookshelves in the winter of 1971–72 were *The Complete Works of Marcel Duchamp*, Shakespeare, Jules Feiffer's *Harry the Rat With Women*, *The Primal Scream*, a selection of Hermann Hesse, *Edgar Cayce on Reincarnation*, and *The Group Sex Tapes*. His varied album collection included the Rolling Stones, Cat Stevens, George Harrison's *All Things Must Pass*, Strauss waltzes recorded by Fritz Reiner, and *Rimsky-Korsakov's Greatest Hits*. He parked a new Mercedes 600 in the driveway but continued to use the battered yellow VW.

Michelle Phillips moved in. Jack Nicholson, movie star, had really arrived.

8

NOTORIOUS

FADE IN ON A PARTY in a New York brownstone. Stretched out fully clothed on a king-size bed, Jack Nicholson is virtually surrounded by females of all ages, shapes, and sizes. "All the women at the party were flocking around him, practically crawling on him," said one of the male guests, B. H. Montgomery. "It was very bizarre. One of them was Iman, who later married David Bowie, but some of them were women that you don't think of in a sexual context. I mean, like magazine editors. They were all horny as hell, and Jack just lay there with a big grin on his face."

Dissolve to . . .

A Manhattan dinner party a few years later. "Jack and I both had our eye on this gorgeous, blond Italian television presenter," said Bob Stebbings, a New York corporate attorney. "Jack was so drunk and stoned that he could barely speak, but he got the girl."

"So I'm sexy. Is that a crime? I know I am sexy, but only in the eye of the beholder. It's as simple as that." Jack had the perfect riposte to those who judged him either as a real-life Lothario or as an actor with a reputation for male chauvinism. He had discovered an interesting phenomenon: "Occasionally you play a character that creates such an impression with the audience that suddenly you are affected by the feedback and it can change your life."

The role that did that for him was Jonathan, the mindless sexual malcontent in the 1971 morality tale *Carnal Knowledge*. He kept saying he did not like the sobriquet of antihero, but it wouldn't go away. Antiheroes were in vogue, and they were replacing the romantic heroes of the silver screen. Jack's attitudes to women and sex were to be examined and pigeonholed largely, as he said, because of his interpretation of Jonathan in this very commercially titled film. *Carnal Knowledge* delivered all the sexual promise that the title suggested, with adventures in lust and love sufficient for some to consider it worthy of being banned altogether. It was one of a number of sexually explicit films that appeared in the wake of the abolition of the Hollywood Production Code in 1969—the one that had enforced the unwritten rule that bedroom scenes must be performed with one foot on the floor.

Apart from putting Nicholson's own sexuality under the microscope, the film also put him in line for considerable abuse, appearing as it did at a time when the feminist movement was emerging as a vital force. Women's liberation had finally found its voice, and it targeted men like Jack Nicholson. In fact, he faced attacks on two fronts, because *Drive, He Said* and *Carnal Knowledge* came onto the circuits at virtually the same time. He was being judged not only as Nicholson, the director of a film whose sex scenes had caused a riot in Cannes, but also as Nicholson, the actor in a film in which, said one critic, "the obscenity and abuse of women continued through scene after scene."

But for all the controversy, the complaints, the indifferent reviews and its lack of quality, *Carnal Knowledge* became one of the big box office successes of the seventies, rating among *Variety*'s list of "all-time rental champs" in May 1977. How much Nicholson deliberately fed to the media for the purposes of publicizing the two films is difficult to assess. It was around this time that he made his eminently quotable quote to *Newsweek*: "I've balled all the women, I've done all the drugs, I've drunk every drink," which he later corrected as being a slight exaggeration.

By then, there was sufficient evidence from his own testimony for the headline writers in the tabloids to begin suggesting that their newfound star had secretly been one of the wildest men of Hollywood. Of course, the secrecy was not entirely intentional; it was merely that, since no one had known who he was until a couple of years ago, they had not taken the slightest notice of his private life.

For many before him, the studio publicity machines had swung into creative activity, inventing positive anecdotes and personal attributes about a particular star while concealing the bad ones.

However, Jack was totally honest with preliminary seekers of the Truth About Jack Nicholson. He made no attempt to glamorize himself—even to the point of refusing to wear makeup for his films—and wanted no truck with the kind of artificial biographies that the studios were used to pumping out. At that time, he did not even have a publicist, which in itself was virtually unheard of for a rising star of his stature. He preferred to tell it straight, the way it was, the way he saw it at that precise moment in time. Refusing to play by the Hollywood rules, he made himself vulnerable.

That very point arose in January 1972 when he agreed to do "The *Playboy* Interview"—the first of several for the magazine—and the interviewer put a very valid question: "Why are you spilling your guts in this interview?" Why, indeed? Jack's reply was this: "At this moment I'm wishing I wasn't. Maybe because I know when the interview is read it will add as much confusion as to who I am as it will reveal the truth."

THE MAGIC appeal of Nicholson the actor inevitably became bound up with his personal and private life. In later years, of course, he began to react against this kind of media attention, treating nosy reporters badly and rejecting questions of a personal nature to the point where he would talk only generally about his work. In this early stage, he did not hold back. He told one interviewer who asked if any areas were out of bounds for questions: "Nothing is out of bounds. You take your chance and I'll take mine." The writer recalled that the smile was flashing cynically by the time the aroma of marijuana had disappeared.

Perhaps in order for him to take his place in the higher echelons of his chosen profession, alongside his hero Brando, it was almost a necessary evil that he should allow his fans and the media (and subsequent biographers) to take a look inside his mind. He opened many doors and displayed a few skeletons. At the time, he seemed more willing to do so than some of his contemporaries and, as a result, assumed a much more colorful and controversial hue, which merely served as an additional boost to his rebel image.

Even a cursory glance at the script of *Carnal Knowledge* would warn its reader that it was full of very prickly thorns likely to sting a varied cross-section of the community, ranging from the unofficial censors to women's libbers. In 1971, when it was released, the battle for women's rights was surging forward. The Pill had encouraged sexual freedom; abortion had become available virtually on demand; women were at last being made generals in the U.S. Army; and organized groups of female campaigners brought their fight out into the open. Fresh from their involvement with the male-dominated antiwar movement, women activists—unkindly dubbed political lesbians in Washington—used that experience to establish their own power base, urged on by such strangely inspiring publications as *The Myth of the Vaginal Orgasm* and *The Politics of Housework* until the call was taken up by the popular women's magazines.

Certain groups named their enemies. The likes of Hugh Hefner and Norman Mailer were popular targets. Nicholson joined them on the strength of his performance in *Carnal Knowledge*, which, he went to some lengths to point out, was a performance played to the script. "I didn't editorialize," he responded angrily when challenged. "I was just doing my job, and anyway, it was a legitimate representation of male attitudes at the time. I myself try to duck conversations about feminism; it is all so dehumanizing." A lot of women thought he was making excuses for himself and for his contribution to sexism through the film role.

Carnal Knowledge was written by Jules Feiffer, then famed for his satirical cartoons and commentaries on modern America in the *Village Voice;* he was also a playwright of note and notoriety. The film was based upon a series of so-called cartoon plays that found popularity off-Broadway in the sixties for the way in which they lampooned trendy people who were up to their ears in self-indulgence, be it in sex, material possession, or political causes.

The film was produced and directed by Mike Nichols, the former comedian acclaimed for revitalizing the careers of Elizabeth Taylor and Richard Burton, both of whom he directed in *Who's Afraid of Virginia Woolf?* (Taylor won an Oscar for her performance.) He chose Nicholson for the lead primarily because he thought he possessed the on-screen presence that would bring the part of Jonathan alive with the necessary degree of devious sexuality. In other principal roles, Nichols cast Art Garfunkel, one of the world's most popular singers, and two of the most attractive female stars around, Candice Bergen and Ann-Margret.

Bergen played the soft and sensitive Susan, who marries Jonathan's best friend, Sandy (Garfunkel), although not before she has fallen victim to Jonathan's bedroom technique. Jonathan describes her as "a good piece of ass," and with lines like that the burgeoning women activists were truly inspired to protest.

Jonathan himself marries Bobbie, the Ann-Margret character. She endures his endless string of affairs, which he records in graphic sexual detail, a color slide show entitled "Ball Busters on Parade." While watching the slides, Sandy discovers the betrayal by Susan and his best friend. Eventually Jonathan discards Bobbie with callous disregard for her feelings, bringing her to the brink of suicide.

Spanning the forties to the seventies, *Carnal Knowledge* is about betrayal and, as one unhappy reviewer submitted, "the impotence of the American male." It provided sufficient offensive matter for the American judiciary to become involved. The film had been banned in Georgia, and the producers fought the ruling all the way to the Supreme Court, where the decision was overturned.

Ann-Margret was nominated for an Oscar as Best Supporting Actress and was bitterly disappointed not to win. She blamed the controversial subject matter, plus a great deal of "jealousy . . . which was to me incredible. I was shocked. I think it was horrendous to overlook the work that was done, and I wish people could get rid of all their prejudices and jealousies and just see it as a piece of work." She praised Nichols to the hilt and was similarly enthusiastic about Nicholson; both knew she was extremely nervous about doing the part in the first place.

"Jack just went out of his way to be helpful," Ann-Margret said. There was one scene that stuck in her mind. While lying on a bed, she had to psych herself up emotionally to portray her fear of rejection by Jonathan. Nicholson solved the problem by bouncing violently on the bed, throwing pillows at her and yelling at the top of his voice. "I actually got frightened of him. I thought he was going out of his mind," she said. "It was just so unselfish of him to help me like that."

Nicholson's character runs into trouble in the very last scene, where he visits the apartment of a prostitute, played by Rita Moreno. Having put his women through various forms of sexual and emotional humiliation, he is now virtually impotent himself. The words Moreno speaks as she indulges his fantasies so he can achieve an erection are tantalizingly provocative: "You are a real man . . . [with] an inner power so strong that every act no matter what, is more proof of that power. That's what all women resent. That's why they try to cut you down. It takes a true woman to understand that the purest form of love is to love a man who denies himself to her . . . a man who inspires worship because he has no need for any woman because he has himself. And who is better? More beautiful, more powerful, more perfect—you're getting hard—more strong, more masculine, extraordinary, more robust—it's rising, it's rising—more virile, domineering, more irresistible. It's up in the air."

The film ends with the camera close on Jonathan's smiling, leering face, reveling in the fantasy world in which, throughout his life, he has expected his women to join him. It was only a movie, as Hopper would say, but the aftermath contained elements of realism for Nicholson. He suddenly found himself being allied with the character to such a degree that he was being questioned deeply about his own sexuality and his attitude toward women. However much he tried, he would never quite live it down, and his mercurial private life in the ensuing twenty-five years merely added to the image.

Carnal Knowledge provided him with the burgeoning reputation as an extreme sexual being. Nicholson himself consolidated that reputation through his most revealing interview with *Playboy.* Its frankness seemed to surprise even the highly experienced interviewer himself, contributing editor Richard Warren Lewis, who asked that telling question: "Why are you spilling your guts out?"

For instance, when Lewis made a fairly innocuous reference to the theme of *Drive, He Said,* Nicholson's explanations turned into an admission of certain sexual problems he had experienced in the past: "Some critics think that I oversimplified by reducing everything to sex, but if you look at the real facts of your life, you'll find if you're not releasing your sexual energy you're in trouble. If you take a trip and you're away for three days and you don't relate to a chick, then pretty soon that's all you're thinking about; within three days in a new town you are thinking, 'Why can't I find a beaver in a bar . . . ?' It's not that sex is the primary element of the universe, but when it's unfulfilled, it will affect you."

Nicholson gave as an example his own recent experiences prompted by the collapse of his long-standing relationship with Mimi Machu. "It ended before I was ready to be out of it. She felt that it wasn't worth her time; she'd had it. It was all very sudden, very abrupt, and I was unprepared. I couldn't cope with all that emotion that was released as a result of being cashiered."

In the weeks that followed, and in spite of his workload, Nicholson subjected himself to sexual therapy to get over the broken relationship. The therapy, based upon the very positive themes of the Austrian psychologist Wilhelm Reich, was structured to eliminate sexual hangups, . . . "to soften and relieve the holding areas of what Reich described as body armor, which comes from pleasure denial or pleasure fear." Nicholson explained: "When you dam up energy, sexual or otherwise, you begin to devour yourself. Our society is unhealthy, according to Reich, because we tend to fragment and separate sexuality. We talk about it in terms of scoring; we have ass men, tit men, cunt men, and lip men. These are partialisms."

This brought the conversation nicely to the subject of *Carnal Knowledge*, because wasn't that exactly the subject matter of the film? It was, Nicholson agreed. Jules Feiffer, whose *Playboy* interview had appeared in a previous issue, had mentioned that he had written the line, "Guys don't really like girls" for Jonathan. It was something Nicholson took issue with because it was only true of some men. "I have an equal number of male and female friends," he said, "and I have many nonsexual relationships with women. I am not trying to get into the pants of every woman I'm interested in. . . . Jonathan in *Carnal Knowledge* is exactly the opposite. I don't think he knows how to communicate with women beyond screwing them."

Nicholson agreed that he had gone through the same stage himself and had experienced a lot of infantilism sexually. "When I began sexual activity in earnest, my point of view was simply to try to seduce everyone I could. At that time, I had trouble with *ejaculatio praecox*. A lot of men have this problem. I had it almost exclusively until I was twenty-six or so. You find yourself making it with a chick and, like, you poke her eight times and right away you're coming. It's a chore trying to go through to the second orgasm and not lose your erection. In desperation you find yourself getting the chicks off without balling them through manipulation of some kind, or you find yourself getting with another chick to share the load with you and to keep yourself from saying, 'I've got a major problem here, man. I'm not fucking for shit.'

"I would never tell you this story now if I was still in that situation. I didn't know the story when I was there. I'd say to myself, 'Well I haven't balled anybody for three days and I'm filled up,' and then I'd have a premature ejaculation, which is really a form of impotence. The root of it all was some kind of pleasure denial; it was pretty unsatisfactory for the women involved. Somehow, in the sexual experience, I was making the woman into a sort of a mom—an authoritarian female figure; that made me feel inadequate to the situation, small and childish. I indulged myself in a lot of masturbatory behavior. I solved none of these problems in therapy. I worked them out for myself, but any of them might reappear."

The sexual scene in general, at least in London or New York or Paris, had taken on startling, new, libertarian tones. Swingers and swappers, singles bars and one-night stands were the norm rather than the exception. Nicholson admitted that there were people around—especially outside of Hollywood and the upper-middle-class set of New York—who were not part of the pervasive sexual environment. *Carnal Knowledge*, though, was about very social New Yorkers, professional men meeting women and having cocktails, having affairs, and constantly judging and rejudging their own sexuality—trying to find some substance in it, trying to make conquests with it. There were millions of men like that in New York and cities all over the world. "Excluding the nonsexual person, I think we must assume that the characters played by Artie Garfunkel and myself are probably far more representative than most people care to admit. Obviously they don't represent people who live in a rural area; a man couldn't be as openly promiscuous as Jonathan in a small-town environment. He would be branded a social outcast and considered predatory."

Given Nicholson's insistence that he did not editorialize and simply spoke the lines, it was a strange blurring of realities that shook him when women activists—and men who saw him as some kind of hero—clearly responded as if Jonathan were the true Jack Nicholson. Nicholson was stuck thereafter with being cast in magazines and newspapers as a leering rebel with two basic aims in life: to fight the establishment and to have lots of women. But it was a picture of his past in many ways; his life had now, when he was thirty-five, become a touch more settled through the positive influence of Michelle Phillips. But Michelle was not a slippers-by-the-fireside soul, waiting by the kitchen sink for her man to come home from work. She was still a free spirit and a model of the age, a woman on the move and one who needed a career of her own so that she wouldn't be the slightest bit reliant on others, especially men. She entered her relationship with Nicholson on "agreed terms," in that neither wanted to be completely tied down.

"I told her up front, 'Look, I don't want to constantly define the progress of this relationship. Let's keep it instantaneous.' It was working beautifully," said Nicholson. "I had spent a certain amount of time completely unattached, and I found that being with someone makes me enjoy my achievements more. I liked sharing things . . . and I discovered that expanding sexuality was not most satisfied through promiscuity but through continuously communicating with someone specifically."

Marriage was discussed, but it was not a proposition that either especially desired, and perhaps especially not Michelle, who had been rather troubled of late by relationships that had become more demanding than she wanted. Asked by reporters about his matrimonial intentions, Nicholson responded: "I don't have a marriage policy." His view was that there seemed little point in anticipating matrimony until it finally became a reality.

The perception was correct in Michelle's case, and they never would come to the point where marriage seemed the right thing to do. Like his previous "communication" with Mimi Machu, this one had its tempestuous moments, often through Jack's inability to stay totally faithful. Perhaps fortunately, they were able to slam doors in each other's faces; Nicholson had acquired an adjoining property, the smallest house in the Mulholland Drive compound, where Michelle could find peace during trying times. "He bought it to try to save their relationship," Robert Towne remembers. "She seemed to be wanting to get out of the affair—a few of us had seen it coming—so he thought that by having her own place she could retain her independence. He was trying hard to keep her, but I could see it wasn't going to work."

Two years after they got together, Michelle decided that she and Jack had drifted apart, largely because of his workload. The affair ended without bitterness or malice, and Michelle moved in with one of Nicholson's best friends, Warren Beatty, reprising what happened when Michelle left Hopper and found companionship with Nicholson. Michelle and Beatty both felt guilty, but they need not have worried on Nicholson's account. He said that they did exactly the right thing in the way they broke the news. Beatty's parents would have been proud of the way their son handled the situation, Jack said. And Michelle, "being the lady that she is, took the trouble to call and ask if I had any feelings about them going together, which I did have—I thought it was fabulous because I am fond of them both. Michelle is a real stand-up lady, incapable of anything dishonorable."

Anyway, it all worked out for the best, because Anjelica Huston was about to come into his life. And if at that moment Nicholson seemed less inclined toward the rakish behavior of past years, there were still some high-profile events waiting in the wings.

PROFESSIONALLY, the year of *Carnal Knowledge* continued with much the same frenetic work schedule as the previous twelve months. He made two more films in quick succession, both of which were with former Corman employees in the rebel alliance at BBS.

The Hollywood establishment was both annoyed and fascinated by these upstarts from independent studios who were trying to break the mold of ultimately disastrous "family audience" pictures, for which demand had ended long, long ago. In the end, the establishment won because the upstarts were eventually carried off by fame and fortune to the point where they would join the old guard. After that, the only sign of their rebellious past lay in a certain superficial unorthodoxy—such as wearing sneakers with their evening suits.

For the time being, Nicholson remained with them in the backwaters of the rebellion, loyal to his BBS comrades. He rejected a role in *The Great Gatsby*, which went to Robert Redford, and similarly turned down an offer from Fred Zinnemann for the lead in the film of Fredrick Forsyth's novel *The Day of the Jackal*, because he did not think the character of the Jackal was suitable for his style. He still talked about concentrating his efforts toward directing—the road taken by Coppola and Bogdanovich with very profitable results.

He certainly confounded the pundits by his next film appearance, especially given the type of films he had turned down. He agreed to play the lead in *A Safe Place*, produced by Bert Schneider and directed by his old friend Henry Jaglom, who had appeared in *Drive, He Said*. This was Jaglom's own first attempt at directing, and he persuaded one of Nicholson's idols, Orson Welles, to costar. The film was about the generation gap, a phrase in such common usage then that it could be applied as a reason for anything—except, perhaps, this particular film, which critic Derek Sylvester described as "an indigestible mound of yesterday's lukewarm whimsy."

Jack had been charitable enough to take on the role for an old friend. He did the same thing the following month for Bob Rafelson, who brought him an intriguing script called *The King of Marvin Gardens*. Nicholson saw instantly that it was in the typical Rafelson style, an enigmatic drama unlike anything that had gone before. Given a touch of luck and a fair wind, it might just capture the audience's imagination as *Five Easy Pieces* had done. At best, it required courage for an actor at such a crucial stage of his career to take it on, but Nicholson did not need to be asked twice. Another of his compatriots, Bruce Dern, joined him. The result was another movie that received "cult status": lots of intellectual analysis but very little reaction at the box office. Nicholson and Dern were highly commended as players providing, in the words of one review, a "superb metaphor for the American Dream—the dream of getting rich quick with a minimum of effort and a maximum of manipulation."

EVEN before those two movies were released, Nicholson jerked himself back on course with his agreement to take a leading role in *The Last Detail*, written by Robert Towne from Darryl Ponicsan's bestselling novel. Towne sent him a proof of the book before it was published, along with an outline for the script. It was a powerful story with strong characters. Jack knew immediately that audiences would like him in it, and events proved him right. The audiences loved him as Billy "Bad Ass" Buddusky, one of two career sailors given the task of transporting a seventeen-year-old recruit from their base in Norfolk, Virginia, to Portsmouth, New Hampshire, to begin an eight-year jail sentence for theft. On the five-day journey, Billy decides to give the young man one last look at life out of sheer disgust at naval officialdom.

The journey develops into a long party of whoring and drinking and swearing, and, largely due to Nicholson's riveting performance, the film achieves a near-perfect balance between tragedy and comedy. It also earned him another Academy Award nomination, but not the Oscar itself—which turned out to be one of the few acting accolades he did not receive for his treatment of this part. Billy Buddusky ran up against the establishment because of his foul language. Columbia, which was financing the movie and releasing it onto the national circuit, even postponed production because executives were nervous over the amount of cursing; they wanted the number of swear words trimmed. Robert Towne refused. Servicemen swore. There was no getting away from that; for some men, every sentence contained an expletive and he could not see the point in cutting the number of "motherfuckers" from forty to twenty. If the word "motherfucker" caused offense, it would cause it whether it was used once or forty times, and the script called for it to be used forty times.

Director Hal Ashby and Nicholson both agreed, and eventually the film went ahead without any major surgery to the script. The lack of cooperation elsewhere, however, did cause further delays. Columbia sought permission to film Nicholson in a drunk scene on the steps of the Supreme Court in Washington. Chief Justice Warren Burger refused, apparently because he had heard that Nicholson had signed a petition for the impeachment of President Nixon. The film's crew was barred from two other locations, and the navy did not provide a great deal of help either, since the brass viewed the subject matter with considerable disdain.

The film brought new praise for Nicholson and confirmed his pattern of not allowing himself to be typecast. Each character he had played since the lawyer in *Easy Rider* had been vastly different from the one before, though all were roles on which his own casual style could be overlaid.

As Mike Nichols had already observed: "He is so good because he brings part of his own life into virtually every scene." He refused to become a Hollywood commodity in spite of the financial rewards that more commercial films offered. Money was secondary to the type of role he would accept. After *The Last Detail*, Robert Evans, who was unsuccessful in getting him for *The Godfather*, would make him an offer he could not refuse—and for which he would take a ninety-degree turn for another enigmatic characterization.

The role was J. J. Gittes, and the movie was *Chinatown*.

9

CHINA SYNDROME

JACK HAD FIRST MET Anjelica Huston when she was a little girl. He had lost touch with her after she moved to Ireland with her mother and did not set eyes on her again until she turned up at a party on Mulholland Drive when she was twenty-one years old. In the intervening years, Anjelica had developed into a striking young woman, a photographer's model with Renaissance features and skin like luminous porcelain set against the ebony of her long, silky hair. Nicholson's playboy instincts were instantly aroused: "I took one look at her and thought, 'There is a woman of obvious grace and refinement. She's got class, real class-s-s-s.'" By the time he was making *Chinatown* with her father, this observation had been tried, tested and converted into the makings of a serious relationship.

The frisson that this triangular situation initially generated among a young woman, her lover, and a domineering father provided *Chinatown* with a powerful undercurrent that helped to make it a classic. Nicholson explained: "I had just started going with John Huston's daughter, which the *world* might not have been aware of, but it could actually feed the moment-to-moment reality of my scene with him." He was referring specifically to one line where the Huston character, Noah Cross, says to Nicholson's private eye, J. J. Gittes: "Are you sleeping with her?"

In addition to its themes of incestuous sex and political intrigue, there was another secret behind the Nicholson characterization in *Chinatown* in that he modeled it sartorially as a sort of memorial to the man who he still thought was his father, John

Nicholson. However, in filmmaking terms, the most significant of all the relationships that happened during the making of *Chinatown* was the coming together at last of Nicholson and Roman Polanski in a professional capacity; the mercurial little director brought to the film a moodiness that turned it from something confusing and average into a work of heroic proportions.

Polanski had left America after his pregnant wife, the actress Sharon Tate, and four other people had been murdered by the drug-crazed disciples of Charles Manson at Polanski's rented home in Beverly Hills in August 1969. The murders had caused the Polish director extreme mental torment, which was exacerbated by rumors that his unorthodox lifestyle was somehow responsible for the massacre, even though he was abroad at the time. Nicholson stoutly defended him and asserted that the "moral majority was out to punish [Polanski] because his wife was murdered."

The two men spent a good deal of time together in the winter of 1972, skiing at Gstaad, the Aspen of the Swiss Alps. Polanski taught him some of the finer points on the piste and, since they were both unattached, introduced him to the conviviality of the après-ski scene. A few months later, Nicholson called Polanski and suggested he should get his "ass over to Los Angeles pronto" to direct a new Robert Evans movie for Paramount, called *Chinatown*. It was his for the asking.

CHINATOWN was the quintessential 1970s movie, embodying some of the major themes of that decade, such as corruption and conspiracy, and commenting metaphorically on Watergate. Robert Towne, during moments of depression on the making of *The Last Detail* when it seemed that Columbia might scrap the whole thing because of the foul language, had dreamed of becoming a director. Bob Rafelson told him he should stick to writing, he was good at that, but Towne had conceived a detective story which he decided he would write and direct himself.

Although born in Los Angeles and the son of a wealthy realtor who had been involved in the L.A. land boom, Towne was a committed conservationist. His *Chinatown* story evolved from research he had conducted into the life of William Mulholland, the pioneering engineer after whom scenic Mulholland Drive was named. Mulholland had brought water to the desert regions of the L.A. basin in 1913 by constructing a 250-mile aqueduct from the Owens Valley in the Eastern Sierra Nevada range. The desert had bloomed, and many speculators had grown rich. Towne based one of his main characters, Noah Cross, on Mulholland but made him a scoundrel rather than a visionary.

His second source of inspiration was a pictorial essay headlined "Raymond Chandler's L.A." in *New West* magazine, evoking a Los Angeles that had almost disappeared. As Towne turned the pages, he felt a sense of loss and realized that he could combine the two themes in a movie that "preserves much of the city's past on film." He would set the story in Chandler's thirties, but retain the Mulholland element from the early 1900s. It would be called *Chinatown*, not after the place but after "Jake Gittes's fucked-up state of mind."

The writer approached his old friend Robert Evans, still the boss at Paramount. They went to dinner at Dominique's, and Evans listened to Towne's idea for a new screenplay, liked it instantly, and gave him $25,000 to proceed with an outline. Evans was, incidentally, also seeking a starring role for his new wife, Ali MacGraw.

There was a proviso to the deal, however. Towne could not direct. Evans said: "This ain't no Roger Corman outfit, you know. This film will cost big bucks. I will want a name director." Towne was in no financial position to bargain. One thing they were both agreed upon was that they should offer the leading role, that of the detective, to Jack Nicholson who was brought in almost from the beginning and was able to offer his thoughts as Towne went along.

A year passed.

The Last Detail was a success, and so was *The Godfather*, which Evans had produced and for which Marlon Brando was up for an Oscar. Evans, Towne, and Nicholson were flushed with pride for different reasons, and great expectations now rode on the bulky script Towne had produced for *Chinatown*. Enter Polanski after the Nicholson telephone call, which had been followed up by a firm proposal from Robert Evans. Evans had also been the backer of Polanski's satanic drama *Rosemary's Baby* and was an old friend.

Polanski's return to Hollywood was greeted by a rather mixed reception, ranging from welcoming handshakes to sidelong glances that said, "What in hell is he doing back in town?" The Sharon Tate murderers had only recently begun their prison sentence, and memories were fresh. Polanski hated the Hollywood syndrome and was paranoid about the personal attacks he had suffered, having been branded a megalomaniac by some of his former colleagues.

He discovered that few of his old friends were still around, which made him even more miserable. He noted also that LSD and the hippy lifestyle that had abounded when he left had faded somewhat. Cocaine and Quaaludes were now the favored substances.

In one of his *Playboy* interviews, Nicholson had already admitted that he had used cocaine but said it did not seem to do much for him; cocaine was in vogue "because the chicks dig it sexually." "The property of the drug is that it inflames the mucous membranes, such as those in a lady's genital regions," he said. "That's the real attraction of it. In his book, *My Wicked, Wicked Ways*, Errol Flynn talks about putting a little on his dick as an aphrodisiac. But his conclusion is that there isn't such a thing as an aphrodisiac. I sort of agree with him, though if you do put a numbing tip of cocaine on your cock because you're quick on the trigger, I guess it is considered a sexual aid." Later, he made some corrective statements to the effect that, although he had made these observations, he was certainly not advocating the use of any drugs.

Nicholson believed that all Polanski ever wanted was to make brilliant movies; he dreamed of art on film. He could never be swayed in his support for Polanski's creative side, though he admitted he did find him a trifle wearing at times. Robert Towne disliked him, not so much as a person, but for his I-know-better-than-you attitude and his abrupt decision to make substantial changes to the script that Towne had been working on for almost two years. Polanski conceded patronizingly that it was a masterful screenplay, brimming with ideas and packed with some sensational dialogue; hidden away in the two hundred pages there was, he thought, a powerful movie.

"But it's too long and complicated. There are too many people in it. It wants stripping down to more manageable levels," Polanski told Towne over lunch at Nate 'n' Al's. "It cannot be filmed as it stands. I am going to take over and rewrite it from start to finish."

"No you're not," said Towne.

"Yes he is," said Evans.

"It should be trimmed," agreed Nicholson.

Towne insisted on making the changes himself, and Polanski went back to Rome while the cuts were made. He returned to discover that the script was almost as long as before, and he was still unmoved in his opinion that there were too many characters who were graphically painted but only confused things and added nothing to the action. Polanski still wanted to do the film; for one thing, he needed the money, and Evans had promised him plenty. He agreed to spend two months with Towne on a rewrite, and they worked long hours for eight weeks until a new draft was finally complete. For moments of relaxation, and to get away from Towne's infuriating habit of finding things to do other than write, like taking his sheepdog for a stroll, Polanski began taking flying lessons at Santa Monica airport. Evans was growing concerned, and Nicholson was getting flack from everyone, especially Polanski, who had moved temporarily into his home on Mulholland Drive. Evans eventually rented a small house for Polanski on Sierra Mar with a soothing waterfall and swimming pool, where he was able to put the finishing touches to the script.

Polanski had altered the thematic base of the story so that it had a very definite Chandleresque quality, with shades of *The Maltese Falcon* and *The Big Sleep*. Nicholson's character, the private detective J. J. Gittes, was in the mold of a smartened-up Humphrey Bogart, smoother and less inclined to talk from the side of his mouth, though still rather monosyllabic. It was a brave 30s piece, allowing Jack to utilize the image of photographs and descriptions of his own father-grandfather, John Nicholson, dapper and smart in his flashy clothes that won him the best-dressed man prize in the Easter parade.

The story was still complicated. Gittes is a cool and cynical former police detective who once worked the Chinatown district and is now out on his own as a private eye largely in divorce actions. He is hired ostensibly by a wife who produces evidence to show that her husband is involved with another woman. But then the story fragments along several different, and eventually converging, paths as Gittes realizes he has stumbled into something big, with subplots by the score—corruption reaching into high places, violence, sex, incest, and death.

The action and the corruption were centered around a huge reservoir, and *Chinatown* provided a feast of nuances, symbolic and real. Towne blurred the facts about the Owens Valley land speculation scandal and added a fiction about a woman who carried a shameful secret.

THE ACTORS who were to join Nicholson in the venture were the subject of almost as much preproduction discussion as the script itself. Ali MacGraw, whom Robert Evans had wanted for the lead, had since decamped with Steve McQueen, who had been her costar in *The Getaway*. Evans then sought Jane Fonda, but she turned it down without discussion—"I'm fed up with people telling me how good Jack Nicholson is"—so he cast Faye Dunaway as Evelyn Mulwray, the beautiful though seriously damaged woman who has borne a daughter as the result of being raped by her own father, Noah Cross.

At the rock-bottom fee of $50,000, the signing was one of the bargains of the decade, but Evans had known that Dunaway needed the work. When she arrived for the first day of principal photography on September 28, 1973, she was, understandably, in no mood to be slighted further. Her volatile temperament, coupled with Polanski's, which had earned him the nickname of the Little Bastard, set the scene for an explosion, and in fact there would be several.

One such occurrence was recounted by Polanski himself. It happened when a loose strand of Dunaway's hair kept catching the light during a scene. The hairdresser made several attempts to flatten it, until Polanski went over to Dunaway and, distracting her in conversation, grasped the offending strand between his fingers and pulled it out, hoping she wouldn't notice. Dunaway burst forth: "I just don't believe it. He's just pulled my hair out." She stormed off the set, with Evans running behind trying to persuade her to return.

Dunaway complained, "That little shit wouldn't talk to me about the part. He would explain nothing and give me no clue as to the motivation of the character. What was I supposed to do . . . read his mind?" When she repeated her question to him about the motivation, he screamed: "Motivation? I'll tell you motivation. All the money you're being paid to do it. That's motivation." Freddie Fields, the mega-agent who represented Dunaway, demanded an apology from Polanski, who gave one half-heartedly and then ruined it by adding, "She's nuts anyway." The star was not pleased, and the Little Bastard was lambasted with some more well-known phrases before work resumed.

Nicholson remained cool. He arrived late a few mornings because early calls were never his forte; old habits die hard, and he was still a night owl, sometimes on the prowl. Occasionally his eyes were bloodshot. Life's like that, he would say; people have late nights, even in the movies; sometimes their eyes get bloodshot, and sometimes they get baggy. So what? He never cared much about how he looked, and in *Chinatown* he spent half the picture with half his face covered by plaster and bandages after Polanski, doing a Hitchcock and playing a bit part as a knife-wielding punk, slit his nose. It looked so effective that some viewers thought it was a real wound.

Peace remained between leading man and director until the very last day, when there was a basketball game on television that Nicholson particularly wanted to see; the Lakers were playing the New York Knicks. Polanski was retaking a shot and could not get it right, because of some complex lighting. Between takes Nicholson kept running back and forth to his dressing room to find out the score, until finally the Little Bastard screamed for him to return.

"I told you we wouldn't finish this scene," Nicholson shouted.

Polanski came back: "Okay, if that's your attitude," and then called, "It's a wrap," hoping that Jack would realize the scene had not been shot correctly and stay until it had been. On this occasion, however, he did not. The Lakers game had gone into overtime, and he shuffled off to watch it. Polanski stormed after him, barged into his dressing room, and smashed the television, which exploded with glass shattering everywhere.

"You are an asshole," he fumed at Nicholson, grabbing what was left of the television set and hurling it out the door. Nicholson also delivered a few choice lines. Later, as they were driving home, they pulled up together at some lights. Jack was in his old VW. They turned and looked at each other. Nicholson mouthed the words, "Fucking Polack." Polanski grinned. Nicholson grinned back, and the fight was over.

When *Chinatown* was finished, Nicholson knew instinctively that he had done a good job. This was confirmed when Robert Evans called him to view a rough cut. "Mogul," said Nicholson, "we've got a hot one. Get those checks ready." Then he called his friend Bruce Dern. "Hey, Dernsie," Nicholson jibed, "I think you'd better retire. I got it all covered, babe—know what I mean?"

The critics were not entirely at one in supporting this opinion. Though they raved about Nicholson's acting, some reviews indicated that they were stumped for appropriate words to describe *Chinatown*, not knowing quite what to make of the undercurrents. There were those who could not resist drawing their readers' attention to the "lurid violence," which suggested, they said, that Polanski was still possessed by the Manson Family murders at his home and his exploration of depravity. The film took off. It was a box office success and received eleven Academy Award nominations for everything from technical merit to acting, with Nicholson and Dunaway nominated for Best Actor and Best Actress. Robert Towne converted his nomination into an Oscar for his outstanding script. But for the moment, an Oscar still eluded Nicholson.

HE WAS happy and cheerful, however, and the mood was not entirely because of his new acclaim. He could now name his own price, and the figure he had in mind was $750,000 a picture plus a piece of the action.

He was happy most of all because Anjelica Huston had just walked into his life. For all his prowling around town with Warren Beatty "skunk-spotting," he was a romantic at heart. He needed to be with someone on a semipermanent basis, although his serious love affairs had also been punctuated by bursts of one-night stands. He boasted to one friend in early 1973 about a highly paid fashion model who was arriving that weekend for a secret assignation. "Jesus," he said proudly, "she's flying ten thousand miles just for a weekend with me."

Anjelica was also a model, having rejected the acting career mapped out by her father. She was slender and willowy, taller than Nicholson; her long hair fell neatly around a classically oval face, and her eyes seemed to have a natural outline, even without makeup. She was also taken by his eyes. "And who isn't?" she said. "They were kind; his whole face lit up when he smiled." He was drawn to her natural sophistication, which was very similar to her father's; as Lauren Bacall said, they could look equally at home and at ease somewhere in the wilds of Africa or in formal clothes at a hunt ball in Galway, where Huston had his castle.

Nicholson's reputation had preceded him; she was fascinated by this older man who was as enigmatic as her father and, by all accounts, just as big a womanizer. As soon as their eyes met, they circled each other like gladiators and became engulfed almost simultaneously by each other's presence.

Jack was in awe of both her father and her father's father, the late Walter Huston; they were two of his old-time heroes. Bogart had nicknamed John Huston "the Monster" while they were filming *The Maltese Falcon*, and this titan of the film industry did indeed dominate a room just by being there. Actors who worked with him were always ready to pass on a horror story about their experiences. Some still blamed him for Clark Gable's death, for having pushed the star into doing his own stunts for *The Misfits*. They believed this had contributed to his heart attack at the end of the film. Others accused him of pushing Monty Clift over the edge in his search for perfectionism during the making of *Freud*; the actor became a shambling, sweating wreck as the director insisted he deliver a long lecture in one take, ruining Clift's confidence and hastening his decline into the drug haze that killed him.

Huston was undoubtedly a psychologically cruel man, but many also testified to his lovableness and generosity. Anjelica loved and hated her father for many of the same reasons given by those who worked for him and who, incidentally, saw more of him than she did. She had also shared the suffering of her mother, Ricki, who witnessed some of his most boisterous bouts of womanizing and gambling before and after they became legally separated in 1959.

John Huston was still married to his third wife, Evelyn Keyes, when Anjelica's mother, Ricki Soma, became pregnant—not with Anjelica, but with her brother Tony. A quickie divorce in Mexico enabled him to marry Ricki before the baby was born. Ricki was then nineteen years old, Huston forty-four. They first met when she was a child of thirteen, the daughter of his friend Tony, who ran a restaurant on West Fifty-second Street in New York. When they met again at David Selznick's home, Ricki was eighteen, a stunning classical beauty who had already made the front cover of *Life* magazine, which classified her as the modern Mona Lisa. Anthony was born in April 1950, and Anjelica arrived just over a year later, in July 1951. At the time, Huston himself was mosquito-swatting in the heart of the Belgian Congo with Bogart and Katharine Hepburn on location for *The African Queen*. Shooting was momentarily interrupted by the arrival of a runner from Butiaba. There was no other form of communication, and it had taken him three days to get to the film crew, bearing a telegram from Ricki's mother announcing that the baby had arrived and that mother and daughter were fine. Huston read it silently and stuffed it in his pocket, then carried on filming the scene.

"For heaven's sake, John," cried an exasperated Hepburn. "Tell us the news. Is it a girl or a boy?"

"It's a girl," said Huston.

Anjelica was often separated from her father, especially after her mother's departure from the marriage. Her early years were spent on Huston's 110-acre Irish estate, St. Clerans; Ricki chose to live in a cottage on the grounds, and Anjelica was taught by local nuns. Her parents split up when she was eleven, and she went to live with Ricki in London, where she was educated at the Lycée Française in South Kensington and at Holland Park Comprehensive. When she was sixteen, her father virtually forced her into acting, casting her as a fourteenth-century French heroine in *A Walk With Love and Death* and announcing that decision to the press before he even told his daughter. It had been a demoralizing experience for a young girl, and Anjelica had shunned acting ever since.

This, Jack Nicholson surmised years later, was just a man clumsily dealing with events in a difficult father-child relationship. Anjelica tackled it courageously, and her father said that, in spite of her fears, she had great talent; she did not agree. She was petrified and for years to come constantly rejected any further thoughts (and plenty of opportunities) of becoming an actress. She saw even less of her father, until tragedy moved them closer together in 1969 when her mother was killed in a car accident in France at the age of thirty-nine. As Huston admitted to Hal Boyle of Associated Press a few months later: "Anjelica was frantic after Ricki died. I just didn't know how to reach her." As the grief subsided, Anjelica went off on her own to try a career in modeling.

In 1973, she was lonely again. A relationship with photographer Bob Richardson, who had captured her as a model for *Vogue*, had just ended. She was more at peace with her father than she had ever been, though the relationship was still tenuous. She accompanied him to the party on Mulholland Drive, where, gazing into Nicholson's eyes, she saw kindness and warmth.

They saw a great deal of each other during the filming of *Chinatown*. It was apparent to Nicholson's closest friends that he was falling in love with the stylish, sophisticated lady who appeared his exact opposite in the way she dressed (impeccably, rather than in crumpled slacks and sweatshirt) and in her aloofness, which was sometimes mistaken for snobbishness.

Before the year ended, Mulholland Drive had become the focal point of her life. She had no other, as it happened, because she did not seem intent on pursuing her modeling career. She had come into Jack's life at exactly the moment he was seeking that superior female figure that seemed so necessary to his psyche.

Soon, she would rarely be away from his side.

10

SHOOTING THE CUCKOO

SWOOPING LIKE A HAWK, Jack Nicholson flew down Ajax Mountain with skis for wings. "Anjelica would be at the bottom waiting for him to come down," said an Aspenite who has known them for twenty-three years. "She never wore any makeup, and she always looked anxious, which is understandable. Jack skis like a kamikaze. He hasn't got great style, but he's a very strong skier, and he can be a total wild man on the mountain.

"He's not into chic, up-market dressing with a $1,000 ski suit and all the accoutrements. He dresses in what look like army fatigues and a big old down parka with a fur-trimmed hood; very funky. He doesn't seem to care how he looks, and you would not recognize him unless you saw his face."

Nicholson's next-door neighbor in Aspen for many years was Elizabeth "Pussy" Paepcke, the Chicago philanthropist whose vision of creating an "Athens of the West" had turned the old Colorado silver mining town into a ski resort with an admirable cultural life. Pussy and her husband, Walter, were the real pioneers of Aspen, but Jack and his friend the actress Jill St. John were the first stars to discover its charm and start a stampede that would turn it into Hollywood-in-the-Rockies.

"When Jack and Jill were the only celebrities, no one bothered them," said my source. "There was only one club in town in those days, the Paragon, in the center of the Hyman Street Mall. That was it; there wasn't anything else except for the bars. Like most of Aspen, the Paragon was Victorian, and as you walked in, there was all this gorgeous velvet, period furniture, and stained glass windows. Jack would always sit in that first room, sit by himself—I never saw him with anyone, not even Anjelica—smoking and drinking and relaxing with his sunglasses on. No one went over and interrupted him. Aspen natives, for want of a better term, have always prided themselves on the fact that they leave celebrities alone. I think Jack likes people; he just doesn't like stupid people."

Nicholson needed a place like Aspen to escape from the Hollywood madhouse. Activity had been nothing less than frenetic in recent months, during which he had overlapped filming *Chinatown*, seeing *The Last Detail* come to its New York premiere in January 1974, and holding endless talks with a small group of other directors and producers knocking at his front door. His telephone never stopped ringing, and the doors were always open to his select but not small band of friends for whom, in his spare moments, he liked to arrange entertainment. He was a great organizer of junkets to first nights in Las Vegas (Sinatra, Torme, Midler), or concerts in New York, or ringside seats at major sporting events, or skiing at Aspen or Gstaad. Opportunities, social and professional, were there for the taking, and he was making the most of everything.

He was incapable of saying no with conviction; he would shake hands with anyone who showed tentative signs of recognition, and he seldom refused to sign an autograph. One of his friends in that set observed candidly that it was if he was afraid he would wake up the following day and find everything back just the way it was in 1967.

And as people with new money often do, he swung violently through the gamut of extreme generosity and high spending to nothing short of meanness. The house, the Mercedes, the skiing trips, and shopping excursions with Anjelica set him back thousands, and he dug deep to help out friends who were less fortunate; yet according to Roman Polanski he was stingier than W. C. Fields, usually on inconsequential things. He kept the Mercedes in the garage and used the yellow VW except when going out with his pals: "I couldn't shove my friends in the back of the VW." They received VIP treatment, with his tapes of the Rolling Stones, Duke Ellington, or Ray Charles blaring away while they indulged in a selection of booze and food from the backseat bar, which always held a correctly chilled bottle of his favorite champagne.

Helena Kallianiotes, who had small roles in a couple of his early films—she was a belly dancer in *Head* and the neurotic hitchhiker in *Five Easy Pieces*—came seeking sanctuary after her marriage broke up and stayed on as his "totally platonic companion," personal assistant, housecleaner, and nagger. "Jack has always protected me—even from the beginning when I showed up at his house with a black eye," she said.

Nicholson retained possessions and memories from his past; he threw every single review he could find about any of his films into a huge drawer. People stayed in his life, too. "There were always lots of friends around," said Helena, who moved into the Mulholland Drive house he had bought for Michelle Phillips. "Not hangers on or bloodsuckers, just genuine people. If he liked something he'd bring it home, whether it was a lampshade or a person. Two or three houseguests were around in any single month."

During this busy period he hired Anne Marshall, daughter of actor Herbert, as his secretary, and they enjoyed a tempestuous but friendly working relationship. He would get mad over minor events, while remaining laid-back if the world was falling in around him. His habit of losing things was a frequent irritant for them both. He lost seven wallets in the space of a year. Once, in Rome, he telephoned Anjelica, who was in London, to ask if she had packed his comb; he couldn't find it but didn't want to go out and buy a new one if it was there.

THE YEARS of shuffling were paying off, and the autumn of 1973 had marked his final departure from that protective, familial environment that had maintained him virtually throughout his career, first with Roger Corman and then with BBS. He was now able to connect his directorial interests with the work he accepted. European directors had always fascinated him, and he would soon find himself working with three of the most discussed and controversial, Michelangelo Antonioni, Ken Russell, and Milos Forman.

The first was Antonioni, who called Nicholson to talk about his top-secret new film, *The Passenger*, even before Jack began filming *Chinatown*. It seemed a prestige approach from the man who had recorded such a bizarre commercial success with *Blow-Up*, a murder mystery set to the beat of Swinging London, rather than his usual habitat—a humorless world of sentimental dismay. Even so, one reviewer commented that *Blow-Up*, starring David Hemmings as a photographer-stud, was "not a mystery but a think-in on the difference (if any) between fantasy and reality."

It was more in the director's interest than in Nicholson's for the actor to become involved, because Antonioni badly needed a bankable star to raise the financing for his new project. The disastrous flop of his last, *Zabriskie Point,* had put him at a low ebb. It took him months to raise the cash, and he succeeded only with Nicholson's name on a contract.

His producer, Carlo Ponti, who had taken note of Polanski's enthusiasm for Jack, was also keen to secure the financial viability of *The Passenger* to help keep at bay the line of creditors who gathered daily at his offices over the Piazza Aracoeli in Rome. He had also noted a new trend emerging in Hollywood, loosely termed packaging, which meant putting together at least two big names who would appeal to nervous distributors and lure the fans back into the half-deserted theaters. Such efforts were badly needed.

In 1973, *Variety* reported that between 1969 and 1972, the major studios had lost $600 million in aggregate. Annual attendances had fallen from 4.06 billion in 1946 to 820 million in 1972. Packaging big names in highly hyped films was taken to quite extraordinary lengths, and by the mid-seventies the major distributors were loathe to back a film without a star partnership. Still, that was not necessarily the answer. One of the most expensive was the packaging of Burt Reynolds, Gene Hackman, and Liza Minnelli in *Lucky Lady,* it was not a success. However, for actors like Nicholson it meant fatter paychecks and the promise of joint billings with the biggest of names.

Ponti and Antonioni teamed Nicholson with the awesome, liberated sex princess Maria Schneider, fresh from her nude entanglement with Brando in Bernardo Bertolucci's controversial essay on male sexuality, *Last Tango in Paris*, a smash hit. With Jack and Maria, Ponti had two of the hottest actors around. Even rumors of them appearing together brought the gossip columnists out in force, though after the several miles of column inches she had endured in the aftermath of *Last Tango*, Maria refused to speak to any of them, much to the chagrin of the publicity department of MGM, the studio that was putting up most of the money.

Jack and Maria Schneider were old friends. He admired her for her company, her body, and her ability: "I always thought of her as a female James Dean, a great natural. Tony Richardson [the director] once told me he asked Maria what she thought of me and she said, 'Jack is a professional. He likes to know what he is doing. I do not.' "

Anjelica needed to be an understanding companion. She had joined Nicholson for part of his location work, which took him to

London, Germany, Spain, and back to New York. She had seen it all before with her father.

The film itself, which Antonioni had cowritten, featured Nicholson as a TV reporter who is fed up with his own life and switches identities with a dead man. It had the dramatic potential of *Day of the Jackal,* but it was a typically obscure Antonioni piece and the drama became secondary. Even Nicholson admitted that some of the gripping, melodramatic sequences were underplayed because of Antonioni's insistence on achieving visual effect at the expense of action. It was clearly not going to appeal to mass audiences.

The director's well-known habit of using actors as items in his cinematographic landscape or furniture in a room, speaking lines and not acting them, was perhaps becoming passé. Nicholson did not mind that too much. He also put up with the director's tantrums, two or three a week. "That's why he's good," said Nicholson. "He drives you crazy when you're working for him, but he's been one on the greatest influences on filmmaking in the past three decades. They told me I was the first actor who got along with him in twenty-five years, probably because I gave him the performance he wanted. The one you see is exactly what he wanted."

Unfortunately, by 1975, Antonioni's film artistry did not command the instant applause it had when he was the darling of the avant-garde, although success with him could never be judged in financial terms. Carlo Ponti's creditors did not agree. *The Passenger* was received with little enthusiasm. Jack liked it, however, and defensively commented that "I know people who have managed to live out double lives."

The Passenger was the first of Jack's four films that would be released during 1975, which meant he was working virtually nonstop almost to the end of 1974. His next date, though, was hardly taxing. British director Ken Russell signed him for a cameo appearance in Pete Townshend's rock opera, *Tommy*. He was the singing Harley Street specialist, and this second attempt at musical rendition remained in the picture, unlike his first for Vincente Minnelli. Nicholson's presence in *Tommy* was brief, but it paid $50,000 for two days' work. He saw old friends and met lasting new ones: The film had Tina Turner as the Acid Queen, Oliver Reed, Keith Moon, Roger Daltrey, Eric Clapton, and, of course, his former costar in *Carnal Knowledge*, Ann-Margret.

Anjelica was with him when he heard he had been nominated as best actor at the Cannes Film Festival for his portrayal of Billy

Buddusky in *The Last Detail*. They hopped on a plane to be there and do some unabashed politicking and glad-handing. He smiled innocently when they handed him the award.

IN HOLLYWOOD, a new package deal was in the making, one to set the town humming. Nicholson and Beatty were being brought together for a film directed by Mike Nichols. Jack's old friend from *Five Easy Pieces*, Carole Eastman, had written the script of *The Fortune,* and with that kind of lineup, funding the project was no problem. It had the makings of a minor blockbuster during a period of depressing box office returns, with a script designed to cheer up the audiences. It was again a thirties setting, a "screwball comedy" in which the two real-life friends plot to entice the overweight daughter of an extremely rich aristocrat into marrying one of them and thus get their hands on his fortune.

It was not one of Jack's best efforts. He and Beatty romped through the story with little of the promised hilarity. Jack even looked different. His hair was frizzed daily and had an Art Garfunkel look to it. Comedy for Nicholson needs to have an edge, not necessarily black but certainly with a touch of the weird so that he can bring the brilliance of his drawl and facial expressions into play. After initial low returns at the box office he and Beatty had to do some personal hyping. He held court in the lobby of a New York hotel, looking slightly disheveled in a Hawaiian shirt and designer stubble (before designer stubble had been invented), and proceeded to talk to reporters about his life.

Helen Dudar of the *New York Post* found him angry over reviewers' claims that no one in the audience had laughed. Dudar said: "I told him I also found it unfunny and had watched it in the company of paying moviegoers who had not laughed much either. Nicholson said quietly, firmly, gently, 'I don't believe you.' Ah Hollywood, the reality factory."

It was while shooting *The Fortune* that Jack discovered that his "sister" June was his mother. *Time* magazine was preparing a cover story on the emergence of Jack the star, and their investigations took them to Neptune in search of old chums. They discovered the secret Mud had kept from him since birth. A *Time* reporter telephoned him on the set in Mexico. Nicholson said he was stunned; he never knew. He asked the magazine to keep his secret, and the facts about his real mother were pulled from the story.

Only a few weeks earlier, Jack had said in response to a publicity interviewer's assertion that his father, John, had abandoned the family when he was born: "My father and mother separated when I was a baby. I saw him extremely intermittently. He was a nice man. He's been dead for some time. My mother is also dead, so I'm an orphan."

He telephoned Lorraine. She confirmed that he was June's baby. "Such is the price of fame," Jack ruminated. "People start poking around in your private life, and the next thing you know your sister is actually your mother." He appeared to shrug off the news, but there is no question that it injected some kind of identity crisis into his life.

He was by then already working on the film that would win him the accolade he so badly wanted, an Oscar. *One Flew Over the Cuckoo's Nest* was adapted from Ken Kesey's explosive novel, published in 1962 and written long before the counterculture movement of the sixties and the antiheroes of the seventies. Antiheroism was one of the keys to the success of the film, fueled with the very considerable contribution of Nicholson and Czech director Milos Forman, who turned an enormously difficult project into a film verging on the classic.

It had been a long time in coming to the screen, and the story of its arrival is filled with uncanny coincidences. Kirk Douglas bought the rights to Kesey's book even before it reached the shops, convinced it would make a terrific picture with himself in the leading role of Randle Patrick McMurphy—eventually played by Nicholson. Douglas got as far as Broadway with his project, where he played McMurphy in a short run; the play flopped badly, leaving Douglas free to accept an invitation from President John F. Kennedy to join a goodwill mission to Czechoslovakia, a trip he had previously turned down.

In Prague, Douglas met Milos Forman, then a thirty-one-year-old scriptwriter and director with the Prague Film Faculty of the Academy of Dramatic Arts, whose family had, like Roman Polanski's, been largely wiped out by the Nazis. It was probably his discussion with Kirk Douglas that eventually led him and his young family to emigrate to America five years later.

Douglas himself was so taken with Forman that, when he returned home, he sent him a copy of *One Flew Over the Cuckoo's Nest* to see if he was interested in joining him in the project. With all hope of Hollywood financing seemingly vanished because of the play's failure, there was a vague chance that it could still figure somewhere in the advancement of East-West cultural relations. For some reason, still unknown to this day, Kirk Douglas's package was never delivered to Forman, who remained in Prague unaware that one of Hollywood's major stars wanted to do business with him. There the matter rested without further progress. One other reason for the delay was that the rights became locked in a protracted legal battle between Douglas and his former partner in the Broadway project. When the property became free again, his son Michael Douglas, himself gathering fame after his successful TV series, *The Streets of San Francisco,* became interested in getting it produced.

He had a new script written to suit contemporary events and tastes. Kirk naturally would still have liked to play McMurphy, but he appreciated that the part needed one of the new young stars who would appeal to a younger audience—someone like Burt Reynolds. As his father had earlier, Michael Douglas found reaction in the major studios lukewarm at best and positively cold at worst.

A few even remembered the play and remarked: "Look what happened when your dad did it." Then he introduced it to Saul Zaentz, head of Fantasy Records, who was so enthusiastic he agreed to put up most of the production money, budgeted at $4 million. In seeking a director, they turned coincidentally to Milos Forman, unaware that ten years earlier Kirk had wanted to send him the book.

In the years that had elapsed, Forman had made a name with films such as *Blonde in Love* (1965), *The Fireman's Ball* (1967), and *Taking Off* (1971), in which he showed a remarkable ability for lampooning authority—so much so that the Czech fire brigade went on strike in protest at his *Fireman's Ball.* As the play was further discussed, it became apparent that Burt Reynolds, though a major box office attraction at the time, was not right for the part, and Mike Douglas approached Nicholson. A further coincidence was in store. "It's funny," Nicholson told him. "When the book first came out, I tried to get an option on the rights and was told Kirk Douglas had bought them."

Forman and Nicholson became instant comrades. Nicholson's interest in and respect for European directors and Forman's admiration of some improvised scenes he had Nicholson perform for him convinced everyone that a certain magic was developing between them. Nicholson kept in touch with preproduction work and marveled at the fact that Douglas and Forman saw more than nine hundred actors to cast a dozen principal roles. One of the chosen few

Dr. Devil with the *Witches of Eastwick, left to right:* Cher, Susan Sarandon, and Michelle Pfeiffer (Archive Photos)

Jack as the Joker in *Batman* (Archive Photos)

Jack and Rebecca Broussard with their daughter, Lorraine, who was born in the spring of 1990
(Daily Mail)

Jack with daughter Lorraine in 1995
(BIG Pictures)

Jack and Alan Finkelstein shopping in Mayfair in July 1994 (David Koppel)

Jack and his eldest daughter, Jennifer, leave the Connaught Hotel during his promotional visit for *Wolf* in 1994 (Nikos)

Jack's three dates tonight are *left to right:* Naomi Campbell, Amanda de Cadenet, and Christy Turlington (Nikos)

Jack in London, 1994 (David Koppel)

was a former native of Neptune, New Jersey, called Danny DeVito.

Forman said: "We told Nicholson we were going for the best we could get. He agreed. Some actors don't like that because they could be outclassed in such a movie where the actor is one of a group, but he said that good actors would enhance his own performance rather than detract from it." As an example of the perfectionist search for the right people, they looked long and hard for an actor to play the large Indian chief who was supposed to be deaf and dumb until McMurphy got him to talk. They found him in Mount Rainer National Park, where plain and ordinary Will Sampson was working as an assistant warden. "Suddenly, two men appeared on horses and offered me a career in the movies," Sampson said later. "I thought they were kidding." They weren't, and he thus became a minor celebrity, appearing later in such movies as *The Outlaw Josie Wales*.

THE STORY of *One Flew Over the Cuckoo's Nest* was based on Kesey's own experiences working as night attendant on the psychiatric ward of the Veterans Hospital in Menlo Park. He wrote much of it, he admitted, under the influence of peyote and LSD, and even endured electroshock treatment in order to describe its effects on mentally ill patients.

In the film, audiences were given a sharply realistic view of life in a mental institution, but it needed Nicholson's humor to prevent it from becoming an abject, depressing tale of woe. He kept the movie bouncing along with his zaniness almost to the dramatic end, when McMurphy is subjected to a frontal lobotomy after trying to strangle his nemesis, Nurse Ratched.

Jack's role is a dramatic portrayal of convicted rapist R. P. McMurphy, who has convinced the authorities that he is mentally disturbed in order to escape heavy prison duties. At the same time, Nicholson had to show the audience that, while feigning insanity, McMurphy has a very definite mental disorder of which he is unaware.

McMurphy arrives at the institution as the epitome of a man who has spent a lifetime baiting the establishment. Once inside the ward, where a controlled calm prevails, he pits himself against the hospital beauracracy in the person of Nurse Ratched, who daily supervises the administration of tranquilizing medication. Naturally, McMurphy resists and begins a one-man rebellion, leading fellow inmates into riot, escape, and a party with smuggled booze and prostitutes. McMurphy's personality is magnetic and destructive, both to himself and fellow inmates.

There was one major hurdle to overcome: The film had to be made without alienating American mental health administrators, and it would be a wise move to obtain their active cooperation. There was also a measure of concern among certain actors who were told that the film might upset a lot of people and that the subject matter might do little to improve their own image.

Among those who turned down the part of the domineering Nurse Ratched, for example, were Anne Bancroft, Jane Fonda, and Faye Dunaway. Louise Fletcher accepted the role and provided Nicholson with the perfect foil as martinet to his rebellious lout. Nicholson himself had not the slightest concern about image; this was not a film to promote him as a romantic idol. He attacked the part with his usually methodical tenacity, analyzing the implications, dissecting the character, measuring its demands and psychological tones. As he read the script, he underlined key phrases in his lines and assigned numbers to certain words to signify beats and phrases.

Before memorizing his lines, he flew up to the mental institution in Oregon that was going to be used as a setting for the movie. There were 582 inmates, most of them classed as criminally insane. He had talks with the chief of staff, nurses, and inmates. He was shown all around the hospital and personally persuaded the hospital's medical chief to let him watch patients undergoing shock treatment. Then he went into the maximum security ward and was sitting in the hallway when the patients were brought out of their cells. They included a number of especially violent cases, among them several murderers. They all thought he was a new patient, and most were anxious to engage him in conversation. One was a handsome blond man who had killed a prison guard three weeks earlier with twenty-eight stab wounds. Nicholson went to lunch with them and continued his conversations, with hospital staff never too far away.

"There were all these mentally shattered, destroyed human beings about you," Jack related. "And I asked one of the orderlies, 'How do you do this as a job?' There were people there that stabbed people, all kinds of horrible things. And he just looked me in the eye and said something I won't forget, 'Well, Jack, some people do get better.' "

When the time came for filming, the hospital's superintendent, Dean Brook, readily gave permission for some inmates to appear in background scenes. Brook himself even appeared in the film; although he later chided the producers for certain inaccuracies, he felt it "a great honor to do a scene with Jack Nicholson, who is an absolute genius in getting across the character of McMurphy, a sociopath, of whom there are plenty around. Jack's performance typified them."

Filming in Oregon was to cover a period of eleven weeks, and Nicholson arranged accommodation for himself and Anjelica. Within a few weeks, however, he had so immersed himself in the role that Anjelica found him increasingly difficult to live with. Nicholson explained, "Usually I don't have much trouble slipping in and out of a film role, but in Oregon I didn't go home from a movie studio, I went home from a mental institution, and there's a certain amount of the character left in you that you can't get rid of; you are in a mental ward and that's it. It became harder and harder to create a separation between reality and make-believe because some of the people in there look and talk so normal. You would never know they were murderers."

In fact, he became so engulfed by the institutionalized life he was acting out that Anjelica started to get worried. His behavior toward her when he came home after a day in front of the cameras was distinctly odd and getting worse as the days went by. Eventually, she challenged him, "Can't you snap out of this? You're acting crazy." He could not, so Anjelica packed her bags and flew back to Los Angeles, complaining, "I'm no longer certain whether you are sane or not. I'll see you when you come back into the real world."

Michael Douglas took the trouble to apologize to her for the difficulties she was experiencing with her lover. "If it's any consolation," he said, "this movie is going to be a smash. I've never been more impressed with any actor in my life." Saul Zaentz, whose $4 million was riding on *Cuckoo*, added his praise: "I can think of only one other actor to compare him with. Paul Muni."

People magazine found less dated comparisons than Muni in a glowing tribute to his acting abilities: "*Cuckoo's Nest*, the trade figures, should bring Nicholson his long overdue Oscar and public acceptance as the first American actor since Marlon Brando and James Dean with the elemental energy to wildcat new wells of awareness in the national unconscious."

The magazine attempted to minimize his connection with the drug culture but succeeded only in drawing attention to it. "Nicholson's reputation as a drug freak has been overblown," the article proclaimed. "He smokes cannabis, occasionally snorts cocaine, and has dropped a good deal of acid—at first under medical supervision, later mostly for kicks. No speed, no heroin. 'Drugs are a social thing with me, a pleasant evening now and then. Nobody's ever seen me slack-mouthed. I'm not an advocate of decadence. I've seen friends extremely negatively affected by coke and heroin. But with marijuana, on the other hand, you're making outlaws of an enormous percentage of the population for no good reason.' "

Nicholson's peers agreed with *People*'s comments, at least about his acting, and the following April they awarded him his first Oscar, for Best Actor, which he accepted with joy. His talents, he believed, were now fully recognized, and he was glad to participate in the system that bestowed this honor. The film picked up nine Academy nominations in all and took five Oscars: Jack for Best Actor, Louise Fletcher for Best Actress, plus Best Film, Best Director, and Best Adapted Screenplay.

Actors, film buffs, producers, and reviewers alike were all completely stunned by the tumultuous audience reaction to *One Flew Over the Cuckoo's Nest* when it opened in America, and these scenes were repeated across the globe. It was not merely the light-hearted moments that brought such stirring participation; even the most soberingly dramatic scene in the movie, when McMurphy is trying to strangle Nurse Ratched, was received with cheers and applause. For that reason alone, while praising Nicholson and Forman's direction, reviewers sounded many notes of caution.

Stanley Kauffmann in *The New Republic* declared quite adamantly that the film was warped, sentimental, and possibly dangerous. Pulitzer Prize winner Roger Ebert, one of the most influential critics in America, was of the view that Nicholson and Forman milked the film so that it became a simpleminded anti-establishment parable. "I think there are long stretches of a very good film," he said, "and I hope they don't get drowned in the applause for the bad stuff that plays to the galleries."

Before Jack took his hard-won trophy home to Mulholland Drive on Oscar night, a reporter asked him, "When you were doing *Little Shop of Horrors*, did you ever think it would lead to this?"

"Yes," Nicholson replied. "I did."

And he wasn't kidding.

11

GUNNING FOR BRANDO

LONDONER LAURA LEVY was a newcomer to Los Angeles when she was invited to a barbecue at Jack Nicholson's place. "I was staying in Coldwater Canyon with Francesca Avedon [ex-wife of photographer Richard Avedon], who had been at school with Anjelica Huston, and we were invited up for the afternoon," she told me. "We drove up to Mulholland Drive and pressed the bell at the gates to be let in, and we were admitted. Nobody had said, 'Go right,' and we went left. We got about fifty yards down the road when these two guys with shotguns stopped us and asked what we were doing there. We said we were expected, and they said, 'Mr. Brando is not expecting anyone.' Unbelievable! I didn't even know he lived there. So we went back, and we found our way to Jack's place, and we had a very nice afternoon."

This little cameo was typical of life in the Mulholland Drive compound: Marlon was under siege; Jack was having a party.

Though they had been neighbors in their lofty commune for more than five years, Nicholson was not yet "close" to Brando, who was often away for long spells on his South Seas island, to which he escaped from the modern world and all its problems. Even when he was at home in Beverly Hills, Brando did not go out of his way to socialize, although the comings and goings in the two households at the top of the hill were indicative of the colorful domestic lives of the two star residents. However, behind the scenes, there were moves to bring them together professionally that would inevitably lead to an inseparable friendship.

The opportunity came when Brando needed money for a variety of reasons, including his considerable alimony payments to two ex-wives, his property venture in Tahiti, and his financial support for his latest political cause, the Native American. This was demonstrated at the end of 1974 when he appeared on television on the steps of a courthouse in Lincoln, Nebraska, announcing that he was going to give away his house on Mulholland Drive—and other property—to the Indians. He had come to court in support of some Indian activists appearing on a number of charges. Though a firm supporter of civil rights himself, Nicholson was nonethless disposed to comment of his idol, "Jeez, what's that sonovabitch doing now? He's crazy."

Neighborly interest in the activities of his professional comrade was more than advanced by some of the happenings at the Brando household. Over the past couple of years, they had ranged through a variety of domestic incidents, often involving tragic and very public battles between Brando and Anna Kashfi over custody of their thirteen-year-old-son Christian, whom Anna once had snatched from Brando's custody only to have him snatched back. The resultant court action cost Brando dearly, both financially and emotionally, and hung out a lot of dirty family linen.

BRANDO'S political affiliations had also attracted a lot of media attention to Mulholland Drive, where he received friends of the American Indian Movement in various rank, ranging from chief to squaw. One of them, a young woman called Sacheen Little Feather, went to the Academy Awards on his behalf when he was nominated for Best Actor for his role in *The Godfather*. "And the winner is," said Liv Ullmann, ". . . Marlon Brando."

He was not there but sitting at home on Mulholland Drive, watching the live television coverage. Sacheen Little Feather, who had been given a seat next to Jane Fonda, ran up to the podium with a long speech Brando had prepared, but since it would have exceeded the allotted time, she was not allowed to read it and thus refused to accept the Oscar from the presenter, Roger Moore. She stated that this was Marlon's protest at the treatment of American Indians in the movies and on television. As Moore politely tried to usher her away, she begged that "in future, we will be met by love and understanding."

An icy silence was followed by some cynical remarks from other presenters and recipients. Clint Eastwood referred to "all the cowboys shot in John Ford westerns." Academy president Daniel Taradash: "If Marlon had any class he would have come down here and said it himself." Michael Caine: "I agree with Marlon's principles, but he should have done this himself instead of sending some poor little Indian girl." Caine added, "A man who makes $2 million playing a Mafia godfather should give half of it to the Indians." Even Chief Dan George, who had given up his Indian life to become a movie star and had won a Best Supporting Actor nomination for his role in *Little Big Man,* said Brando's protest was ten years out of date because movies were more accurate now.

Coincidentally, the director who made *Little Big Man,* the admirable and scholarly Arthur Penn, now wanted Brando for his next film. He had heard through the grapevine that Brando was short of cash and looking for work. This seemed incredible after *The Godfather* and *Last Tango in Paris,* but Brando had invested heavily in a South Seas project that went bust the following year. Having offered to give away his property to the Indians, he also stood costly bail for some activists for the Indian cause, two of whom were later charged and convicted of first degree murder. Amid a ceremony complete with tribal drums, he handed over a gift of forty acres of land west of Los Angeles, worth $200,000, to the local shaman; it was land that originally belonged to the Chuwala Indians before the settlers forced them off.

After the publicity from this gesture had died down, Brando suffered dire humiliation when newspapers revealed that the land was heavily mortgaged and the Indians would face huge repayment costs. He promised to clear the mortgage and did so ten months later after earning sufficient funds to cover it by signing with Arthur Penn for his movie with Nicholson. "That's how it came about," the director told me. "They talked about it over the garden fence." Ironically, the film was a western.

Nicholson was the junior partner in the alliance; producer Elliot Kastner had promised him $1.25 million for ten weeks' work plus 10 percent of all gross receipts in excess of $12.5 million. This was a landmark in Nicholson's career—the first guaranteed salary exceeding $1 million and the prospect of more to come. Apart from achieving his goal of playing alongside Brando, it also provided him with the opportunity of working with another of the directors he most admired. Penn's string of new wave films included *The Left-Handed Gun*, *Bonnie and Clyde*, and *The Chase*, all controversial documentaries on the conflict between violent outsiders and the law.

The new western, *The Missouri Breaks*, contained similar offbeat elements. The script was written by novelist Thomas McGuane, who lived in Montana. It was based upon his research into the historical significance of the cattle business and the skilled system of rustling that accompanied the settling of northern Montana; he said it showed that some basically decent people perpetrated some pretty awful things. Brando made a cursory study of the script and characteristically asked for $500,000 a week for the duration of filming with a million to be paid immediately. He settled for $1 million for five weeks' work and 10 percent of the gross takings after the first $10 million, thus giving him a potential for $3 million or more if the film was a success, plus overtime if filming ran over the five-week limit.

PENN had not seen Brando lately and was shocked when they finally came face to face. Marlon had ballooned to a considerable 250 pounds and hardly looked the man they had in mind for the role of an eccentric, buckskin-clad gunfighter hired to track and kill a band of cattle thieves led by Jack Nicholson.

However, from the point of view of a box office package, Penn felt he could not have done better: Brando, the greatest draw in the business, and Nicholson, the most talked-about new star of the age. When they all moved down to Billings, Montana, for location shooting they discovered the preproduction crew, angry and upset, sweltering in temperatures of 112 degrees Fahrenheit.

The location village had been set up on a sprawling ranch twelve miles outside of town. Penn had assembled a relatively small cast of extraordinarily good actors, including Nicholson's old chum Harry Dean Stanton. There was also a supporting crew and cast of 112, dressed in a variety of headgear and heavy footwear that kept the dangerous rays of the sun off their heads and the fatal fangs of the rattlers off their feet and legs. Penn had known exactly what to expect. "I'd been to Montana before," he told me.

Brando's huge, air-conditioned trailer had EXECUTIVE painted on the side in silver against a pale blue background; there was also a candy-striped awning to shade the side that got the most sun. In conformity to Hollywood protocol, Nicholson's trailer was slightly smaller because he was a slightly lesser star. Many of the discussions about how to play a scene were to go on in the Brando wagon.

Tempers were already short before shooting began because, as usual, Marlon wanted some changes to the script—nothing substantial, he said, as he unfolded his copy covered with a mass of notes and crossed-out lines over which he had written new ones. He wanted it at least to include some propaganda for his Indian cause. Tom McGuane was furious, especially because he knew the area well and his research had been meticulous. Penn wasn't too happy, either. And neither was Nicholson when he discovered that Brando wanted Jack's part to be played as an Indian. McGuane refused point blank. Penn said he did not care for the idea, and Nicholson, less partisan, calmly proffered the opinion that he did not think it would work. Brando sat back in his chair, pondered for a moment, and announced that he was quite unhappy with this lack of cooperation.

Nicholson was keen to get started. He turned up bright and early on the first day ready for his first scene with the great man. He, too, had put on a touch of weight, and he had a straggly beard and greasy hair and lounged about in sandals, baggy jeans, and an open-neck brown shirt. Brando appeared wearing riding breeches and a battered brown hat, looking like a renegade from the Australian outback.

Brando and Nicholson tried a couple of scenes together and spent some time in Brando's trailer with Arthur Penn. The crew outside were becoming impatient in the broiling heat as the minutes ticked on into half an hour, then an hour. A muffled voice over someone's walkie-talkie summed up their feelings: "Has God's gift to the world appeared yet?" He had not.

Nicholson was slightly bemused by it all; everyone was, even those who had worked with Brando before. They held him in awe. Some were scared of him, especially the producers and the publicity people. Few argued with him for fear of upsetting him or throwing him off his line of thought, although more often than not he wasn't even thinking of the scene. At that time, the intricacies of wind power were occupying his thoughts; he was designing a wind-driven electricity-generating unit for his house in Tahiti and often sat sketching a new idea. He also spent a good deal of time collecting grasshoppers and studying their curious leg movements.

On the first day of serious filming, Nicholson was to discover another of Brando's eccentricities.

"Cue cards?" said Nicholson to Penn, mystified. "Who are they for?"

"Himself."

"Marlon?"

"Yes."

"Why does the greatest actor in the world need cue cards?"

"Because he hasn't learned his lines, that's why."

The cue cards, written in large letters, might be held up in strategic positions off camera, pinned to the anatomy of other actors, or affixed to Brando's shirtsleeves or inside his hat. But cue cards they were, and there would be moments of pure comedy because of them. Once Brando was doing a scene with John Liam and asked if he could stick his lines to Liam's forehead while they were doing the shots over Liam's shoulder.

Liam replied: "I don't mind, but I would like to see your face."

"Okay," said Brando, "then we'll punch two holes in the paper."

Even that didn't work, so new cue cards with letters four inches high were stuck on a wall behind Liam. The cameras rolled, and Brando started speaking, then interrupted himself.

"Shit," he said, "there's an airplane coming into shot over your left ear."

On another morning, a gale blew up as they were filming in what was supposed to be the garden of a wooden shack. Brando's cue cards were blown into the cabbage patch, neatly planted the day before, and he couldn't see them properly. In this particular instance it did not much matter, because he was changing the lines almost to the point of ad-libbing. The scene was aborted when it became plain it wasn't going to work, and Brando rode off into the prairie in disgust.

"Oh well," said Nicholson, trying not to sound bored, "another day, another twenty grand."

The Brando halo slipped a little, and after a couple of days, Nicholson was giving a cheeky impression of Brando being filmed while reading cue cards. "Watch the eyes," said Nicholson, moving his own from side to side. "That's what happens when you're reading cue cards."

Brando later claimed that the cue cards were part of a policy of noncooperation he had pursued because the producers hadn't signed his contract yet. Once they did, "I started remembering my lines."

Nicholson was full of admiration for Brando as an actor, especially for the sparseness of his mannerisms and the power of his voice; even though it did not sound powerful, it carried across the set once he had decided how he was going to say that line. His walk and his movements were graceful, like a dancer's almost, despite his gross physique. The crew liked him, too, especially when early on in the proceedings Brando successfully protested the long workdays the producers had scheduled. Unfortunately, the crew spent their extra leisure time drinking and dancing at the War Bonnet Motel two miles out of town, where they were housed. The management began to get upset.

The night Nicholson hosted a party there for the crew resulted in the whole crowd being given notice to quit by the manager—and not simply because of the drinking. By now, the crew had moved in for the summer with their wives, girlfriends, in-laws, children, and pets. On the notice outside, someone had added UN to the sign that read WELCOME MISSOURI BREAKS. The lieutenant governor of Montana became involved, and a compromise was eventually worked out, whereby half would leave the motel for other accommodations.

ANJELICA flew to Montana for the summer and stayed with Nicholson at the house he had rented outside of town. His daughter Jennifer, now twelve, also came for a visit during the school holidays, and Nicholson spent half his time trying to dissuade her from playing poker with the crew. With Jennifer verging on her teens, Nicholson had decided upon an open and honest relationship with his daughter, whom he idolized, but not obviously so. He did not duck her embarrassing questions about his affairs, nor would he necessarily hide other aspects of his lifestyle. Poker with the crew was good fun, and she was not overawed by the position of her father, whom she never seemed to regard as a star.

On the set, Brando remained the center of attraction. He had gone on a diet, eating only raw vegetables, and boasted that in the first two weeks he had lost three inches around his waist—much to the concern of the wardobe department, who had visions of having to make up new gear for their star as he shrank in stature before their very eyes.

Nicholson worked hard, and was generally a solid citizen, though he did have a row with Arthur Penn over the interpretation of one scene. The producers publicly accused him of holding up production for five hours at a cost of $20,000 an hour. Jack denied their claim. He actually saw little of Brando, who was there for only five weeks of filming while Jack was required for ten. Most of the time when he wasn't on set, Marlon was either riding on the prairie in search of grasshoppers or sitting alone in his trailer tapping away on his bongo drums or phoning his Indian friends.

His involvement with the Indian activists had deepened, and proceedings on the set of *The Missouri Breaks* were enlivened with gossip for a day or two when a carload of FBI agents swung their car onto the set and their leader spoke to Brando urgently about two renegade Indians. They were on the run from the police, and the FBI had reason to believe they were using a mobile home belonging to Brando. The actor was decidedly uncooperative but later admitted he had indirectly assisted the two men in their escape.

So that was Nicholson's first and last professional encounter with Brando. Brando himself later commented: "Poor old Jack. He was running around cranking the whole thing out while I'm zipping in and out like a firefly." And he added a note of vitriol about his next-door neighbor: "I actually don't think he's that bright—not as good as Robert De Niro, for example." As Jack had disposed of Brando in the film by cutting his throat, a little backstabbing of this kind was, perhaps, understandable.

What did the critics make of it all? *Newsweek* went for the populist view, billing it as the great shootout between Brando and Nicholson facing each other not merely as characters but as magic icons; Brando had become a symbol of lost innocence, while Nicholson radiated the new kind of beleaguered innocence, "grinning hedonistically against the moral confusion of our time."

Nicholson himself seemed unsure of the picture's box office appeal. Although his original deal for making *The Missouri Breaks* gave him $1.25 million plus 10 percent of the gross receipts over $12.5 million, he obviously had second thoughts as to how successful it would be after viewing the final cut. On May 14, a week before *The Missouri Breaks* opened in Los Angeles, he sold back to producer Elliot Kastner half of his 10 percent for $1 million to be paid within ten days. However, when the money had not been received by the agreed deadline, Nicholson's company, Proteus Films, filed a suit for breach of contract in Los Angeles Superior Court. The case was eventually settled amicably.

BRANDO's comparison between Nicholson and Robert De Niro was timely. Both actors were possible choices for the lead in *The Last Tycoon*, based loosely on the life of the legendary boy mogul Irving J. Thalberg as told in F. Scott Fitzgerald's unfinished novel. It was being heralded as a new blockbuster from the same team that brought Brando to the screen in *On the Waterfront*, producer Sam Spiegel and director Elia Kazan, with the backing at Paramount of Robert Evans—the living legend and clearly, some said, the very last tycoon.

The added ingredient this time was the famed British playright Harold Pinter, who had been commissioned to write the screenplay about the sexual misdeeds and power struggles of old Hollywood. Nicholson and Spiegel were good friends, and Jack's name was being pushed by the producer for the lead. Kazan had other ideas.

"I told Sam to forget Nicholson for the role of Irving Thalberg," he recalled. "I wanted Bobby De Niro. I knew very little about him, but I was playing a hunch." Sam Spiegel gave Kazan his head. His hunches had been good in the past. He chose Brando for *A Streecar Named Desire* as well as *On the Waterfront*, and James Dean for *East of Eden*, to name just two stars he had pulled from virtual obscurity.

"It was much the same now," said Kazan, "because I had to transform De Niro from a New York Italian kid into Hollywood royalty. That wasn't easy. Thalberg was a thin, somewhat sickly Jew with erudition and culture. But we came together on instinct, his and mine."

Spiegel still wanted Nicholson in the film, so he was offered a cameo role as the radical union leader, thus joining such other good names as Ray Milland, Donald Pleasence, Tony Curtis, and Robert Mitchum. He was paid $150,000. Spiegel got more than his money's worth, using Jack to batter Kazan all the way through the making of *The Last Tycoon*—and afterward, when met with a lukewarm response both critically and commercially. Spiegel kept saying that the leading man was a problem and that Nicholson would have done it better. He said De Niro was "common," once describing the actor as a "petty punk," which Kazan insisted was grossly unfair. At the end of it, Kazan wrote in his diary: "The picture hangs together; the performances are good, outstanding in the case of De Niro and Ingrid Boulting, and the film has class, beauty, humanity, and sublety." That, Kazan admitted, was "the only supremely favorable notice we were to receive."

NICHOLSON was also talking to Sam Spiegel about the financing for a new film called *Moon Trap,* his own project, which he wanted to direct but not appear in. This ambition was proving difficult to achieve. United Artists, which had released *The Missouri Breaks*, was disappointed at the initial box office results, and by the time contracts came up for discussion, the studio was wary of the film's viability.

As always in Hollywood when large money is at stake, negotiations went on and off for several months until UA said it would consider the project only if Nicholson himself took the leading role. "If the picture goes into millions, then we've got to have Jack in it; otherwise it is too much of a gamble," said the studio bosses. Nicholson said he was not prepared to do that; he wanted this picture to be a demonstration of his directing skills, and he could not give directing his full attention if he was also in the starring role. There matters rested, and Nicholson took off for Europe in anger, though more at recent developments in his personal life than UA's attitude.

He and Anjelica had moved apart quite suddenly. Only a couple of months earlier the gossip columns had been suggesting that they were considering marriage, though longtime friends of Nicholson like Harry Dean Stanton said they would believe it when they saw it. Stanton was convinced that Nicholson had made up his mind never to marry again. Two deep involvements (with Mimi and Michelle) that had ended badly had left him leery of full and legally binding commitments.

Later, he did want to marry Anjelica, but it was she who refused him and for exactly the same reason: She had seen too many marriages fail, including three of her father's. Anjelica and Jack agreed on one thing, however, that she had been good for him. On location in Billings, he had been a model of decorum and cooperation. He had certainly come out of his shell—into which he had retreated after the split with Michelle Phillips—with Anjelica on his arm, becoming a frequent attender of some of the more establishment social functions and parties.

FAME: Paul Simon, ad-libbing about a party in Annie Hall*: "It'll be mellow. Small. Jack and Anjelica will be there."*

They appeared warm and "frolicsome," as one observer put it. Anjelica seemed to be devoted to him. When Jack was doing his important-person bit, holding court to a group of people who hung on his every word, she assumed a position of quiet attentiveness, sometimes sitting at his feet like a geisha. There appeared to be a strong bond between them, reinforced by the fact that Anjelica had no demanding career of her own, although therein lay one of her own deep personal concerns. All too often these days, she was being referred to either as John Huston's daughter or Jack Nicholson's lover—Anjelica Huston, the person, did not appear to exist in the eyes of the media. She did not want to become an adjunct to the life of a man in order to gratify his ego as her father's wives had done.

Anjelica had become important in Nicholson's life, but perhaps he did not appreciate just how much she had moved toward being the supportive companion in a solid relationship. Nor did he appreciate entirely that there should be two-way traffic and that Anjelica needed something in return, so that she would not brood about being just Jack Nicholson's girl. She was probably also getting a bit tired of his continual assertion that he understood women—a by-product that had lingered from his battles with women's libbers after *Carnal Knowledge.* He was forever in the papers with patronizing quotes such as: "I knew how to be friends with women before I knew how to be sexy with them."

Anjelica was becoming moody, and certainly less enamored of the aura of enigma she once saw around him. She was experiencing what had happened with other long-term relationships in his life, and those looking in at close range could see it coming. Don Devlin, writer and producer friend of Nicholson's from the earliest days on Sunset Strip, recalled: "The long-term ones were very strong and filled with huge emotional ups and downs, and every one fell into the same identical pattern. Jack is such an overwhelming character that girls love him. Then he starts to behave fairly badly, then he starts to lose the girl, then he goes chasing after her again, then the relationship changes and the girl gets the upper hand. Then he becomes like a little boy."

Anjelica had reached the second phase of the scenario described by Devlin. Whispering to a friend, "What's good for the gander, . . ." she took off for London with Ryan O'Neal, another of Jack's good buddies with whom a certain closeness had been developing for some months. "He had it coming," seemed to be the general consensus among mutual friends, leaving Jack so devoid of sympathy he took off to Aspen and holed up in one of the two houses he had purchased in the ski resort with the money he made from *Chinatown*.

Later, he followed O'Neal and Anjelica to London. Nicholson checked into the Mayfair Hotel. When an interviewer caught up with him, Nicholson, still spitting with rage, said all he knew was that Anjelica was in London and she wasn't with him; furthermore, he did not want to be mentioned in the same sentence as Ryan O'Neal. He hung around for a while and dined with Jerry Hall, but she was Bryan Ferry's girl then, and Jack was not going to do to Ferry what one of his best friends had just done to him—at least, that's the way he saw it at the moment.

He had mellowed when he later said: "If you told me that some woman could go off and fuck one of my best friends and I'd end up reading about it in the newspapers, and that four years later I wouldn't give a shit, I'd have said, 'You're talking to the wrong guy here.' That's not the way I am now." Anjelica's departure hurt him more than he had imagined it might, and certainly it came as a greater blow than the earlier goodbyes of Mimi Machu and Michelle Phillips. In August, he caught a plane to the south of France to join Sam Spiegel on his yacht.

Sam was sympathetic but also the bearer of bad news. United Artists had canceled its planned financial backing of *Moon Trap*. The paparazzi who had followed Jack to the quayside at St. Tropez, where the Spiegel craft was tethered at the up-market end, had surrounded the berth upon hearing that Nicholson had just arrived. His response demonstrated his sadness and his anger: He dropped his trousers and mooned them over the side.

The Nicholson-Huston row rumbled on all summer in the gossip columns. First there was a reunion, and then it was all off again. Jack, in the meantime, was being linked to a variety of other contenders for a room with a view on Mulholland Drive. Then Anjelica suddenly rejoined O'Neal, who was filming the World War II epic *A Bridge Too Far* in Holland. On September 23, she received a call from Nicholson "ordering" her back to America. John Huston had advised him to "be firm with her." They met in New York three days later and agreed they would never again separate. In the highly public aftermath, she said that when Jack called her she realized how much she had yearned for him and that she "felt so crummy abandoning him—men like Jack you just don't find anymore."

Jack professed his undying love and insisted they would never part again, not even for separate vacations. "We are side by side now and that's the way it is going to stay," he said. He added no bitterness toward his friend Ryan O'Neal, left licking his wounds in Holland and wondering what had gone wrong.

"It ended as quickly as it had begun, which was a pity," O'Neal confessed. "I really loved her—even Tatum [O'Neal's daughter] liked her."

12

FRIENDS

ON THE EVENING of March 24, 1977, Her Royal Highness Princess Anne, president of the British Academy of Film and Television Arts, was attending the annual presentation of the British Oscars and fully expected to meet Jack Nicholson. He had been nominated as Best Actor of 1976 for his role in *One Flew Over the Cuckoo's Nest*, but when his name was duly read out as the winner, the cameras swung around to reveal an empty seat where he should have been sitting.

Hasty excuses were made, but there were rumors that Nicholson, in the mold of other Hollywood rebels like George C. Scott and Marlon Brando, had simply refused to honor the London occasion with his presence. Later that evening, a spokesman for United Artists, the film's distributors, announced apologetically that he had not, in fact, arrived in Britain as expected and was still in California "going about his normal routine."

In fact, at the time that Princess Anne should have been presenting Nicholson with his award, he was holed up in Aspen surveying the sensational mass of world press headlines that dragged him into the worst Hollywood scandal since Errol Flynn's infamous rape case. His friend Roman Polanski had just been arraigned before the Los Angeles Superior Court on six charges alleging he drugged, raped, and committed an act of sodomy on a thirteen-year-old girl, identified only as Sandra, in Nicholson's house. Anjelica Huston was out on $1,500 bail after being arrested on the same day as Polanski for alleged possession of cocaine.

The sequence of events that brought the world's media to Mulholland Drive had its beginnings fourteen days earlier, on March 10. Nicholson was already in Aspen; his relationship with Anjelica had struck another bad patch, and he went off to do some skiing while she prepared to move her belongings out of Mulholland Drive. Nicholson did not expect her to be there by the time of his planned return late in March, when he was to fly to London for the British Academy Awards. In the meantime, Polanski entered stage left with the impressionable Sandra, whose mind he had filled with dreams of stardom.

Polanski, then forty-four, had returned to Los Angeles shortly after Christmas, claiming to have been commissioned by the French magazine *Vogue Homme* to do a photographic feature on the adolescent girls of America. He suggested to Sandra that they should drive to Jack Nicholson's house to shoot some pictures. Polanski knew that Nicholson was in Aspen, so he called Helena Kallianiotes, who was at home working on a screenplay. Polanski said he was sure Jack would not mind if he used the house for his photographic sessions; Helena agreed. Polanski had, after all, only recently been a houseguest and had been given the complete run of the place.

"Is there anything to drink?" Polanski asked Helena on arriving.

"Champagne in the fridge," she said. "You know where it is. Now if you'll excuse me I have to get on with my own work."

She waited to take a glass of champagne from the magnum of Cristal Polanski popped, then left him with the girl. They sat drinking for a few minutes. The young model was apprehensive. She said the last time she drank champagne she was ill. Polanski reassured her; this was good champagne and would do her no harm. She claimed he told her that Nicholson would be arriving soon, knowing full well that he would not, but playing on the fact that she desperately wanted to meet him.

"I don't know how much I drank," the young model was to tell the police. "I just kept drinking it for the pictures he was taking." The photographs were posed in various parts of the house. In the kitchen, for example, he had her sitting on the table licking an ice cube, and in Nicholson's main living room, he photographed her in the bay window overlooking the canyon.

They moved to the Jacuzzi area; the girl was intrigued by the clouds of steam, and Polanski suggested she should go topless.

He also produced some Quaaludes, the fashionable tranquilizers usually taken after cocaine. He took one himself and persuaded Sandra to take a half.

The scenes that followed, ostensibly for photographic purposes, had the girl topless in Nicholson's Jacuzzi, where Polanski joined her. Feeling the effects of the champagne, the heat, and the pill, the girl wanted to lie down, so Polanski took her to what used to be the spare room, where he once slept. Now it housed Nicholson's huge television screen and his stereo, with sloppy couches against the walls.

"I can barely remember anything that happened with any clarity," the girl said in her police statement. Polanski followed her into the room and began having sex with her almost as soon as she lay down on the couch, first orally, then vaginally, and finally anally. There was a knock on the door.

Anjelica had returned to Nicholson's home. Polanski called out to her, and Anjelica shouted back: "Roman?"

He opened the door slightly, and Anjelica could see he was naked. She had never cared much for Polanski, and now she was angry that he should be using Nicholson's house for what appeared to be sexual purposes.

"What are you doing here?" Anjelica asked.

"I'm doing a picture session for *Vogue*," Polanski replied.

Anjelica was not convinced and went to find Helena to complain about his presence in the house. Undeterred, Polanski returned to the couch and attempted to have sex with her again. The girl froze; she wanted to go home. Twenty minutes later, they both emerged from the room, dressed and ready to go. Polanski made a half-hearted attempt to introduce Sandra to Anjelica, then took her home. Sandra ran straight upstairs to her bedroom, too ashamed, she said, to face her mother.

Later that night, however, the girl broke down in tears and described what had happened in Nicholson's house. Her mother immediately called the police.

The following day, Polanski was walking across the lobby of the Beverly Hills Hotel, where he was staying. "Mr. Polanski," said a quiet voice as he strode toward the exit doors on his way to a theater date. "I am from the LAPD. I have a warrant for your arrest." Polanski protested loudly and denied everything but was arrested nonetheless.

Two other officers arrived at Mulholland Drive carrying a search warrant just as Anjelica was leaving the house. "I'm sorry," she said, "but I can't stay. Anyway, I answered a detective's questions earlier when he called about Roman Polanski being here yesterday. It isn't my business."

"I'm sorry. It is your business. You live here, don't you?"

"It isn't my house. I have been staying here."

"Is Mr. Nicholson still in Colorado?"

"Yes, I spoke with him on the telephone a few minutes ago. He doesn't know anything about this."

"Well," the officer said, taking Anjelica's arm, "we have court-authorized papers for a search, and we have to ask you to step back inside."

"Where do you want to start?" she asked, resigned to cooperating with them.

"Your handbag. We'll start there."

Half an hour later Anjelica was charged with possession of cocaine. Detectives also removed various items from Jack's house, including a small brick of hashish; the police made it known that they would like to take Nicholson's fingerprints and check them against those on the hash container. Nicholson remained in Aspen, refusing all approaches from the near-frantic journalistic activity that had blown up around him. His lawyers and advisers told him to stay away from Mulholland Drive at all costs so that he did not become even remotely involved in an official manner.

When he had not returned to Los Angeles by April 1, police requested a warrant from Santa Monica municipal judge Robert Thomas authorizing detectives to obtain his fingerprints. Nicholson agreed to have his prints taken by Aspen police. They did not match those found on the hashish container, and on April 19 the police announced that he was cleared of any suspicion in the case. The charge against Anjelica was also dropped.

When police developed the film Polanski had taken of the girl, they found the pictures were poor quality and certainly unusable in a major magazine such as *Vogue*. Then *Vogue* spokespeople said they had "no knowledge" of Polanski being commissioned for the feature. One executive described the idea as "an unlikely prospect—we are not into pedophilia."

Faced with the possibility of imprisonment followed by deportation, Polanski telephoned a couple of his friends and then drove to Los Angeles airport, where he purchased the last remaining first-class seat on British Airways flight L598 to London, departing at 5:57 that afternoon. From London, he flew on to Paris, where he knew he would be safe from the law. He held a French passport, and it was unlikely that the French authorities would allow his extradition on a charge of unlawful sex. He was, however, barred forever from returning to Hollywood.

The Polanski affair turned the public against the director despite Nicholson's attempts to play down his degree of guilt. Nicholson should have been warned by the sheer volume of publicity, but it did not appear to alter his own lifestyle up on Mulholland Drive.

One of my informants described the goings-on at a "huge party" there during the summer of 1977: "There were lots of drugs, lots of drinks. I remember that on the coffee table in the reception room there was one of those wood-and-silver fish-shaped dishes that holds smoked salmon. One half was filled with marijuana and the other half with cocaine; it was extraordinary. Jack was charming. You get an image of him from the press, but he was actually a fairly ordinary kind of person. Normal. Not like some stars you meet who are completely carried away with themselves. He seemed much more regular than that. He was in much better shape [than later] and had a lot more hair. He was a very good host. I was a bit dubious, to be quite honest, because he already had a very fast reputation. I was young and it was a bit frightening, but he was very nice.

"The party wasn't one of those megacelebrity parties, it was more the people he was hanging out with at the time. The furnishing was Santa Fe–type stuff, comfortable not flashy, and there were wood floors and big bleached-wood tables. Apart from some very nice art, there was no feeling of opulence; just lots of people running around having a good time."

Soon after this party, Jack packed his bags and cleared off to Mexico to begin work on his next project, *Goin' South*. He would both star and direct.

POLANSKI was one thing; John Belushi quite another. Nicholson met Belushi in August 1977 when Belushi signed a contract to make a cameo appearance in *Goin' South* for $5,000. It was the beginning of a friendship between the future cult star of *The Blues Brothers* and Nicholson; after a shaky start, it lasted until

Belushi's death from an overdose of heroin and cocaine in 1982, when he was at the height of his fame.

John Belushi was just one of a number of new actors recruited by Nicholson for the film, and the project had more to do with Nicholson's determination to direct another picture than anything else. *Goin' South* was built on a slender story and had no other famous names in the cast to help drag it along. Its whole success or failure rested wholly on Nicholson himself as director and leading man.

Why did he put himself in such a position?

For a man who had just won an Oscar and whose name was on everyone's lips in Hollywood—even before the Polanski debacle—it was a surprising choice. By then he could virtually name his picture and his price; he did neither. It was an act of arrogance, or hubris, for him to assume that he could single-handedly produce a satisfactory product in the style expected of him by his now substantial following of ardent fans.

But that was Nicholson then, and now: a bucker of the system, outwardly confident that his own abilities would pull him through. He was also honest enough with himself to realize that a lot was riding on the outcome of *Goin' South*. He said in an interview: "If it doesn't work, it's doubtful whether I will be able to direct another film. One unsuccessful film is okay, but two and you're in trouble."

Hollywood has a long memory, and *Drive, He Said* was not a commercial success. But *Goin' South* was a risk he was prepared to take, and he put himself in charge of every aspect. It was a fairly simple story about a scruffy, smelly cattle thief named Henry Moon, who is saved from hanging by an old custom that allowed any single woman to take a condemned man as her husband. The script was one Jack took from the pile when United Artists finally pulled the plug on *Moon Trap*. Nicholson turned to his old friends Harry Gittes and Harold Schneider, brother of *Easy Rider* and *Five Easy Pieces* producer Bert, to coax some financing from Paramount. They, like UA on *Moon Trap*, wanted him in the picture and he agreed, apparently intent on showing his hand as a director.

"Why not?" he replied to questions about his ability to pull it off. "It didn't hurt Molière, Shakespeare, or Pirandello." After failing to recruit Jane Fonda for the leading female role, he hired a completely unknown actress named Mary Steenburgen, who until that point in her life had failed to land a single screen role and was working as a part-time waitress at Magic Pan by day and performing for no pay onstage by night. When she tested at Paramount, it was the first time she had ever been on a sound stage; at the end of it, she was so unconvinced about her performance that she went down to the pay office to get her expenses to return home to New York. She was flat broke. "Forget it," she was told, "you're on the payroll."

Though he had never made a film before, John Belushi was better known than any other supporting actor in the picture by virtue of his appearances on *Saturday Night Live.* Nicholson had enjoyed one of Belushi's most recent routines in which he had done a cruel imitation of Nicholson playing McMurphy in *One Flew Over the Cuckoo's Nest* with Raquel Welch in the role of Nurse Ratched.

He and Nicholson had one other contact in common, a past friendship with Candice Bergen, who had appeared in several *Saturday Night Live* sketches with Belushi. She joined him in the early days when his humor was wicked, sharp, and fresh. Later, when she went back to do another show, she was disappointed to discover that he relied heavily on drugs to help him through the pressure of work. He had become addicted to Quaaludes and cocaine, and his personality had become dangerously manic instead of spontaneously and delightfully mad. Nicholson had chosen him for one reason only: He had heard Belushi do a brilliantly comic impression of a Mexican, and there was a small part for a Mexican deputy sheriff in *Goin' South*.

Location work was in the central Mexican town of Durango, where seventy or more westerns had been filmed in the past. John Wayne made four there, and the set built for *Chisum*, in 1969, was used by Nicholson for *Goin' South*. The crew moved down in the early summer, and Nicholson appeared to slide without a hint of schizophrenia between his two roles. Dressed in the character's mangy clothes and bent black hat, he would peer through the camera lens at a shootout and then hop in front to become Henry Moon, sleeping in a barn with pigs. His actors were full of praise. "Most directors feel they have to tell you how to do every line," said Danny DeVito, who was one of the supporting actors. "Jack lets you alone. His style is 'less direction is better.' "

Steenburgen agreed. "He taught me the art of acting on film down there. He told me to eliminate the obvious and keep it simple and natural. He directs by asking helpful questions and suggesting another way of approaching a particular scene." He was a seducer of his cast and crew in terms of work, while his own efforts were quite tireless. Not every day was sweetness and light. As the weeks wore on, Nicholson looked tired and at the end of one long and arduous shoot, he angrily chastised himself: "I will never direct myself again."

John Belushi arrived toward the end of August. Nicholson was thrilled, but surprised, that he had agreed to do the part; Harry Gittes wished he hadn't. The comedian turned up, sweating, in a suit that was crumpled as if he had slept in it for a week. He complained bitterly about the hotel they had arranged for him and asked if he could stay at the place rented for Nicholson, a sprawling bungalow in the mountains overlooking Durango, which had been set up partially as Nicholson's personal accommodation and partially as offices and editing rooms.

"I've gotta get out of here," Belushi was mumbling to himself inside the office part of the bungalow where the car had dropped him. "The hotel is suck-o, man." Harold Schneider tried to pacify him, but Belushi appeared scared and disoriented. He continued to rant and shout; he picked up a kitchen knife and appeared to be contemplating jabbing the blade into his own heart.

"I don't need all this," he said over and over again.

Schneider kept trying to calm him, and then Harry Gittes, who had hired him in the first place on Nicholson's orders, arrived. He was firmer and stronger.

"You're acting like a complete asshole," he told Belushi. "You're going to put us all in deep shit."

Belushi slumped into a chair in contemplation, then fell into a deep sleep, snoring and blowing like a tugboat.

"What's this?" snapped Nicholson when he arrived back from the set. "A crash pad?"

He left Schneider with the task of getting Belushi to his hotel. They were brawling and shouting insults at each other. Schneider, furious, had to be physically restrained from hitting

Belushi; Nicholson remained in his quarters studiously ignoring the commotion.

The following morning, Belushi arrived on set looking hung over and sheepish. He apologized to Gittes for the trouble. Nicholson had been told: He was the director and had to bawl him out; it was expected of him.

"You asshole. Any other producers would write you out. You only stay in because they're my friends. If Paramount people were here, you'd be kissed off, and your career in movies would be totally fucked."

Belushi hung around for four weeks waiting to deliver his few lines of dialogue. His contract stipulated that he had to be free to start a new season of *Saturday Night Live* in mid-September. As Jack hadn't managed to shoot his scenes by then, Belushi had to fly to New York and then return to Durango at the end of the month to complete his work on *Goin' South*.

It was a year before the movie was ready for release, and it turned out to be a minor disaster for Nicholson. His direction of the film, and especially of himself, was loose and uneven. The critics went for the jugular. Pauline Kael of *The New Yorker* called him a "leering leprechaun." Comparing this work with his previous roles and recent dramatic performances, she said: "Here there's nothing hidden and nothing hell-bent or sinister—he's just a fatuous actor. . . . [He] keeps working his mouth with tongue darting out and dangling lewdly; he's like an advertisement for a porno film."

Several reviewers appeared to be going for Nicholson on a different count, as well. "He talks as if needed to blow his nose," Kael also said. "Nicholson plays the role like the before half of a Dristan commercial with nasal passages blocked. Why, I don't know and don't care to ask," wrote Charles Champlin in the *Los Angeles Times*, while *New York* magazine noted his "peculiar nasal voice and fogged manner." To this obvious implication about drugs, Nicholson responded lamely: "I was merely trying to do my Clark Gable bit."

John Belushi had found the entire experience of making the movie a torment and had caused his employers to share his suffering. He was on screen in the finished version for two minutes and forty-eight seconds, but it was a tantalizing taste of his unique talents.

The net result of *Goin' South* was that questions were being asked in high places about Nicholson's judgment.

AFTER the Polanski affair, discretion should have counted more than valor in Jack Nicholson's private world. As the paychecks and the media attention rose in equal proportion, he realized that he needed to protect himself from the tabloid press, and that meant being more cautious about the company he kept. But he had to learn the hard way that he was a prime target for scandal no matter where he was or who he was with. Just a year after Polanski's fall from grace, he let his guard down momentarily while he was in London to make *The Shining* with Stanley Kubrick and lived to regret it.

The femme fatale who kissed and told was Margaret Trudeau, former wife of the Canadian prime minister Pierre Trudeau. Nicholson tried to dismiss Mrs. Trudeau's version of events as nonsense. However, his reputation as a womanizer was so widely known that her claims of lovemaking were given a good hearing, and she was quite adamant that they were, albeit briefly, passionate lovers.

There had been other lovers since she had left Trudeau and their three sons two years earlier after seven years of marriage. She had embarked upon an embarrassingly childish swirl around the world with men several years her junior, ogling Mick Jagger like a love-starved groupie and standing around at posh people's parties eyeing the local talent.

Filming of *The Shining*, an adaptation of the Stephen King novel, was due to start early in 1978, and it was expected to be a long task. Notwithstanding a salary of $1.25 million plus a percentage of the gross, the producers provided Nicholson with a house rented for £850 a week, which in those days was sufficient to acquire a four-bedroom, four-bathroom, four reception-room minimansion with a covered garden on the Chelsea embankment, and a Daimler with a driver named George outside the front door. For the next eighteen months—with time off for good behavior and occasional sorties back to Los Angeles—Nicholson enjoyed stylish London life and regularly attended parties given by the alleged elite of English cafe society.

Margaret Trudeau met Jack at a party given by antique dealer Martin Summers and his wife, Nona. He was alone and, she said, she was immediately attracted by the leering twinkle in his eyes. She was with a younger rock musician identified only as "Tommy from Texas," who had a penchant for staying up all night and drinking champagne in bed; it was he who had introduced her to a sleazy world of drugs and sex. She escaped from him that night by fleeing with Nicholson in his Daimler, crouching down in the back so that she would not be seen.

That night of their first meeting she discovered, as they drove around London behind "the inscrutable George, just how much room there was in the back of a Daimler." She ditched Tommy for good and spent some time with Nicholson. They made love all night, she said, and she joined him regularly at his Chelsea home for some "flirting." Margaret should have got the message, though. He kept telling her he was in love with Anjelica and gave the former Canadian first lady an unceremonious brushoff when he said one evening with apparent glee: "Guess who's coming tomorrow?"

It was Anjelica, joining him for the duration of his stay in London. Mrs. Trudeau settled for a brief encounter with Jack and went off to find Ryan O'Neal.

Anjelica was slightly gloomy when she arrived in London and had been for some months. She did not much care for the kind of sickeningly patronizing people who she knew would be surrounding Jack at parties. She felt trapped in a phony existence of famous names and sycophantic hangers-on that had swirled around her since she was a child; few were true friends. Her relationship with Nicholson was back on terra firma, and he had even asked her to marry him. She refused because she thought it was an offer made out of sympathy.

Not only that, she was afraid of marriage. She had seen too many bad ones. She felt her life was going nowhere. She had no career, no major ambitions. If she had once become fed up with being described alternately as Nicholson's longtime girlfriend or Huston's daughter, she now positively detested seeing these descriptions of herself in print.

The Huston dynasty still haunted her, and she reacted by staunchly rejecting the opportunities that came her way because she was a Huston; she saw them as a "baggage of nepotistic embarrassment." Nor could she dispose of the bundle of fears that had engulfed her since her father forced her into her first acting role so many years earlier. All this pent-up uncertainty affected her relationship with Nicholson just as much as his flirtations. To compensate, he would set up auditions and suggest her for film roles; he even offered her a part with himself and Beatty in *The Fortune.*

Anjelica rejected everything. "Absolutely not," she said. "I don't want handouts." Nepotism again. He tried taking her back to her roots at her former home in Ireland, which she had not visited since her mother's death. Her father had sold the castle, but she wandered the grounds of St. Clerans and talked to a gardener who was there when John Huston was squire; she and the gardener both cried. Anjelica admitted to feeling demoralized, almost paralyzed.

"When I first met Jack, I decided I did not want to work for a year," she said, "and then it became two. Before I knew it, I hadn't worked for five years and when I was living with him it was to all intents and purposes as a housewife without my own center. Not that I didn't have a good time. I traveled a lot on his films, but at a certain point I became thoroughly disillusioned with myself for not having an aim, and this was merely aggravated by the fact that we were surrounded by very motivated people all day long."

There was nothing in London to change her perception of life. Another source of strain was that once again she had to endure the personality changes that came through the role Jack was playing. He was working hard on *The Shining,* often not coming home until late in the evening. They seldom went out, and on one occasion when they did, they were an hour late for an engagement to meet Princess Margaret. It was all very similar to the time he was filming the traumatic scenes of *One Flew Over the Cuckoo's Nest* and would come home desperately overwhelmed by the demands of that day's work.

In London this exhaustion was emphasized by his appearance, because by then he was into that part of the film where his character was unshaven, unkempt, and totally mad. He was feeling the pressure of the role now, and there were times when he wished he'd never met Stanley Kubrick. There were indeed some very heavy scenes requiring character changes that he could not shed simply by walking off the set.

Kubrick had a reputation for being methodical and meticulous in everything he did, although not everyone shared the view that the end result was worthwhile. An excellent writer on the cinema, David Thomson, opens his entry on the director in his *Biograph-*

ical Dictionary of the Cinema by saying, "Kubrick is the most significant and ornate dead end in modern cinema. . . . He is most impressive to the uninformed, speculative visitors to the art." Such controversy over his merits had dogged Kubrick through his interpretations of such films as *Spartacus*, *Lolita*, *Dr. Stangelove* and *A Clockwork Orange*, and from that standpoint he and Nicholson appeared to be an ideal partnership.

When Kubrick called just as Nicholson had finished the script of *Goin' South*, he asked: "Have you read Stephen King's new novel?" Jack hadn't, but got hold of a copy of *The Shining*, read it, and sent a "Yes" message to Kubrick back in England, whence he had retreated from Hollywood in 1961, vowing, "I'll never work in that town again."

The Stephen King story was that of aspiring novelist Jack Torrance, who takes the job of caretaker of a seasonal hotel in the mountains of Colorado. The Overlook is a vast place, snow-blocked and kept closed during winter. Built on an ancient Indian burial ground, it is apparently haunted by ghosts from atrocities in American history.

The most memorable and quoted scene from the film is when Torrance hacks his way through a door with his axe while his wife cowers on the other side. He cuts a hole big enough for his face to be seen and cries out: "Heeeeeeeere's Johnny." That line was not in the script or the book. When Nicholson suggested it, Kubrick did not understand what it meant; having lived in England for so long he was not familiar with the introduction to the Johnny Carson show on television. It was a line that brought a sudden injection of light relief into a particularly terrifying moment when audiences were being brought to the very edges of their seats. It was clear that Nicholson put a great deal into the part, though one criticism of the film when it was released was that he had grossly overacted and was often too camp.

He said afterward he had played the role just the way Kubrick wanted it. Even while they were filming, Nicholson challenged some moments and said: "Jesus, Stanley, aren't I playing this too broad?" Kubrick said he was not; he wanted a semicomical villain who was also essentially very evil.

It was this play between humor and horror that most confused the critics. Some were judging Kubrick, some were judging Nicholson, while fans of Stephen King were assessing the overall merit of the film of the book. However, as Nicholson always answers when he runs up against a critic of *The Shining,* it got into the Top Ten Warner Brothers "all-time highest grossers."

NICHOLSON continued to live dangerously by agreeing to appear in three films for friends, all set for release in 1981: *The Postman Always Rings Twice,* directed by Bob Rafelson; *Reds,* for which producer, director, and star Warren Beatty had handed him a six-thousand-page treatment; and *The Border,* which director Tony Richardson was about to bring to the screen. The workload was horrendous; the rewards immense. He was gleefully receiving box office reports that *The Shining,* in its third week of release in June 1980, was second only to *The Empire Strikes Back.*

The Postman Always Rings Twice had been made by Tay Garnett in 1946, with Lana Turner and John Garfield in the leading roles. Nicholson was convinced that it contained tremendous potential for a remake because the censors had never allowed the book to be accurately portrayed. Also appealing to Nicholson was novelist's James M. Cain's unique approach to thriller writing: There were no detective heroes; the protagonists were all criminals. But, above all, it was the sex theme that most attracted Nicholson; he wanted to highlight and extend the provocative scenes first made famous by Lana Turner as Cora. Rafelson hired the Pulitzer Prize–winning playwright David Mamet for the screenplay and world-class cinematographer Sven Nykvist, and then looked around for an actress to play Cora.

One of the actresses Rafelson seriously considered for the part was Susan Anspach. During his deposition in 1996, Nicholson was asked: "Did you ever tell Bob Rafelson that you would not work with Susan Anspach on *The Postman Always Rings Twice*?" Nicholson replied: "I don't recall." However, Susan clearly remembers the occasion. "Bob told me he thought the friction between Jack and me was perfect for the part," she said. "But Jack intervened to stop me getting it. He also blocked Candy Bergen for the same role." A new young star, Jessica Lange, whom Nicholson later described as "a cross between a deer and a Buick," was chosen instead.

The story in essence is one of passion, murder, and deceit. Frank, the Nicholson character, is an ex-convict and mysterious drifter in the days of the Depression, hitching across America. He comes upon a roadside cafe run by a Greek, who befriends him, and his sexy, younger wife, who falls in love with him.

When it came to playing the sex scenes, Nicholson was intent on making them as realistic as possible, even to the extent of spending forty-five minutes upstairs, away from the crew and fellow actors, trying to achieve and sustain an erection—"a full stinger," to use his own words. He did not normally have any problems on that score, especially when playing with one so attractive as Lange, but he had some difficulty in front of the assembled crew and cast. The scene, he felt, was sufficiently important to virtually portray the sex act, and he needed an erect penis—his own—for the full effect. "They had never seen that before in the movies," he explained. "I just knew that odd image would be a stunner."

Nicholson was obviously pleased with the result. According to the gossips on set, he retained a personal video of this particular encounter with Lange to take home and show his friends. In an odd sort of way, however, all these modifications and the increased sexual content actually detracted from the impact. The film turned out to be *not* as sexy as the original and *too* grimy and *too* tacky.

Anjelica Huston had a bit part in the picture, absurdly cast as a German lion tamer, but at last she was working and had done something positive toward bringing a sense of purpose into her life other than being around for Jack's pleasure and companionship. She had picked herself up and stopped her weepy calls to friends who had turned their telephones off because they no longer knew how to deal with her. The last few months had been bad, and made worse by Jack's day-and-night schedule.

The moment of decision came while she was convalescing from a car accident at the start of 1980; a drunk driver on the wrong side of the road had hit her car head-on at the bottom of Coldwater Canyon. She was not wearing a seat belt and went through the windshield, breaking her nose in three places.

"That's it," she said to her father. "I'm going back to acting." He was pleased.

While Nicholson was working, she began to take acting lessons. Her tutor and mentor, Peggy Feury, was as good as a therapist, teaching her to disperse her emotional difficulties, which related directly to her relationships with the two demanding men in her life, her lover and her father. Feury built her confidence and helped her stand apart from everything and look back to analyze her life and begin to make some adjustments. One of the other pupils under Feury's tutelage at the time was a promising young man named Sean Penn, who would later direct Anjelica in one of her most challenging roles.

WARREN BEATTY called one day and said: "Jack, I'm desperate. I'm looking for the right actor to play the part of Eugene O'Neill in *Reds*. Any ideas?"

Nicholson, who had listened endlessly in the past to Beatty's plans to film the life story of John Reed, author of *Ten Days That Shook the World*, replied as Beatty had hoped, "It's got to be me." Beatty had been working on *Reds* for ten years, and by 1979 the projected budget stood at well over $30 million. According to insider reports, it eventually cost nearer $50 million.

It was an all-Beatty extravaganza. He produced, directed, wrote the screenplay (with Trevor Griffiths), and starred, along with some of the biggest names around: Diane Keaton, Maureen Stapleton, Gene Hackman, and, of course, Nicholson himself. Being a close pal, Jack got caught up in the tailwind of this much-discussed Hollywood epic.

The subject, John Reed, had become Beatty's total fascination. A dashing young all-American boy from Portland, Oregon, Reed joined the Greenwich Village radical circle of the early 1900s, where the talk was of revolution. As a writer, he discovered Pancho Villa's struggle in Mexico and happened to be in the right place at the right time to witness Lenin's rise to power. *Ten Days That Shook the World* made him famous, and he became even more famous when he died in the Soviet Union and became the only American to be buried within the Kremlin's walls.

While politics formed much of the story, it also had a strong romantic theme that grew out of the long love affair between Reed and Louise Bryant, the wife of an Oregon dentist. Louise followed him around the world through all kinds of adversity, breaking off only briefly for an affair with the sad, alcoholic playwright Eugene O'Neill. Indeed, the heart of the film is the relationship between Reed and Bryant, which paralleled the off-screen romance between Beatty and Diane Keaton.

To the gossip could be added Nicholson's own enigmatic comments that he had developed a real crush on Keaton, which he felt bad about because she was his best friend's girl. He let it develop, he said, to help the realism of the film, even to the point where the poem he handed Louise in the film was actually one he had written for Keaton. It was a love tangle that, not surprisingly, got into the gossip columns at exactly the same time as the film was being promoted.

The moment Jack finished *Reds* there was one more film that he had pledged to make, *The Border.* He enjoyed Tony Richardson's company and his work, notably *The Charge of the Light Brigade* and *Tom Jones*, and the money was reasonable, of course, because Jack now had a set asking price.

The Border had none of the social glamor of *Reds* or the controversiality of *Postman*; it was a violent film into which Nicholson introduced an uncanny artiness as Charlie, a tough border patrolman engaged in halting illegal immigration into the United States. Although Richardson had been joined by Oscar-nominee scriptwriter Deric Washburn (*The Deer Hunter*), *The Border* was a flawed and depressing movie. The backers, Universal, tried to cheer up the ending, but even that failed to save the film.

For Nicholson, however, the year had ended on a very cheerful note indeed, and he had no need to share Charlie's lament: "I guess I gotta feel good about something I do."

No one could have done more for his friends—even if, in Roman Polanski's case, the price was unacceptably high.

13

ANJELICA'S HONOR

HE WAS FORTY-FOUR YEARS OLD, chunky, with a receding hairline and a face that did not hide the crow's feet; it was the face of a man who had been working hard. He did not try to mask the signs of age. Like Woody Allen, he allowed the reality of thinning hair and slashed temples to show; it is all part of his style of revealing yourself and mocking images of deception and perfection.

As the decade turned into the eighties, life in the Dream Factory was filled with the same kind of uncertainty, indecision, and retribution that had dogged the industry for the previous ten years. There were many casualties lying around Hollywood. Some of them were Jack's friends, and some of those he helped with cash loans during hard times to remind himself that fame and fortune could disappear as quickly as they had arrived. One of the objects in his home attracted the attention of every visitor: It was a silver platter containing a pile of shredded money, bills of all denominations. He had placed it there to make plain his attitude to wealth. "You just have to remember that John Wayne was broke in 1960 to see just how ephemeral movie money can be," he said. "It doesn't matter how much you make, you still can't save anything unless you're one of the landed gentry."

Or possibly Hugh Hefner.

Nicholson was at that time a regular visitor to the Playboy mansion, set in five and three-quarter acres of lush gardens on Charing Cross Road in the suburb of Holmby Hills. Hefner allowed close friends and show business people free access to the mansion, especially on Friday nights, when he gave lavish dinner parties. There was a movie and drinks afterward, followed by disco dancing or other entertainment.

Hefner's personally approved guests could arrive for dinner at nine, or for a 2 A.M. party, or for champagne and breakfast. Heady opulence exuded from the pools, exotic saunas, bars, game room, and theater; behind the mansion itself, the massive Jacuzzi was located in an area of Polynesian design with private guest rooms and bungalows. That was what wealth provided for Nicholson: the freedom to choose and the opportunities for involvement in this kind of lifestyle if he felt so inclined. He collected some of the trappings himself, more for comfort and pleasure than display.

Jack's own Jacuzzi, in an enclosure that took three years to carve out of the rock face, was his first move toward laid-back luxury. Off his living and dining rooms, he built an enclosed patio that led onto a wooden deck with cantilevered swimming pool. There were two Mercedeses in the driveway now, a red one and a blue one. There was a Cadillac convertible, which he hardly ever used, in the garage; he still preferred to drive his VW convertible.

The interior of the handsome white stucco house had an artistic feel, though one with a lived-in atmosphere. His living room was beamed and rustic and invited his visitors to relax and be comfortable. In winter, aromatic pine logs crackled in the hearth. Long, low sofas were placed around the walls. Throughout the house, he had on view his increasingly important art collection—"I'm not so much a collector, I just buy what I like"—which eventually included works by Matisse, Tiepolo, Magritte, Picasso, and Tamara de Lempicka. Though he denied being a collector, he attended art auctions in London and New York and sometimes asked friends to bid on his behalf. The collection grew to such a size that he ran out of hanging space and had to store a number of canvases in a cupboard.

In front of one sofa, he had an onyx coffee table edged with silver and trimmed with silver ashtrays and a silver cigar box for his Cuban Montecristos. The guest bedroom, where Polanski used to stay, had long ago been turned into the den; it boasted a wall-sized television and VCR, for watching favorite movies or replays of Lakers games. Another wall contained a bank of the best stereo equipment for his vast music collection. There were two bedrooms. His own, the master suite at the end of the corridor, had a balcony overlooking the pool; he had installed the balcony to "give myself an escape route if ever I needed it." Anjelica had been using the other bedroom while convalescing since breaking her nose in the car accident.

He kept to a fairly strict regime while working, though that did not stop him from staying up half the night if friends came to call. New friends like John Belushi and Ed Begley Jr., who came into his sphere while making *Goin' South*, dropped by occasionally. Belushi's life was a mess because of drugs, and he sought Jack's advice about how much money he should charge per picture. Nicholson had one answer for Belushi, which was not necessarily true for others. "John," he'd say, "just remember this: Without you there'd be no fucking picture. Charge them a million and a quarter." Nicholson admired Belushi's unique comedic talent; Jack was known among his close friends as being generous with his time in giving others a helping hand or advice based on his own hard-earned experience.

For example, when Mary Steenburgen won an Oscar for her role in *Melvin and Howard*, she said in her acceptance speech that she owed everything to Jack Nicholson, who cast her as his costar in *Goin' South* when everyone else said he was crazy to do so. Without his generous support, she would have gone back to waiting tables in New York. The next day, after the Oscar presentations, Mary received a huge bouquet of flowers from Nicholson with a message reading, "Dearest Chair"—his nickname for her because her film character hung chairs on the wall—"Congratulations on Oscarhood, motherhood, and for me, sainthood."

Sometimes, though, even friends would not be allowed to disturb the Nicholson routine. Though the likes of Nolte, Belushi, and, of course, all his more long-standing friends knew they could call at virtually any time, Nicholson jealously guarded his domesticity from unwanted interlopers. He was adamant about knowing everyone who came to his parties and always insisted on learning the names of the guests they might bring along. He had a strict rule: There were to be no crashers. Maintaining the atmosphere of good friends enjoying themselves in a completely private environment was his goal.

He wanted no gossip column items about what happened at a Jack Nicholson party, and indeed few appeared. In interviews, he himself released snippets to keep the newshounds happy. Apart from the Polanski scandal, which attracted some meticulous media keyholing, there was only one serious occasion when some private details got out. That occurred when *Washington Post* journalist Bob Woodward began his investigations into the "life and fast times" of John Belushi, which became a bestselling book.

It was inspired by Belushi's widow, Judy, who contacted Woodward soon after John's death; she requested all of Belushi's friends to cooperate. Nicholson was among the many whom Woodward interviewed in 1982. Woodward was already famous for his role in exposing the Watergate scandal with colleague Carl Bernstein in the bestselling *All the President's Men*.

Nicholson said he did not especially want to talk about Belushi after his death but did so because Judy had asked that he should. He spoke merely about his friendship with Belushi and of his talents; he was less inclined to discuss the comic's drug problems. Like many others, he seethed with anger when the book was published, in 1984. As he must have anticipated from an investigative professional like Woodward, it was a compellingly chilling book, entitled *Wired*. In following Belushi's life and brief career, it tracked his astonishing appetite for drugs; the word "cocaine" appeared in just about every other paragraph. It demonstrated the forces that worked against his wife, friends, and managers who tried to stop him. In doing so, it exposed the extent of the cocaine culture that had Los Angeles and the entertainment industry in particular in its grip.

Those who cooperated with Woodward found themselves tainted by association with a morbid and awful tale. Nicholson's contribution was a fairly innocuous account of the Belushi he knew. He recalled that on one occasion Belushi had turned up about 5 A.M. "on a terror and trashing the place." He used the Jacuzzi and then sat around in a bathrobe, talking about how he wanted to do a musical with Ken Russell with himself playing God.

Nicholson's anger over Woodward's work stemmed not merely from the overall tenor of the book. Interviews given by others enabled Woodward to put some famous names in a drug environment, and the passage that stung Nicholson into a rage referred to his ambivalence about friends using drugs while in his house and claimed that he "at one time kept two kinds of cocaine—the 'downstairs cocaine' for visitors and acquaintances and the 'upstairs cocaine' for special friends and women." Nicholson said of Woodward: "The man's a ghoul. He's an exploiter of emotionally disturbed widows. I only talked to him because Judy [Belushi] asked me to."

NICHOLSON had canceled 1982. He was tired. He had been telling everyone as he neared completion of filming *The Border* that he had worked virtually every day for the past three years, which was true. He wanted a sabbatical; he wanted to go to bed, get up at the crack of noon, lie on the couch, slumber after a late breakfast, and then go and lie by the pool.

When he had done enough loafing, he wanted to go to Aspen and do lots of skiing and travel again to the sunshine of the south of France without having to plug a film or appear in front of the cameras for days on end. And for the next year or so, the gossip columnists tracked him on his various excursions to fashionable spots and wrote occasionally of the women he encountered, such as Princess Caroline of Monaco, Cathy Wolff, the seventeen-year-old daughter of Petula Clark, and the *Thorn Birds* star Rachel Ward.

Sometimes, Anjelica turned up at his side and they resumed their apparently open relationship, which allowed them to go their separate ways whenever either of them wished.

Susan Anspach disclosed to me that she had made love with Nicholson at his home on Mulholland Drive several times during the eighties. "Anjelica wasn't living there," she said. "He had bought her a house nearby, and theirs wasn't a monogamous relationship by any means—as far as I and, it seems, the rest of the world knew. Jack didn't live with women, but he did live with his drugs. That was a commitment he seemed to have no problem making."

Anjelica had already come to terms with life, and the car accident had prompted her to make some decisions of her own. She moved wholeheartedly toward forging her own career so that she was no longer a sidebar in Nicholson's life. She began talking to directors and producers about auditioning and sought additional coaching to improve her performance. She secured small parts in two films in 1982, *This Is Spinal Tap,* a satire on a British rock group touring the United States, and *Ice Pirates,* in which she played a space-age Amazon. Neither served any other purpose than to give her work experience. She also appeared on television, notably with Penny Marshall and Cindy Williams in their hit television series *Laverne and Shirley*. She began scouting around for her own house, and eventually Jack bought her an attractive, palm-fringed home not far away from his own. No, she told reporters, this did not mean she and Jack were splitting up.

"There is not an area of my life that has not been touched by Jack's influence," she said. "He is a very rare and special being, sensible and at home with himself. When I'm with him, I feel as if I've come home. He's family."

IRONICALLY, family life was the subject of *Terms of Endearment*, the movie that brought Nicholson back to the screen after his long layoff and also provided a significant stepping-stone in his professional life, more so perhaps than anyone realized at the time. James L. Brooks, better known in television for producing *The Mary Tyler Moore Show*, *Rhoda*, and *Taxi*, had been trying to get Jack on the telephone for ages. Brooks owned the rights to the Larry McMurtry novel and intended to make a film of it, with himself producing, directing, and writing the screenplay. He'd had difficulty raising the money because the studio people he had talked to all had reservations about its commercial potential. It was the first big-screen movie for Brooks, and because the story had an unhappy ending, they challenged its viability. "Could it be that we are in danger of doing some original work?" said Brooks with a well-earned note of sarcasm.

Paramount eventually agreed to back him, subject to cast approval. He had signed Debra Winger and Shirley MacLaine as costars and desperately needed a middle-aged male star who would take third billing in a supporting role to play a pot-bellied, slightly balding, hard-drinking, girl-chasing former astronaut without worrying what it might do to his image. Burt Reynolds had already turned it down.

Nicholson read the script and said instantly that he would do it. "How many scripts make you cry?" he said. "I read hundreds of screenplays every year, and this one made me think, 'Yeah, I know just how this guy feels.' It was a terrific screenplay."

It offered him the very type of role he had been seeking to take him from being a thirtysomething renegade involved in sexual and psychopathic activity into a more mellow style that would allow him to grow as a person and an artist. "I could not keep on playing thirty-five-year-olds," he said. "Apart from giving me a more redeeming character to play, I was interested in the transition from a personal standpoint. It's an area of life that had only been explored in sullen lime-green tracts about midlife crises or in situation comedy. Whereas, in truth, it can be different. People have written great novels, for example, during this period of life."

The story had a Chaplinesque blend of comedy and pathos in which Nicholson excelled; it was exactly his kind of humor. He played Garrett Breedlove, who has retired from spaceships to a less-than-quiet existence in the wealthy suburbs of Houston, Texas, where the squeals and shrieks of his unending parade of one-night stands upsets his neighbor, played by Shirley MacLaine. Her character is the neurotic widow Aurora Greenaway, who has remained sexually inactive since her husband died fifteen years earlier.

She is at first appalled by her obnoxious neighbor and then touched by him when she discovers that he has possibilities. This bittersweet romance was secondary to the main theme of a remarkable mother-daughter relationship marked by lighthearted moments punctuated by tragedy. It was a warm and enjoyable film that earned excellent reviews. *Terms of Endearment* also won eleven Academy Award nominations. Nicholson won the Oscar for Best Supporting Actor to go with his award for Best Actor in *One Flew Over the Cuckoo's Nest*, a double achievement matched only by Jack Lemmon and Robert De Niro. Shirley MacLaine won Best Actress, and *Terms of Endearment* was voted Best Picture for 1983.

Nicholson's role bore an uncanny resemblance to the scene-stealing attributes of George Hanson in *Easy Rider*, and he got some of his best reviews in years. He sauntered casually to the podium on award night, wearing his sunglasses, clasped a fist, and said, with typical nonchalance that masked his glee: "All you rock people down at the Roxy and up in the Rockies, rock on." Later he went to Europe, where the film picked up more awards, and France voted him Best Actor; he always had been a particular favorite of the French.

He was jolly and working well in the promotional interviews until *The Sun*, the London newspaper, upset him with allegations of drug use and claim that he had had a "string of drug busts in America," which was untrue. He had never been arrested in his life and had encountered the law only once, when police requested his fingerprints over the Polanski business—and cleared him. He also objected to *The Sun* reporting that he "liked to get high four times a week." The paper had to pay him substantial damages.

The general tone of press coverage in Europe cut deep, and when he returned to America he was fed up. "They blew this drug thing out of all proportion," he complained. "I gave a press conference, and I said some great stuff about the fucking picture, *Terms of Endearment*, and all they wrote about was cocaine, which I didn't even say anything about! They said stuff that they just assumed because of my reputation."

By the time of the accolades for *Terms of Endearment* he was already well into two other projects. The first was *Prizzi's Honor*, which he had agreed to make for John Huston, with Anjelica in a supporting role. After that, he was planning the sequel to *Chinatown*, entitled *The Two Jakes*, with his friends Robert Evans and Robert Towne.

JOHN HUSTON was now seventy-eight years old. With his health fading through periodic bouts of emphysema, he knew that there would not be many chances left to make another film with his daughter. And Anjelica, overcoming her anxieties about nepotism, wanted to work with him. Huston also was eager to direct Nicholson, and Jack was just as enthusiastic. That did not stop him, however, from questioning the choice of screenplay that would finally bring the three of them together.

Huston had taken an option on the novel *Prizzi's Honor* by Richard Condon, an old friend from Ireland. Nicholson did not immediately see the new project in the same light, and Huston needed to persuade him; without Nicholson it was doubtful that he could raise the money to make the film.

"I don't understand it," Nicholson said to Huston after reading the novel and the screenplay and still not appreciating that the overall tone would be one of satirical black comedy, a parody of *The Godfather*.

"I think," said Huston, "we've got the chance of doing something different here." It was exactly the sort of film in which he would have placed Bogart and Bacall. Nicholson was not entirely convinced but said he would trust Huston's instincts, especially as the director was so keen to make the picture and give a major role to Anjelica. A fee of $3.6 million provided an added incentive, although Nicholson told friends that he agreed to participate as a favor to Anjelica and her father.

Once again, he found himself taking on an intriguing, if unattractive, role. He had to play a Mafia hitman named Charley Partanna with a strong Brooklyn accent and, like Bogart, a stiff upper lip. As usual, his preparation was impeccable; this time, it included personal involvement in buying Charley's strange wardrobe from secondhand clothing shops in Los Angeles.

Like *The Godfather,* the film opens at a wedding, but there the similarity ends. Unlike the romantic, charismatic characters that are *Godfather*'s Corleone family, the Prizzis are a weird, gloomy, and psychotically greedy lot. "We'd rather eat our children than part with money," Charley explains. This portrayal upset the Italian community of New York to such a degree that they complained to 20th Century–Fox. Once again, their nationality was being shown as Mafia-oriented, and now they also appeared to be dumb!

Nicholson, as the Don's grandson, played it very dumb indeed. He was the monosyllabic, implacable hitman who killed without remorse and whose character was so unattractive that Huston wanted Nicholson to wear a bald wig. Nicholson said he would prefer not to do that; he needed to administer his own interpretation, which *Time* magazine judged to be "one of his boldest performances" with a subtlety and nerve that matched Huston's. In the opening scene, at the wedding, he discovers a beautiful blond stranger (Kathleen Turner). There is an instant chemistry between them—not unnaturally, perhaps, because she is secretly a hired gun for the Mafia.

As their love affair develops into passionate sex, Charley confides in his cousin and former fiancée, Maerose Prizzi, played by Anjelica Huston, who is plotting to win him back; ironically, Anjelica's part reflected her relationship with Nicholson in that she was seen as being seduced, abandoned, shrewish and spinsterlike, and finally an exceedingly efficent woman in her own right. During location work in Brooklyn, Anjelica and Jack stayed at separate hotels. As usual, Nicholson had become consumed by the part, and there was, according to Anjelica, "too much of the hitman in him when he came home."

Altogether, it was an odd story that played with American criminal folklore and attempted to present a group of ordinary people who performed callous and murderous deeds in pursuit of sex, money, and power as a matter of routine. The message was that organized greed corrupts all. In composing this somewhat clinical parody, Huston constructed a film that laughed at itself and its characters in a black, almost bleak, way.

To Nicholson's fans, it was unquestionably another test of their loyalty. He liked it. And he liked Anjelica's performance as the sedate and Machiavellian Mafia princess. So did her father. Huston called to tell her she had done well. "Afterward, I realized I'd been waiting to hear that from him," she said. After the premiere, Nicholson said he could smell an Oscar—for Anjelica, and he was right. The Academy awarded her Best Supporting Actress in what was her first major acting role since childhood, and thus the movie industry ensured the continuing Huston Oscar-winning tradition for one more generation. Jack was jumping gleefully and whooping support for his lover.

14

JACK'S SECRET SON

"NOTHING CROWDS A ROOM as much as a teenage boy," Jack Nicholson said when making excuses to avoid meeting his son Caleb. Friends said he found teenage boys threatening; they took some of the limelight away from him. Could this have been one of his problems with public recognition of Caleb—too much sharing of attention? Fortunately, his aversion to adolescent youth did not extend to girls, and he had always performed his fatherly duties toward his daughter Jennifer, who volunteered the opinion that he was "a sweet and good man."

After Jack and Sandra Knight had split up, he had entered Jenny's private world "by invitation only," as he put it, and the little girl was always delighted to welcome him. Throughout her childhood, she had enjoyed carefree holidays with Jack and one or another of his girlfriends, though mainly Anjelica Huston, on Mulholland Drive and then returned to Hawaii bursting with stories to tell her mother about how Daddy was faring in wicked old Hollywood.

When she was nineteen, she had joined him in Los Angeles to enroll at the University of Southern California, studying fine arts. Her goal was to enter the movie world, though on the production side rather than as an actress. Father and daughter had developed what Nicholson himself had described as a very adult relationship in which he had adopted a "very open policy." He had not tried to hide anything from her; she knew he indulged in drugs. He explained: "I felt that we could only have a good relationship if I was totally honest with her about what I'm like and what I do." Jennifer agreed that the policy had brought them closer. "Everybody knows all the family secrets, so they don't bother you so much," she said.

There was, however, the unresolved issue of Caleb Goddard to consider, and that was a much trickier subject. For one thing, Nicholson had never mentioned Caleb to Anjelica. Her brother, Tony Huston, said: "She didn't know Caleb existed until he was thirteen years old." Asked about his relationship with Susan Anspach in an interview published in *Rolling Stone* on March 29, 1984, Jack described her as "an avant-garde feminist who—when I met her—was proud of the fact that she already had a child whose father no one knew. She didn't mention her second child to me until six or seven years later."

Q You've never spoken with her about it? Have you ever met the boy?

A No.

Q Did you ever call and say, "Susan, can I see this kid? Can I talk to you about this?"

A I actually made a call a couple of times, but I've never reached her.

Q So you're not convinced that this is your son?

A No, I'm not. But I haven't had the opportunity to look into it. I know Susan slightly and feel she's an extremely respectable person, who is powerful, smart, and, I'm sure, in very good control of what she does. And I guess I like the idea in a certain way.

Q The idea of her son being your child?

A Yeah, if it were true. Hey, I'm ready to meet anybody. Do you know what I mean? And that's all I can say about it.

In fact, Susan had been trying to effect an introduction between father and son for more than seven years. When she separated from Mark Goddard in 1977, she realized that the time for Jack to meet his son was long overdue. "I'd been to a couple of parties at Jack's house on Mulholland, and I called him and told him Mark and I had split up," she said. "It seemed like the right thing for him to take some fatherly interest in his son.

"I wasn't totally stupid. I knew that I had been married and hadn't given him a son when the child was born and that I was at fault there. I was just doing the best I could in terms of having a family. That was the choice I'd made, and I'd have to live with it, but now I was giving him a choice to accept this gift. He said he'd think about how he felt. He was hesitant, and we had this discussion many times."

Nicholson was questioned about his relationship with Caleb at his 1996 deposition:

Q Did she [Susan] make any request at all with respect to Caleb at that time?

A I don't actually remember. I mean, I have a feeling about it. I don't know if that means anything. I don't have a specific recollection about it.

Q Is there anything that you did after this conversation to establish some kind of relationship with Caleb?

A At that time? No.

Q Other than being suspicious, as you have testified before, did you have any other feelings about the information that Ms. Anspach gave you at that party concerning Caleb?

A Well, I mean, I was very pleased that Susan had a son. I felt mildly stung that it hadn't been mentioned to me before.

The matter had assumed an urgency in Susan's life because Caleb had grown into an exact likeness of his father. "When Caleb was becoming a young man-child around the age of thirteen, I really fell in love with Jack in a way that I'd never felt before," she said. "I started seeing him in all Caleb's playfulness, in his goofiness, in his intelligence, in his wiseness. I think that was healthy—that's what you're supposed to do: put it back on the father instead of falling in love with your son. It's a really sane, well-adjusted way to go."

At one point, Susan issued a direct challenge to Jack over the question of fatherhood: "How can you not want to be a father? Don't you know your son needs you?"

"I had no father," he said, "and I'm a big star."

Susan said: "He was saying that fathers weren't important. I'd send him pictures of Caleb and keep him in touch with what we were doing, and we'd talk on the phone. When Caleb came out of the hospital after some treatment in 1984, I drove him up to Jack's place and called from a pay phone. I said, 'I'm bringing him up, and you can decide whether you open the gate or not.' That was when they met for the first time. He acknowledged

Caleb right away when he said, 'You've got my eyes.' After that, I would drop Caleb off at Jack's place or we'd all hang out."

According to writer Martin Torgoff, who visited Nicholson that summer, "with his hair disheveled, sticking up like wild antennae, Jack looks like an unmade bed. He slumped back on the raised couch in his den, engrossed in the tape of yesterday's Celtics-Bucks playoff game, wearing a red Cadillac Cafe T-shirt, his tanned, muscular legs protruding from a pair of baggy gray gym shorts." Jack rarely climbed out of bed before noon, when a cook served him brunch. In the afternoon, he read scripts, shot baskets, played music, swam in his pool, and tried to come to terms with suddenly having a young boy around the house. Caleb was a devout Celtics fan, which gave him and Jack an immediate area of father-son rivalry. They went to watch games together at the Forum.

"I know that Jack absolutely acknowledged Caleb and they would get together for social occasions," said actress Sharron Shayne, a long-standing friend of Susan's. "To tell the truth, I never thought that Jack *didn't* acknowledge Caleb as his son. He's the spitting image of Jack—an incredible kid, very honorable, with a wonderful character, and he was like that as a child."

Caleb was a student at St. Augustine-by-the-Sea in Santa Monica, and Jack followed his scholastic and athletic progress without ever offering financial support. "Susan never asked Jack for a penny," said Sharron. "She didn't believe in that—she was pretty much a feminist all her life." True, there was a huge gap in the father-son relationship that would take time to fill, but this was a healthy beginning. Jennifer had also adopted Caleb as a younger brother, and they grew to love each other, a bond that has never weakened despite the troubles between Jack and Susan.

However, as Nicholson entered a new, mellow era as a father, an experience abruptly intervened to turn his hopes and aspirations into shattering disillusionment.

THE TENTH anniversary of *Chinatown* had been the starting point for the first attempt at the making of its sequel, *The Two Jakes*, which became an obsession that captured him for years to come. The three men who had been responsible for the original—Nicholson, screenwriter Robert Towne, and Robert Evans, now the former head of Paramount—formed a new partnership to make the second film of what had been envisioned as a trilogy; the plan was to revisit the subject every eleven years.

Nicholson and his two friends set up a company called TEN Productions (from the initials of their last names) and were full of high hopes. The partnership deal stipulated they would make the film without salaries and take their recompense from a high percentage of box office receipts. If *The Two Jakes* became as successful as *Chinatown*, it promised to bring in many millions of dollars.

Sitting around the inlaid mahogany conference table in the projection room of Evans's $15 million Beverly Hills mansion, they put their hands together in a bond of trust. As they planned it, *The Two Jakes* would be their film, owned by the triumvirate and made without outside interference: just the three of them, the Irishman (Nicholson), the Beener, (Towne), and the Kid (Evans). There would be no agents, lawyers, dealmakers, or producers linked to the financing. The idea admirably suited Paramount because it would save considerably on the outlay. Work on scripts and sets went ahead, with filming scheduled to begin in early 1985.

Nicholson, of course, would star as the detective Jake Gittes. Towne, whose *Chinatown* screenplay had won him an Oscar, would write the new play and direct the film, since Polanski, the original director, was unavailable. Evans, who was an actor before he became a studio head, was to be the producer and would costar in the role of the other Jake, Jake Berman, a builder of tract homes in Southern California in the postwar housing boom. For the rest of the year and the early part of the next, the three men worked furiously toward their rarely achieved Hollywood coup, a film of their very own. A million dollar's worth of sets were built at Culver City, location geography was carefully mapped out, and a rapid shoot of a few initial scenes was planned to get, as Nicholson put it, Paramount on the hook.

Somewhere in the sayings of Confucius there must be some advice about starting a partnership of three. Nicholson explained: "The main problem is that when you get too many egos involved, including mine, there's going to be friction—but that's normal in filmmaking." Robert Evans became the odd man out as they progressed toward the day that actual filming would begin.

The story handed down in the aftermath was that the Beener came to the Irishman and complained that the Kid wasn't up to it; he could not cope with the demands of the role. They simply had to tell him he was off the picture, news which Nicholson correctly forecast would not be well received.

Towne had nothing against Evans personally. In fact, he was once quoted as saying that Evans set a "standard for every kind of human generosity and one I have yet to see matched in this town." In the movie business yesterday's favor is not necessarily a consideration when ruthless deeds have to be done for the sake of the picture. Evans was mortified by Towne's suggestion that he step down. For one thing, having just come through the very worst two years of his professional life, he needed the money.

ELSEWHERE in Los Angeles, the name of Robert Evans was being mentioned in a sordid murder inquiry in which the protagonists had links to a consignment of stolen cocaine and, ultimately, connections stretching to a Colombian drug cartel. How could Evans have become involved with such a set of people? Before very long he was asking himself the same question. Everybody in Hollywood was asking it, too, because the story was on television newscasts as often as it was plastered all over the newspapers. Suddenly, life looked grim for the former golden boy who was Tinseltown's true-life Last Tycoon.

Nicholson, who went to the Evans mansion most weekends to play tennis on one of the best courts in Beverly Hills, sometimes called him Mogul in recognition of his erstwhile exalted status. Their friendship stretched back to long before Nicholson made *Chinatown*. That was just one of a string of successful films produced at Paramount when Evans was in charge. Others included *Love Story* (he married the star, Ali MacGraw), *Rosemary's Baby*, *The Godfather*, *The Great Gatsby*, and ironically *The Last Tycoon*. Some of the less successful included *Darling Lili*, *Finian's Rainbow*, *Paint Your Wagon*, and *Urban Cowboy*.

The cynics and the avengers ganged up. Bob Evans had it coming to him. Hadn't he just been in the right place at the right time, like the subject of any Hollywood success story, real or imaginary?

He was discovered by Norma Shearer, who thought he was the image of her former husband, Irving Thalberg, and Evans had taken the role of Thalberg in *Man of a Thousand Faces* at her request. He then won a part as the matador in the film version of Hemingway's classic *The Sun Also Rises*, but after these early successes, he struggled as an actor and returned penniless to his family home in New York to work in his brother's lingerie company.

By a stroke of good fortune, the brothers sold the business for $2 million in 1964. With his share, Robert set himself up as a producer. By another stroke of luck, the late Charles Bluhdorn, creator of the Gulf + Western conglomerate, had just bought a company that owned the virtually bankrupt film studio, Paramount. Bludhorn knew nothing about the film business, and he hired Evans after reading a profile of him in the local newspaper. Six months later, Bob Evans was made worldwide head of Paramount.

In the coming decade, which he described—as he did virtually everything—as magic, he became the new miracle worker of Hollywood, the Man With the Midas Touch, and by holding frequent press conferences, he made sure that everyone knew it. He surrounded himself with all the trappings of great wealth inside Woodland, a vast reproduction French Regency mansion with a mansard roof. There were thirty-two telephones, countless rooms, a personal bathroom in sheer black marble, a sable bedspread on his double king-size bed, a swimming pool with eighteen fountain jets that looked like something from a tropical island, and his collection of Etruscan artifacts, each illuminated by an individual spotlight.

At dinner, the food was served on china designed by himself, showing a naked girl riding a centaur; after Ali MacGraw walked out, he decorated his arms with gold bangles and the latest models. He was on intimate terms with the rich and famous. In Hollywood, his party guests were the elite of the profession, especially the new wave of stars—Hoffman, Nicholson, and Beatty.

In higher circles, Henry Kissinger and Edward Kennedy were among his friends. His became the supreme success story. He modeled himself on his hero, David O. Selznick, even down to a flirtation with stimulants. In 1980, he pleaded guilty to possession of cocaine, and one of the conditions of his probation was that he should make a $400,000 antidrug film at his own expense.

When Barry Diller was made corporate head of Paramount, Evans departed quite suddenly after they met for breakfast at the Bel-Air Hotel. People asked, "Did he fall or was he pushed?" a frequent question in Hollywood. It mattered not. The Mogul had followed the route of other moguls through the door marked EXIT. He wanted to produce his own highly individualistic movie—just as Selznick had done with *Gone With the Wind*—and for him it was *The Cotton Club*, written by Mario Puzo with the later assistance of Francis Ford Coppola, the same team that had given him *The Godfather*. Richard Gere, the latest male star to appear in the firmament, had tentatively agreed to terms.

Evans said it was going to be a masterpiece, but for once the supersalesman was unable to convince the backers. He was financing preproduction costs himself, running at $140,000 a week, and he had sold the last of his Paramount stock to pay his debts. His search for backers took him into discussions with a variety of possible partners, including Adnan Khashoggi and his brother Essam, but they could not come to an agreement.

He finally agreed to go into partnership with an unsavory New York promoter called Roy Radin, with the objective of making movies. However, Radin double-crossed the drug cartel of which he was secretly a member and was murdered by contract killers in a disagreement over a missing consignment of cocaine. His body was discovered, riddled with bullets, in a remote canyon in California. Thus, in April 1984, Robert Evans found himself in the middle of what became known as the *Cotton Club* case.

The investigation took the Los Angeles police force the ensuing five years, virtually putting Evans's career in suspension. His reputation suffered amid rumors that he would be charged with conspiracy to murder. Nasty stories surfaced about his private life: among them that on Christmas Eve he showed porn movies in his mansion with actors depicting Jesus and the Virgin Mary in anything but evangelical poses.

Then there were the antics of Denise Beaumont, a stunning brunette playgirl from Palm Springs who drifted into the Evans set and stayed to party. A Hollywood socialite told me: "Denise and Bob Evans's friendship has always been based upon the fact that her unofficial job was to bring girls over to the house and her real job was to break them in for three-way sex, which Denise was more than happy to do. So she knew Warren Beatty and Jack [Nicholson] very well—the regulars over at the house.

"Before Warren got married to Annette Bening, he and Jack were like the two studs, and Robert Evans was the glue that held it all together because he had the house. Warren did eventually buy a house near Jack up on Mulholland Drive, but for years he lived in the penthouse at the Beverly Wilshire. Jack's not the kind of guy who wants people up at his house, and he doesn't have a screening room. Evans's was always *the* place. He had the screening room . . . he had the girls—what more could a guy want?

"It was always fun over at Evans's place. Evans could always get girls because he was a big motion picture producer, so there was never a shortage of great-looking, sexy women over there."

A former stripper, who knows the Evans scene well, said: "Denise Beaumont thought that Robert was going to put her in movies, so she was always bringing great-looking girls up to his house for him and his friends. The truth was Denise couldn't act. Robert put her in *The Cotton Club*, but all of her scenes ended up on the cutting room floor. He liked her there because she was wild and crazy, and his pals like Jack Nicholson and Warren Beatty liked her and the girls she invited over. But Denise always got out of control because she drank too much and did too many drugs."

An L.A. actress, who lived with Denise for two years, said: "One time she heard that Jack Nicholson, Warren Beatty, and Robert Evans were all talking about how many times they had screwed her. She got really pissed off and vowed to get revenge. Well, first she went to Robert Evans's home and screwed him, then she went over to Jack Nicholson's and screwed him, then she went to Warren's and had sex with him. After Warren had oral sex with her, she began to laugh and told him that Bob and Jack had just been there. At first they were all mad at her, but then Robert Evans thought it was funny, and it became the big joke of the group: how Denise Beaumont got even with them."

The district attorney's office, of course, knew none of this at the time of the investigation. But having first indicated that Evans might be implicated in the slaying and then having failed to produce any evidence to prove it, the DA listed him as a chief prosecution witness. The Hollywood cold shoulder was turned with vigor, and he was an outcast to all but a few of his closest friends.

Evans, nevertheless, had found backers for *The Cotton Club*, principally two Lebanese casino owners from Las Vegas, but he lost control of the picture. It also went millions over budget and flopped badly. He blamed Coppola while Coppola blamed him. Evans was close to financial ruin, which he hoped to stave off through his partnership with Nicholson and Towne.

When acrimony exploded between Evans and Towne four days before principal photography was due to start on *The Two Jakes*, he was understandably in no mood to go quietly. He blew his top, as Nicholson said he would. In a series of standoffs over the next three days, Towne moved that Evans should be fired; it was the only way he thought they could save the film from disaster. Nicholson refused to treat their partner "like shit," but Paramount, by now listening to the jungle drums about Evans's other troubles, pulled out.

Production of Nicholson's great hope ended before it had even started. The million-dollar sets stood idle and had to be destroyed. The partners were sued by creditors, which cost them $3 million and created a lot of bad publicity. The three friends, who had joined hands in a bond of trust and faith, parted in an acrimonious dispute. Nicholson astutely summed up: "What you have to realize is that a lot of people were anxious to see *The Two Jakes* fail because of all the rumors about the problems we were having making it."

Nicholson felt especially sorry for Evans. His friend was clearly in dire straits, having to sell his mansion and lease it back to raise some capital to live. Towne also suffered. The furor in the press over *The Two Jakes* damaged his reputation, and it was two years before he managed to get another film to write and direct, the flawed but intriguing *Tequila Sunrise*. For the moment, *The Two Jakes* seemed doomed.

ALMOST on cue as *The Two Jakes* collapsed, Mike Nichols was looking for a male lead for his film adaptation of *Heartburn*, Nora Ephron's screenplay from her bestselling roman à clef based on her marriage to the Watergate reporter Carl Bernstein.

Nora's tale was one of a charismatic professional couple who fall in love, have a child, and live a wonderfully witty life, with nights of pepperoni and show tunes until she discovers he is having an affair. The other woman, in real life, was Margaret Jay, daughter of former British prime minister James Callaghan and wife of the man whom the PM sent to Washington as British ambassador, Peter Jay.

In Washington, it was a great talking point because of the personalities involved. Nora Ephron was so bitter about it all that she wrote a thinly disguised, autobiographical novel that became a bestseller. A wife so badly scorned writes in blood, and the blood was Bernstein's.

The alleged fictional husband was painted as an insensitive, sex-mad male chauvinist "who was capable of having sex with a Venetian blind." Bernstein said that when he heard about it, he made a deliberate decision to say nothing to fellow journalists. Instead, he took it in his stride, and after his initial anger he was man enough to admit that Nora had written a perfect obituary for the Me Decade: "It is a clever piece of gossip that owed its success to who we were. *Heartburn* is a book of our times. It is prurient and it obliterates everybody's dignity." He was none too happy when he heard there was a movie in the offing, and he telephoned his lawyer.

Bernstein was worried that he would become a laughingstock. "From now on," he said, "I'm going to be hard-assed about this in terms of what can be in the movie and what can't." In an out-of-court settlement, Nora and the filmmakers agreed to give Bernstein the right to see the script and consult with the director, Mike Nichols, on matters he found distasteful.

Nicholson came in with a $3.5 million contract two weeks after filming had started. He was doing a favor for Nichols, whose first choice for leading man, Mandy Patinkin, had found the constraints of the legal maneuvers too much to handle. Nicholson was given specific instructions from Nichols that he must *not* play Bernstein, whom he had met a couple of times in the past at political events. He had to create the husband character himself.

"I probably wouldn't have considered doing the movie," Nicholson said, "but I'd never been hired *not* to play someone before. I was hired not to play Carl, and I liked the idea. It's a provocative idea for an actor." He thought the part had been written as an uninteresting sort of a cad, though a likeable enough fellow. He said, "If you play characters for charm, it's most often cloying, so here was an opportunity where you had to bring a little bit of quality . . . make it a little bit show-boaty."

His own personal stock of tricks, such as the way he might enter a room or get up out of a chair or put his feet on a table—plus the revolving eyebrows, the catlike grin, and the occasional flash of his scary fierceness—were all brought into play in creating his un-Bernstein-like character. Meryl Streep as Nora found herself pushed to keep him from acting her off the screen. His moments are filled with humor, and even when he is not in the action, his presence is felt. Never did the audience get the impression of the near villainous Venetian-blind-shafter portrayed in the book.

Jack was having fun, as an actor and in his character, but the onus of making the picture work fell on Meryl Streep, the star of the show. She, unlike Nicholson, based her performance on a real person. She copied Nora Ephron down to her mannerisms and facial expressions; Streep had the constant vision of Nora in her mind. Even though her performance might be more imitation than creation, Streep did carry the film along, and there were some funny moments in which, with Nicholson as the feed, she excelled. These better moments tended to come in scene-length clips rather than hang together as a whole.

Critics had mixed reactions to the film, and so did audiences; most seemed to think that the actors had been limited by a poorly structured script that went tangentially into other confusing areas. The film did not do justice to the book, nor to the actors in it, and box office response was decidedly low-key.

AFTERWARD, a lot of gossip centered around a certain chemistry that had developed between Streep and Nicholson during filming. Director Mike Nichols had tried to induce it by keeping them apart until the very last minute—they had never met before—but Nicholson spoiled that scheme by barging into Streep's dressing room looking like something the cat had dragged in and saying: "Hi, do you mind if I use your toilet?" However, it was certainly obvious in the early scenes of happier times in the marriage that they had quickly established a rapport. It brought out the unexpected comedienne in Streep. Her crackling, wisecrack responses to Nicholson fairly sizzled.

Word reached the outside world that Nicholson was totally smitten by Streep, who was happily married to sculptor Don Gummer. As the film hit the circuits, Nicholson gave an interview to *Vanity Fair* that merely added a touch of spice to the mystery. He often chooses to chat to the megamedia during the launch of a new movie. He talked of his "experience" with Streep: "Meryl is my idol. She was so good [in one particular scene] . . . I was all at sea, floundering around, but I could see that we would be fine because she was doing great. You do fall in love with . . . certain . . . creative situations."

Read into that what you will, because that is why it is there; it is part of the image, and there was more: A life-sized portrait of Meryl was hung in the Mulholland Drive house, and Anjelica was so angry that Jack had to buy her an $85,000 bracelet to pacify her, so it was whispered. Was this true desire, or was it just that some juicy gossip would give his box office percentages a bit of a lift? One thing was certain in an era in which teenage-oriented pictures were all the rage, pictures Nicholson did not much care for: He was beginning to feel his age. During a break one night, he went to the movies and watched *Ferris Bueller's Day Off*. He came out feeling "totally irrelevant, 119 years old, and that my days were numbered."

He went home to Anjelica, his ever understanding and unmarried companion. Apparently untouched by the message of fidelity in *Heartburn,* he continued to behave like the cad he might have portrayed in the Nora Ephron story if Carl Bernstein hadn't threatened him legally. He made some self-serving remarks about a culture that fears total freedom; he said that rigid moral principles relating to sexual fidelity needed adjustment to suit personal situations—like his own, no doubt.

Anjelica drifted into his house and bed and then back to her own and looked the picture of a relatively contented woman. Unlike Nora, she managed to come to terms with the lifestyle of her man, though it was difficult at times.

15

BEWITCHED

IN THE SPRING of 1986, Jack Nicholson accepted $5 million to make *The Witches of Eastwick*. The producers for Warner Brothers were a pair of young whiz kids, Peter Guber and Jon Peters (the same two who would offer him the part of the Joker in *Batman* a year later). For a man of a certain reputation, it was not unfair to observe, as many did, that it was a role for which Nicholson had been practicing all his adult life, and his later self-caricature as Dr. Devil owed a great deal to his portrayal of Daryl Van Horne.

Nicholson seemed such a natural for the role of Lucifer in the guise of the mysterious, violin-playing Van Horne that the film's director, George Miller, who hadn't met him at this stage, expressed some doubts. "When I read the screenplay," he told me, "it was so like Jack that I thought, 'It's too obvious, it's too on the nose.' But I happened to be speaking to a friend of his, Carol Kane [an actress who had known Jack since she made her screen debut in *Carnal Knowledge*], and she said, 'No, the Jack you see—the public persona—is different from the real Jack. He's got quite a spiritual dimension to him.'

"That really surprised me, and when I eventually met him, I understood what she meant. He's a very evolved human being, very evolved. He's not so much cosmic as someone who's learned from life. When you look at his career, you realize that most of the roles he takes on are pretty evil characters, and I've since learned that you can't really take on those roles and make them sympathetic unless you're a pretty substantial human being."

Anjelica was called in to do a screen test for Miller for the role of one of the three witches, but she was unaccountably struck by nerves. She knew as soon as she had completed the test that she would not get the part. Cher won instead to join Michelle Pfeiffer and Susan Sarandon in a sex comedy written by the Pulitzer Prize–winning playwright Michael Cristofer and loosely based on John Updike's bestselling novel. Miller had directed the successful Mad Max trilogy, but this was his first Hollywood feature film. He was, he said, absolutely astounded by the turmoil that occurred before he could start filming that summer. "It was very difficult because of the madness of the producers, Peter Guber and Jon Peters," he said. "They were just competely morally, organizationally, and in every other way chaotic. Peters had blowups with anybody, big, blustering things, and then got incredibly apologetic. It happened several times, and I just ignored him after a while. But it was crazy. Over half my energy went in politics with the studio. Their inefficiency put huge costs on the film just by craziness. [They were] completely erratic—worse than erratic; they had no idea how to make a movie.

"No one wanted to know about Michelle Pfeiffer until we tested her, because at the time she wasn't regarded as big-star material. People didn't think she could act, but she did a magnificent screen test, so she came in as a kind of junior. They didn't want Anjelica, either—none of them wanted Anjelica—but I thought it had worked so well with Michelle that I said, 'Okay, let's test her.' [The idea] was to get some cohesion, some focus from the studio and the producers. We tested Anjelica for the role the day after she won the Academy Award. Unfortunately, the test wasn't very good. Jack was incredibly gracious about it. I mean, Anjelica could have done it much better than Cher. Cher was the odd one out in the sense that she and I didn't get on and she and the producers didn't get on; I didn't think she was right for the role, and we switched roles between Susan Sarandon and Cher. It was not something I enjoyed being part of, but it was necessary to keep the film going."

Thus, at the eleventh hour, Cher became Alexandra, the chief witch who sculpts fertility idols, while Sarandon switched to Jane, the number two witch who teaches music. Pfeiffer remained as Sukie, the junior witch, who writes social notes for the local newspaper.

Even before they had shot a single scene, Miller was impressed by Jack's total commitment to the project. "He said to me before we started, 'You don't just get an actor [with me], you get a moviemaker.' He didn't mean the fact that he'd directed and produced, he meant that he would do whatever's necessary to get the movie made with the highest degree of excellence."

Jack threw himself into research for his part by reading Dante's *Inferno* and vast mounds of witchcraft material from the Middle Ages to examine the nature of evil, declaring to Anjelica that he wanted his audiences to think that Jack Nicholson was the Devil himself. That, she assured him, should not prove too difficult, even without the research.

It was going to be Nicholson's show. Everyone could see that; he was positively drooling in the publicity photographs. With three beautiful women wrapping themselves around him at every turn of the page, *Witches* offered the type of role that best suited him, sexy comedy with a touch of menace—once the producers decided exactly what sort of film they wanted. George Miller struggled to meet the edicts of Guber and Peters, shooting some scenes eight or nine different ways. The three actresses were occasionally near tears and were said to have tried some amateur witchcraft themselves to inflict the men on the other side of the cameras with a heavy rash of herpes.

Miller, a thick-set, quiet-spoken Australian, said: "I kept it on the rails, but I was going to quit two or three times, and it was Jack who said, 'No, we're doing good work here, hang in.' He advised me to make them all think I was a bit crazy. He said, 'You're too nice. If they think you're crazy, they'll be frightened of you.'

"He's incredibly loyal—the most loyal person I've ever met in terms of his friends. He doesn't take power, he kinds of surfs power—he goes with the wave, he goes with the flow, which I find very female. 'Male' and 'female' are words you have to be careful of; I certainly don't mean effeminate. I mean that very nurturing, affiliative, go-with-the-flow approach that's female. If you characterized bull-at-a-gate behavior as male, well, that's not Jack. You can't be a great actor like him unless you've got that great flow. He loves the group, and he's very nurturing in that way. I think that's why females are attracted to him. He was nurturing toward the three actresses, toward me, and anyone else he thought was doing a good job on the film."

"We all looked forward so much to working with Jack," said Michelle Pfeiffer, "and then we were reduced to weeping because of the demands of these conflicting forces running the picture. I seriously considered walking off. I might well have, if it hadn't been for Jack." He provided the shoulder to cry on, but since he had only two, there was always an odd girl out.

Nicholson plowed on regardless, having a good time in the role. In Eastwick, a conformist New England village, Daryl Van Horne has been invoked by three bored women seeking more pleasurable experiences than the local male population can supply. He buys a big mansion on the outskirts of town, and no one knows who he is or whence he came; the women who summoned him, meantime, are delighted to discover that he can provide all they desire of him.

Nicholson displayed his usual flair for relaxing his comrades to good effect, playing a sort of Devil's advocate with director, producers, and costars. Cher was especially grateful: "I wanted to be in *Witches of Eastwick* because of Jack. He was like the jewel, and we women were the setting. I remember getting ready to do the buffet scene on the lawn, and for some reason I got an anxiety attack. I could hardly move. I was terrified, and he put his arm around me and said, 'Look, it's free-floating anxiety, nerves. Nobody's gonna do this scene until you're ready.' And the minute he said that, I really started to feel good."

Miller greatly appreciated the magic that Jack worked with the cast. "We had to work incredibly hard with Cher to get that performance," he said. "She was a bundle of nerves. She's the opposite of Jack; she's not a very evolved human being. She's got too much unresolved stuff, a lot of baggage that goes back to childhood. The other three, Jack, Susan, and Michelle, understood the ensemble. But, in her case, she felt somehow she was the star. Years later Nick Nolte said that if someone is used to being a performer, either a comedian or a pop star, the entire show depends on how they do, so they can't see the ensemble, they can't see the group effort, they can only see the individual work. So she had no broad view of the movie, whereas Jack was the opposite. He was doing everything he could to get the movie made. He worked his butt off to get a performance out of Cher. He'd do the most outrageous things behind the camera. Whereas most stars would be off set, he'd come in when he wasn't shooting and just feed off-camera lines to the actresses. He was fantastic."

The Witches of Eastwick became one of the great box office success of 1987, taking in more than $125 million. George Miller survived his Hollywood baptism of fire but did not make another feature film for five years. "It was a terrible experience, but it was also one of the best I've ever had because of the experience of getting to know Jack," he said. "He was very lovely to me. Jack was the one who held it together. He not only has the ability to live in the moment, he somehow uses his experience to see what's valuable and important in life. Even though he won't sit and have long philosophical conversations like people might do on college campuses, he is deeply philosophical."

NICHOLSON collected another $5 million to star in *Ironweed*, the film adaptation of William Kennedy's bestseller about the decline and fall of a baseball star. It was scheduled for filming in Albany, New York, during the spring of 1987. The director was to be Hector Babenco, famed for his portrayal of human degradation in South American slums and prisons in such films as *Pixote* and *Kiss of the Spider Woman*.

There was an added bonus in that his costar was, once again, Meryl Streep, whom he loved as an actress and, it was said, as a woman. He had been planning to cut back his commitments but went on working because, he said, Anjelica would be tied up in the coming months, working with her father on a film version of a James Joyce short story, *The Dead*.

Anjelica had made great strides toward establishing herself as a leading actress. An Oscar was fine, but she still needed more work to show that it was not merely a fluke. Francis Ford Coppola cast her in his Vietnam War movie *Gardens of Stone*, with James Caan, and her father wanted to involve three Hustons—himself, Anjelica, and his son Tony—in *The Dead*. Tony had already been put to work writing the script. John Huston was largely incapacitated; he was often confined to a wheelchair and had a permanent supply of oxygen on hand.

However, there was one family reunion that did not come off as the gossip columnists had hoped. Jack had suggested that Caleb should audition to play the younger version of his character in *Ironweed*. Dozens turned up for the casting call, but Caleb was not among them; he had no intention of following his mother and father into the movies. Jack's invitation, though, was a welcome sign that the father-son relationship was working, even though Jack still refused to speak about him in interviews.

Nicholson made it a condition of his contract that the producers provide him with a house with an indoor swimming pool, where he could keep up a new fitness regime he had recently commenced after his weight had shot up to 210 pounds. Fitness was an important consideration because he was at that psychological point in life of the Big Five-Oh, as he called it, and he did not care to be reminded of it when he looked in the mirror. It was only during these periods of working that he looked strictly at his diet; otherwise his food tended to consist of a wide mixture of tastes and styles, ranging from junk food to the best Italian cuisine around.

Anjelica flew in for a birthday celebration during the weekend of April 18, and on his actual birthday, the twenty-second, she joined the cast on the set of *Ironweed* to toast him with champagne. It had to be a brief interruption, though, because shooting was scheduled until late in the evening, often until the early hours of the morning, largely because Nicholson's contract stipulated a sixty-nine-day schedule with a $70,000-a-day penalty for overtime.

The movie itself wasn't exactly smooth going. *Ironweed* was a gloomy saga about dropouts from society in which alcoholism triggers a despairing weight of memory, guilt, and hopelessness. It was also an arty film, full of silences and moody location shots. The scenes were heavy but lacked drama or suspense, even though Babenco had tried to extract some kind of Brandoesque performance from Nicholson. There were moments that were as good as, if not better than, anything he had ever done. However, the film recouped only a fraction of its $27 million budget despite costarring the two most sought-after and highly paid actors in the world. Nicholson and Streep received Best Actor and Best Actress Academy Award nominations for their performances in *Ironweed*, but neither won.

Between *The Witches of Eastwick* and *Ironweed*, Jack had also found time to do a cameo role in *Broadcast News* for his friend James L. Brooks. Nicholson played the conceited anchorman on a network TV news program in a satirical comedy about a trio of young TV hopefuls: a feisty, truth-seeking producer (Holly Hunter), an ambitious though ultimately deceitful newsreader (William Hurt), and a rapid-fire young war correspondent (Albert Brooks). Written and directed by Jim Brooks with tremendous verve, *Broadcast News* stripped the gloss off TV news reporting from first newsbreak to station signoff. The finished product must have appealed greatly to Nicholson, who makes no secret of the fact that he detests television. He agreed to do the part provided he received no off-screen billing, explaining that it would have been unfair to his fans who might go to the movie on the strength of seeing his name on the marquee and then discover that he had only a minor role.

However, Nicholson figured that once it became known he was one of the cast, it would become a selling point for the film. The zero advertising strategy worked. Audiences actually cheered when Jack was spotted on screen, and he chalked up a triumph that sent a chill through Madison Avenue: how to sell a movie without spending a dime.

HE APPEARS on TV reluctantly and then only for special programs, such as the Oscar ceremony. He has said that never, never would he go on talk shows, which he hates. His TV appearances are unscheduled and always at basketball games. He supports the team of Magic Johnson, and later Shaquille O'Neal, with an ardor verging on fanaticism.

At the Forum, he invariably arrives as tension is mounting in the capacity crowd and heads toward his courtside seat. A mild cheer goes up. He is wearing one of his two dozen pairs of designer sunglasses, a crumpled white suit, black shirt, and sneakers. He waves and clasps his hands. In spite of his closeness to the action, a pair of binoculars hangs around his neck. Normally, he slips in during the national anthem to avoid a fuss. Then he shuffles his feet, clears his throat, and gets ready for some loud deliveries of support for the home team, taunts against the visitors, or insults for the referee.

This is the Nicholson ritual, three hours of devoted, throaty, passionate support for the basketball heroes whom he watches, work permitting, fifty nights a year. He is their number one fan and has been for so long that no one awards him special status, except for a ribald welcome from the crowd to which he impolitely responds. Visiting fans and officials eye him cautiously.

He often travels with the Lakers to away games, but when he can't make it, either at home or away, they videotape the game for him and send it overnight to wherever he may be. The Lakers have plenty of celebrity followers, but he doesn't join in the backslapping routine in the dressing rooms.

The tales of Nicholson the basketball fan are legendary. One of the most memorable was back in 1980 when the Washington Bullets were playing at the Forum and a lively exchange broke out as the visitors' coach, Dick Motta, began shouting at an official and headed toward the scorer's table. Just as he passed Nicholson, the star grabbed him by the legs.

"You touch me again and you won't need a frontal lobotomy," screamed Motta.

"You're breaking the rules," Nicholson shouted back.

"Say, pal," Motta responded, "if you wanna be a coach, buy me a team and I'll make you my assistant. Now sit down."

"Sit down yourself," Nicholson came back. "I pay money for these seats, and by the way, pal, it'll take somebody bigger than you to make me sit down."

His best, or worst, encounters have been with his son Caleb's team, the Boston Celtics. At the Forum one night, Boston star Larry Bird came close with the ball to where Nicholson was sitting with his godson, Nicky Adler, son of the music mogul Lou. Jack turned to the boy and urged: "Hey, babe, bite the son of a bitch." Bird looked up and winked at the boy.

That was good-humored banter, but sometimes a note of bitterness creeps in. One of Boston's officials described him as "an embarrassment to the game and a nuisance to the players." This criticism came after Nicholson dropped his trousers and mooned the Boston Garden home crowd.

Since then, Nicholson has been the target of animosity whenever he turns up for a game in Boston. When he flew in for the finals, in 1984, he heard there might be a reception committee waiting, so he threw Celtics fans off the track with the elaborate dodge of making reservations at every major hotel. One of the local radio stations, WBCN, was urging anyone who had a ticket for the game to take a sign reading JACK FLEW EAST, JACK FLEW WEST, FLY JACK BACK TO THE CUCKOO'S NEST.

WBCN said the idea was submitted by a Celtics fan who was fed up with Nicholson's face and the bad-mouthing he gave the home team and its officials. When he arrived at the arena, he found T-shirt sellers touting a great new line in slogans, FUCK YOU, JACK. He laughed and bought a dozen to take home.

Inside, there were more anti-Nicholson posters than pro-Boston signs, among them HIT THE ROAD, JACK and CHOKE ON YOUR COKE, JACK. As he arrived to take his seat, he stood up and held his hand around his throat in a choking sign and made obscene gestures to demonstrate his view that Boston had no chance.

He lived to tell the tale.

16

REBECCA'S LOVER

AT A PARTY ONE frosty night at his Aspen home, Jack Nicholson met Karen Mayo-Chandler, a British model and aspiring actress. After playing a minor role in Woody Allen's *Play It Again, Sam* in San Francisco, Karen had moved to Hollywood in search of a full-time career in films. Having been married briefly, she was unattached when she was introduced to her host on February 13, 1986. Jack's Dr. Devil grin indicated that a new, tempestuous affair was about to happen.

That night was fairly typical of the parties that Nicholson held in the Green House, a desirable Victorian residence in town near the corner of Monarch and Hallem. He opened the door personally to the party of six with whom Karen had arrived. Hanging their coats in the closet, he showed them where to change out of their snowboots into evening shoes. Some Irish friends were among the guests, including a priest who had known Jack's family in New Jersey. The priest played the fiddle, and everyone danced and sang. Nicholson, said Karen, was the perfect host, polite and sober. He drank Louis Roederer Cristal champagne, but not to excess. There was a buffet supper laid out in the kitchen, and guests wandered through the three downstairs rooms.

Those outside his circle, Karen observed, might have been surprised to discover that one of the world's highest-paid film stars ran a fairly modest household, relaxed and informal, with few obvious signs of his wealth. He dressed in clothes that looked slightly disheveled, but a closer examination would reveal that even his baggy sweatpants carried an expensive designer label.

Karen and one of her friends whom she had accompanied to Aspen from Los Angeles were invited back to Nicholson's house the following evening, St. Valentine's night. There was a log fire crackling, and the open curtains revealed a stunning view of the Aspen landscape. More champagne was drunk, and, according to Karen, Nicholson made a guarded suggestion that the three of them should retire to his room, at which point, she said, she and her friend decided to leave.

Back in Los Angeles, Jack virtually snubbed her in a chance meeting at Helena's nightclub, then apologized when they met again at a $500-a-ticket charity night at the Hard Rock Cafe. They eventually came together when Karen went to the house on Mulholland Drive for another party.

Jack later showed her off to his friends, taking her to dinner at Robert Evans's mansion and to Warren Beatty's home for a showing of *Mona Lisa*. Nicholson's friends could see what was happening between Jack and Karen and did not need to ask what this meant as far as he and Anjelica were concerned. Their relationship was the same as it had been for the past five or six years—an understanding that allowed him the latitude to continue another life just so long as he did not make a fool of her.

Karen visited Mulholland Drive often that summer. As she would later describe in detail, he took her on an exciting voyage of sexual discovery with long, passionate nights of lovemaking—she loved the messages he left for her on her answering machine, "Hi, babe. It's raining. Come up to my place and we'll do it in the rain."

Nicholson was having fun, but Karen took it seriously. She knew that Anjelica was still in the background of his life somewhere; perhaps even he did not know where. "If he had been married, I would not have agreed to see him," said Karen. "I believed his relationship with Anjelica had become merely a friendship thing."

Karen insists—using the words "in all honesty"—that he was going to make some kind of commitment to her. When she asked him about his intentions, she pointed out that he was old enough to be her father and that there were many younger, more attractive, and possibly more virile men around with whom she could find sexual satisfaction, if that was all she wanted. She said her feelings for him were powerful and she hoped they were reciprocal. It all sounded a bit like wishful thinking, yet in those hot summer months around the Nicholson pool, even if Karen only half-believed that she and Jack would form a permanent relationship, disappointment would soon loom large.

THE SUMMER fun for Nicholson was shattered by the death of John Huston, who had remained active long enough to achieve his ambition to complete *The Dead* with his two children. They had had happy times during the spring and early summer of 1987, and the children felt closer to him than ever before.

Huston had hoped it would be like that, because he knew he was dying and this would be his last film. The subject matter was carefully and poignantly chosen. Huston could quote the Joyce short story from memory, and he would be writing his own epitaph with one line from it: *Better to pass boldly into that other world, in the full glory of some passion, than fade and wither dismally with age.*

The film was to be his final testament, not only to his family and his profession but also to his beloved Ireland. Translating the story to the screen was difficult because so much of it consisted of a man's thoughts, and the result was not especially successful in the way that Hollywood judges success. It was, however, the best film that Huston could possibly have left his audience before passing boldly on. Critics acclaimed it as a triumph, with Anjelica winning many of the plaudits.

Huston died on August 28, 1987, at the age of eighty-one at a house he had rented in Newport, Rhode Island.

If there was one unexpected legacy, it was that Anjelica's own confidence had been given the final boost she required. As Tony Huston saw it, their father had spent his last two years in a quest to pass on the knowledge he had acquired in a lifetime. "It was almost like shift work," Tony recalled, "going from one to the other to work in collaboration—first Anjelica, the actress, then me, the writer, and then Danny, the youngest, to whom he gave the director's eye."

To Jack Nicholson, John Huston bequeathed an instruction that he should look after Anjelica. Nicholson promised he would. Jack served as moderator at the memorial service for Huston arranged by the Directors Guild and could not hold back the tears as he spoke his tribute. He said he would cry for the rest of his life.

In the days following Huston's death, Jack was asked to contribute to many newspaper and magazine articles assessing his idol's life and career. Coincidentally, a festival of John Huston's films had been arranged in Sante Fe from September 16 to 20, and it became a memorial to him instead. Jack, who had stayed closer to Anjelica after her father's death, was to have accompanied her to the festival, but at the last minute she decided not to go. Tony and Danny went, along with Lauren Bacall, E. G. Marshall, Zsa Zsa Gabor, Jacqueline Bisset, and Brian Keith, to talk about Huston and his films. Anjelica herself was due to fly to New York at the end of the month to begin rehearsals for the stage production of *Tamara,* which was due to open on October 12. She went to New York but then dropped out of the play. She had decided to concentrate on films and get on with her life with or without an accompanying male.

It was at this time that Susan Anspach's declining career went into freefall. She had turned down so many roles as being incompatible with her artistic standards and political beliefs that the phone had stopped ringing. According to Dr. Paul Fleiss, "She sacrificed her career in order to provide a good home for her children."

Susan said: "I was so in love with being a mom that I really wasn't paying that much attention to my career. I was going to the zoo and cooking dinners, and I didn't have any time for the fast life even if I'd wanted it. I definitely had a reputation for being a feminist, and I had the image of a liberated woman. The parts I had chosen, such as Catherine Van Oost in *Five Easy Pieces,* and the parts I had turned down proved that.

"Hollywood likes to typecast. In *Play It Again, Sam,* I played this woman who said to Woody Allen, 'Get lost unless you shape up.' In *Blume in Love,* it was 'Hello George, goodbye George. You're screwing around, go to hell.' I remember one magazine writer said, 'Anspach is that woman who knocked down Jack Nicholson, Woody Allen, and George Segal in one fell swoop.'

"All the parts I was being offered were bitches, because Hollywood translated a woman who stands up for herself and makes the male lead suffer for his love as 'bitch.' It went from these decent parts that I liked to edgy, nasty women, and I started turning them all down. There was an interaction between my private life and my career throughout the seventies. People were just rude to me sometimes because I had turned down one of their movies. I knew I had turned it down for sociopolitical or aesthetic reasons, but they just felt rejected and held it against me.

"My career had reached that point partly because of these rejections, which I naively never thought they took personally. To me, it was a business. What I learned is that they took it very personally indeed and held grudges. A perfect example was the time a certain studio head came to talk to my agent at lunch and totally ignored me during the five minutes he was visiting our table. He walked away fifteen feet, turned around, and said, 'By the way, Susan, what have you turned down lately?'

"I had turned down a wonderful series called *Family Ties* because I thought this is a woman in an apron saying, 'Yes, honey, no, honey, yes, kids, no, kids,' and that wasn't my idea of a mom. I would have made $6 million from that role, but I didn't think in those terms. I thought in terms of what's going to help the image of women.

"When I did *Blume in Love,* they called me the first truly liberated woman in Hollywood movies. Several writers likened me to Katharine Hepburn, yet saying that Katharine always wound up with a pat on the fanny at the end but what I was doing was true liberation. They said I was the first woman to be doing for the new Hollywood what Pacino was doing for the guys: this sort of antihero, this witty person who isn't quite beautiful but is real. And that just didn't sit well with the big boys. It caught up with me. I married my second husband, Sherwood Ball, in 1983. He was a rock-'n'-roll singer and songwriter with his own band, called Gumbo. The band didn't do all that well, so he turned to jingle writing and became very successful. We broke up in March 1987, and soon afterward the bottom fell out of my career.

"I did another TV series, *Slap Maxwell,* but it didn't run very long. I did about five more movies, but they were turkeys, and I felt this lack of attention from the industry. I had a standard of living that demanded I earn at least $200,000 a year, which I had been doing. You can't suddenly go from that to zero without panicking. It was torture.

"Michael Douglas, whom I starred with in *Running,* and Dustin Hoffman, whom I'd starred with on Broadway, were earning in the millions—and deservedly so. The men I'd worked with at the Actors Studio in New York suddenly got to middle age and were having wonderful careers. Harvey Keitel is a prime example—he was coming into his own; he had matured, but I just got older.

"I called Michael Douglas and said, 'Come on, help out.' He said, 'I'll get you a reading on *Fatal Attraction*. But I think you're going to hate the script.' I was frankly cutting my nose off to spite my face and just thinking I was being true to myself. But I'll never forget Michael said, 'Watch out. You sound desperate to me, and nobody in this town likes the smell of desperation.' That was very painful. I thought, 'I'm talented, I'm hard-working. Who cares if I'm desperate? It's logical I'm desperate!' That moment was just horrible.

"Anyway, I read the script and, in fact, hated it. The character was named Eve, of all things. I went into the meeting with the producers, Sherry Lansing and Stanley Jaffe, and they asked me what I thought of the script. I sat there willing to be respectful and said, 'Well, are we really going to call a career woman who destroys all things wholesome and good in the family, Eve?'

"Everybody just looked at me. They didn't say anything. Then one of them asked if I had any questions. I said: 'Well, are we really going to believe that a guy who graduated tops in his class at Harvard can't find some more intelligent way to get rid of a woman who's bothering him than to kill her?' I blush to tell you now, I was just so naive to think that everybody should see the world politically the way I do. You don't make a woman into a bitch, thank you very much, just because she's a career woman. But at least they changed Eve's name; they called her Alex. I know I hurt myself; I did stay true to myself, and I paid a price. It was really something else to be faced with this incredible plunge. In 1987, I went to Jack for help to send Caleb to Georgetown University, and he agreed to pay. It was shortly thereafter that everything just sank."

LIFE was looking up, however, for a wannabe actress called Rebecca Broussard. Born in Kentucky on January 3, 1963, the blond former beauty queen had landed a job as cocktail waitress at Helena's nightclub. Nicholson happened to call in one evening and was introduced to the new member of staff whose swimming-pool-blue-eyes caught his in a moment.

Rebecca admitted some time later: "The first time Jack touched my hand I almost blacked out. I saw stars, flashes of light. The minute I was introduced to him, I knew something was there. We'd sort of vaguely known each other for ages because I'm a friend of Jennifer's. I said to myself, 'Stop, Rebecca, he's a movie star,' but the attraction was too strong for both of us."

Helena's was at Silver Lake, which was strictly off the beaten path for the movers and shakers of Beverly Hills and Hollywood. A former member of the private club told me: "I was one of the first people who went there when it opened. There were six people there, counting myself, and two of the other five were Harry Dean Stanton and Virginia Madsen. By the time it had been open a month, it had become *the* place. There was a restaurant area and a dance floor that were just crammed with A-list celebrities: Eddie Murphy, Madonna, Prince, Sean Penn—whoever was happening was there—and, of course, Warren Beatty. Girls outside were crying and begging the doormen to let them in. It was the scene."

Although the name on the door was Helena's, Nicholson was the secret owner. "All Jack would admit was that he was an investor, but everybody knew that it was his place," said my source.

Before Nicholson had a chance to get serious with Rebecca, she was attracted to another regular customer, Warner Brothers record producer Richard Perry. "He was very wealthy and extremely successful—he managed the Pointer Sisters, who were very hot at the time," said my source. "Richard was also famous for having after-hours parties because all the bars and clubs here close at 2 o'clock in the morning. It was always open house at Richard's after the clubs. Again, always big-name stars—Nicholson, Stallone, Sting, Rod Stewart.

"Richard and Rebecca had a very brief courtship and got married on July 18, 1987; then they showed up at Aspen at Christmas. As usual, there was a big Hollywood contingent there. Here's this little cocktail waitress who's been serving drinks to these people, and now she's hobnobbing with them. She'd moved her position up about ten notches from being 'a cocktail waitress'—and with attitude to boot. I took one look at this woman and thought, 'She looks quite innocent.' She was tall, she was lanky, she had big eyes and big lips. I would never have called her stunning or sexy, but I'm a woman; I don't see what men see. But there she was, one of the mistresses of the manor, a Hollywood wife, if you will.

"Just before Christmas, there was an invite-only party at Tom O'Gara's home in Little Woody Creek next to Don Johnson's place.

Tom O'Gara is the son of Beverly Hills millionaires who do all the customized interiors on people's automobiles. Jack and Anjelica were there, and so were Michael and Diandra Douglas—and Richard and Rebecca Perry.

"The house was a two-story New England farmhouse with big rooms with a lot of exposed wood . . . nothing cutsie like a chalet. Eight days later, the O'Garas held a New Year's Eve party there. An ember from the fireplace blew on to the roof, and the whole house caught fire while everyone was inside. No one was hurt, but the house burned down and had to be rebuilt.

"Anyway, the fire was an omen of sorts because over that holiday period, Jack and Rebecca got together and Richard found out about it and *boom!* After the vacation was over, so was the marriage. It was history. Hollywood is run on the BBD—the bigger, better deal—and BBD people always want to trade up. As good a catch as Richard was, Jack was better."

The Perrys separated on January 12, 1988. Seventeen days later, Richard petitioned for a dissolution of the marriage through his lawyers, Mitchell, Silberberg and Knupp. As the couple had entered into a prenuptial agreement, there was very little to argue about. In a property settlement signed on May 2, 1988, it was stated that "irreconcilable differences have arisen between husband and wife which have led to the irremediable breakdown of their marriage." All wedding gifts were amicably divided, and Richard agreed to pay Rebecca a total of $8,100, of which $2,000 had already been paid.

A sum of $500 was to be paid upon the execution of the agreement and the balance handed over at the rate of $700 per month for eight months. The divorce would not become final until May 17, 1989, and in the interval Rebecca moved into a house on Westwanda Drive owned by one John J. Nicholson.

"He had Rebecca ensconced in this little house on Westwanda off Benedict Canyon, which is a stone's throw from his house," said my source. "The way Jack drives, it would probably be a one-minute ride, because he drives like a maniac. He's known for that—he loves speed. A lot of neighbors verified to me that they had seen Jack there.

"He was still having his very public relationship with Anjelica Huston. Jack and Anjelica had an understanding that 'so long as you don't put it in my face, it's cool.' Their relationship was still going on, and he was seeing Rebecca on the side. He told Rebecca as well, 'This is who I am. It's take it or leave it time.' He was having a great old time. This is Jack. He makes his own rules, he marches to his own beat, and he does what he wants to do, and the rest of you be damned."

THROUGHOUT these months, there had been intense behind-the-scenes activity at Warner Brothers, where it had become a matter of supreme importance that Nicholson should be persuaded to play the Joker in *Batman*. Ten years earlier, in 1979, executive producers Benjamin Melniker and Michael Uslan obtained the screen rights from DC Comics, which launched the Caped Crusader in 1937. In those early discussions, *Batman* creator Bob Kane had personally selected Nicholson as the Joker. Kane had an image of the character superimposed on a publicity photograph of Jack in *The Shining* to show how right he was for the role.

Worries about the $20 million cost of producing *Batman* as a movie when repeats of the television series were still running all over the world meant that the project was kept on the back burner until, in the mid-80s, it was brought to Jon Peters and Peter Guber, who were coming up in the fast lane among the newest new wave of Hollywood producers. Their record was already impressive in their solo careers. After they joined forces in 1980 and established Polygram Pictures, their string of successes included the cult classic *An American Werewolf in London* and Paramount's top box office earner of 1983, *Flashdance*. They sold Polygram that year and formed a new company, Guber-Peters Entertainment, committed to high-quality, bigger-budget pictures, which eventually included *The Color Purple*, *The Witches of Eastwick*, *Gorillas in the Mist*, and *Rain Man*.

Guber and Peters could do no wrong, and Warner Brothers committed themselves to going ahead with *Batman*. They announced that filming would start at Pinewood Studios in October 1988.

A new young director, unencumbered by too much previous experience, was sought, and they found him within the Warner organization. Tim Burton was a thirty-year-old ex-Disney animator, who had worked on two recent smash hits, *Pee-Wee's Big Adventure* (1985) and *Beetlejuice* (1988), the latter starring Michael Keaton (now to become Batman). They were both imaginative, if somewhat oddball, films. Burton immediately saw the potential. It was his view that the new *Batman* should get away from the Biff! Capow! Holy Crimewave! image of the television era. He wanted to take it back to a "darker vision, a dark melodrama with almost absurd black humor."

The recruitment of an actor for the Joker was seen as more important than casting Batman himself. Peters was deputized to persuade Nicholson to take the role they felt he was born to play. Those in charge of the finances looked with horror at the projected costs, which had doubled from the original estimate. Warners executives were pretty well agreed that it could not succeed without Nicholson. Lines of communication had been opened while they were filming *Witches of Eastwick*, and Peters' approach found him still decidedly less than enthusiastic.

Had not Brando and Gene Hackman taken a lot of flak for their "demeaning" appearances in *Superman*? Ah yes, but was not Nicholson's chum Warren Beatty already well advanced with plans to appear as a comic-strip hero, recreating for the big screen the adventures of Dick Tracy? And for Beatty, who had made only three films in the last decade, this was no trivial pursuit.

"At least let me fly you to London to see for yourself what we are doing and what our commitment is," Peters pleaded. Nicholson agreed, and he was flown in a private jet, the Warner Gulfstream 3, to London to view the sets, which were already being built at Pinewood Studios. The construction was to be in four stages; the first was already underway, and designer Anton Furst showed Nicholson his plans. There were literally hundreds of drawings already in existence, sketches of Batman and his armory, of his Batcave and his Batmobile, of the Joker and his paraphernalia.

The awesome skyline of Gotham City and its interiors would mean building the biggest movie set since the multimillion-dollar fiasco *Cleopatra* in 1963 and would cost well over $5 million. Nicholson was impressed. He also talked with Tim Burton, whom he had never met before, and they struck up a rapport; he liked the young director's ideas. Jack flew back to Los Angeles still undecided. Peters had been told by Warners production chief Mark Canton to make him an offer he could not refuse, so Peters was talking very big money indeed for what he said would be three weeks' work.

Nicholson was making no commitments, not to anyone. Anjelica was still working hard, and they had seen little of each other these past few months. On his return, he and Anjelica were suddenly thrust into the headlines when news of Jack's friendship with Karen Mayo-Chandler leaked out. She had been seen on his arm at a couple of high-profile social events in Hollywood, including a recent visit by the Duke and Duchess of York.

On March 14, 1988, they found themselves the subject of gossip columns around the world when it was widely reported that Anjelica had said enough was enough and they'd split up, less than a year after he promised her dying father that he would take care of her. She "finally ditched him after discovering that he had taken Karen skiing" in Aspen three weeks earlier, one such column reported. Anjelica was quoted as saying that she and Jack had had a great time together, but she was now bent on achieving the things she most wanted in life—to be a wife and mother.

It was rumored that Nicholson was devastated by Anjelica's decision and that he had made repeated telephone calls to try to patch things up. Unable to get more quotes from either party, reporters asked "close friends" to confirm that Anjelica felt her time was running out to start a family of her own and that the discovery of his dalliance with Karen was the last straw. Two days later, Karen Mayo-Chandler weighed in with the revelation that her affair with Nicholson was already over; she claimed she had called it off. Oh, by the way, she was prepared to tell all if any newspaper or magazine cared to make an offer for her story at somewhere in the neighborhood of, say, $150,000.

JACK'S interest in *Batman* had been whetted. With the customary thoroughness with which he approaches any task, he checked the library and did his homework. He then invited one of the movie's three screenwriters, Warren Skaaren, to Mulholland Drive to discuss the part. Skaaren noted later, "He was like an encyclopedia of culture and history and art. I threw out a line from Nietzsche, and Jack threw out a line from Nietzsche." Nicholson, in fact, later described *Batman* as "Nietzsche for kids."

From these initial discussions, the Joker's role grew; far from a mere three weeks' work, it would run to a hundred days. Jack was making a bigger commitment than Warners had dared to hope for, and the project was developing exactly the way Peters had hoped, into a true Batman vs. Joker scenario. Some said Nicholson had made an artistic takeover bid for the picture and had succeeded by his sheer presence—and given his time on screen, he must have had a pretty good idea that he would steal the show.

It was a hijack. Serious money talk had been going on in the background, and Nicholson eventually put his name to a contract for a $6 million fee plus a percentage of gross box office receipts, as well as a cut of record royalties, merchandising, and other ancillary income from the film. *Batman* earned $200 million in America alone in the first four weeks of showing, and children and adults were scrambling for Batman outfits and souvenirs. In total, Warners estimated, Nicholson would receive somewhere between $30 and $90 million. By 1994, it had reportedly reached $60 million.

He also gave his nod of approval to the casting of Michael Keaton in the starring role of Batman, which had sparked off such a storm of controversy worldwide. Keaton, well known but not exactly famous, was an unorthodox choice, a dramatic departure from the muscle-bound mold of previous comic-strip heroes. Warner Brothers received fifty thousand letters from Batman fanatics all over the world, protesting the choice and the exclusion of a Robin. "I knew there were dissenters," said Peters, "but I also knew that casting Michael Keaton as Batman would automatically make the film twice as interesting and original than if we had cast a traditional hunk. Batman is not your usual hero, and Keaton is not your usual actor."

The producers began to get worried as the protest movement grew louder and threatened to damage the picture's reputation even before it was released. Though *Batman* had been filmed in intense secrecy, Warners released a trailer, which was aimed at both quelling the fears of Batman fans and providing an excellent marketing exercise in prerelease hype. A documentary was also made during shooting, called *The Making of Batman*, in which most members of the cast appeared—except Nicholson. He knew it would end up on television, and he has always refused to do television for anyone, not even the suppliers of what was probably going to be the largest paycheck for a single actor in the history of Hollywood.

Otherwise, he threw himself into the production with amazing energy. Tim Burton found him a model of cooperation, and clearly Jack's portrayal of the Joker had been the subject of meticulous planning on his part. He personally consulted Tommy "the Tailor" Nutter of Savile Row, friend of the Beatles and outfitter to Mick and Bianca Jagger, about his $30,000 wardrobe. Burton said, "Jack gave the entire cast the confidence and courage—that's not an overstatement—to make this film. He was terrific. I had heard people talk about him before, but to watch him work was a pure education in the true art of filmmaking. In an instant, he could amend his performance at a particular time to give more menace, or less, as directed. He could alter his facial expression at a stroke, without having to reconstitute himself."

At the *Batman* premiere, which attracted many of Jack's peers, Eddie Murphy summed up their thoughts: "He was brilliant. Nobody can mess with that guy." Reviews were mixed about the film, but most were complimentary about Nicholson's creation of the Joker. Tom Green, writing in *USA Today*, was typical of the praisers: "Combining incendiary demonics with an impish harlequin flourish, Nicholson's nifty knack for over-the-top performances reaches a zenith in the Joker, cementing his reputation as the best actor working in Hollywood today."

Nicholson was said to be underwhelmed by the movie, but he remarked during and after filming that it was one of his own best performances. Would he appear in the sequel, which at some time or other there would surely be, if only to reuse the multimillion-dollar sets rusting at Pinewood? During the coming winter, there was much talk of him starring in *Batman II*. He was finally asked point blank as he walked into a Lakers game in Los Angeles. "The Joker's dead," snapped Nicholson. "Didn't you see the movie?"

17

BETRAYED

It is early summer 1989, and lines of kids are waiting excitedly by the roadside in a rundown industrial zone of Los Angeles because they've heard that Jack Nicholson is coming. As his limousine comes into view they start shouting, "Joker! Joker! Joker!" He steps out, wearing the ubiquitous jet black sunglasses. His hair is combed back, parted slightly in the middle.

The hot Los Angeles sunshine beats down from a cloudless sky, only slightly hazed by smog. Almost instantly beads of perspiration appear on his high forehead. He's wearing a gray checked suit, carrying the coat over his arm, slacks that look rather old-fashioned, a smart pale blue shirt, and a tie that is also slightly 40s-ish. Wait a minute, that's not the Joker. Isn't that guy what's-his-name, the detective? Jake Gittes.

In that month, twenty years earlier almost to the day, he had stood watching the audience reaction to *Easy Rider* at the Cannes Film Festival and said to himself: "I'm a star. I'm a movie star."

What he did not know was the scope that lay before him. Nor could he have possibly judged the new mood in society, the new attitudes to politics, the renaissance of the American film industry, all coming together to thrust him forward. The circle was completed at the beginning of the year when finally he pulled all parties together and reached agreement to start filming *The Two Jakes* again.

Past troubles had been set aside but not resolved. Robert Evans still languished under the cloud enforced by the L.A. district attorney's office over the *Cotton Club* case. Robert Towne—the screenwriter who was the one who wanted to sack Evans the actor in the first place—was no longer to take an active part in the direction of the picture. Conflicting press statements said he was either unwanted by Paramount as its director or too busy with his own commitments. From that original partnership of three friends good and true who shook on the deal and swore no one would come between them, Nicholson stood alone, although all three would benefit financially, but to a far lesser degree than might have been the case back in 1984 when it was first planned.

On his shoulders fell not just the leading role but also the task of directing, because that was the only way he could get the picture made. Other directors had been approached, including Mike Nichols and Bernardo Bertolucci. Jack even considered trying to bring Roman Polanski back from Paris. In the end, the decision to go ahead with the film or give it up for good rested with Nicholson, and he insisted that he would not let it die, even if it meant directing himself. There were those in Jack's inner circle who were brave enough to remind him that after *Goin' South*, he had vowed he would never again direct and star in a picture.

Many asked why he was returning to old ground, especially at a time when sequels to other first-time hit films had not done so well. Furthermore, *Chinatown* had become a classic of its age because it reflected one of the most horrendous examples of political corruption in modern times. Where could it pick up a decade and a half later? For Nicholson personally, it was like a good book that he could not put down and, as Anjelica had once said, his obsession. The characters were the same, or at least Gittes was. He was still a detective but a more upright member of the community, a war hero and member of the Wilshire Country Club. The story was set in 1948, eleven years after the events in *Chinatown*.

THE ELEMENTS of sexual infidelity, betrayal, greed, and the lust for power were still there, overlaid onto a new scenario in which Gittes has become disillusioned with his life. Jack and Robert Towne never wanted it to be seen as an updated copy of *Chinatown* or as *Chinatown II*. *The Two Jakes* had to have a life of its own if it was to become as successful as its predecessor. It was, said Nicholson, a very difficult film to make because the script did not express in words the undertones he was trying to convey. It all had to be done by implication. This may explain why it took him such a long time to complete the work. Nicholson had to be involved at every stage, right through to the delivery of a final print, and he was not letting it out of his hands until he was satisfied it was as good as it could possibly be.

Every problem associated with the actual shooting was his to solve. He had to handle the hundred-strong crew and direct his actors, guide them, cajole them, and nurse them. He had to make sure the producers met the allotted $25 million budget. He personally had to check locations after the scouts had been out and ensure down to the smallest detail, as is always the case in a period piece, that nothing came into shot that identified it as a later setting. One morning, for example, when they were shooting a scene using original cars of the era, Packards, Chevrolets, Nashes, and Hudsons, he suddenly noticed in the background a parking lot full of modern vehicles.

"That wasn't there yesterday," said Nicholson angrily. One of his assistants plucked up the courage to tell him that it wasn't in the shot yesterday, but it was there; it had become visible because the city parks department had unexpectedly trimmed the trees overnight. The same thing happened at another location, an important one: Orange groves had been there when they scouted the locations but had been cut down by the time they came to film them.

And then, switching from director to actor, Jack had to look through the camera lens at the shot in front of him, dash to the other side of the camera, position himself, shout "Action!" and let the cameras roll, focusing largely upon himself. It was hard, unremitting work and also anxiety-provoking. Who was going to tell him if he needed more violence or less, or a bigger grin or a lesser one? Well, there were some old friends around.

Luckily, Jack had personally asked for Vilmos Zsigmond, the cinema-tographer he had worked with on *Witches of Eastwick*. He always liked to have a buddy among the actors, and Jeff Morris was here again, just as he was in *Goin' South*, *The Border*, and *Ironweed*.

Jack dismissed the studio moaners who would say: "Jack's bringing his cronies in again." These people, he said, were part of his life. He had known them and worked with them for twenty years or more, and when he took them into a picture, he did so because they were good.

REBECCA Broussard had been given a small role as Jake Gittes's secretary, Gladys, and that entitled her to hang around the set or go out on location with her lover. Thus she had quickly achieved what all of Jack's longer-term companions had, with the exception of Michelle Phillips: appearing with him on the big screen.

Rebecca made herself scarce when Anjelica showed up. She and Jack were "friends" again; sixteen years of relative togetherness could not be ruined by the fling he'd had with Karen Mayo-Chandler. Whether or not she was aware of Broussard's presence in Jack's life at this point, Angelica was well aware what *The Two Jakes* meant to Nicholson. She turned up during location work at the bungalow he was using as his base while filming scenes at the country club, bringing a hamper of food and flasks of iced tea to ease the grueling twelve-hour-day shooting schedule he maintained for almost four months.

Unlike Anjelica, Jack's daughter Jennifer had no particular qualms about nepotism. Having completed her courses at USC, she was now a fully qualified production assistant, and she worked in that capacity on *Jakes*.

Filming was wrapped up in late summer of 1989. Jack had succeeded in maintaining a degree of secrecy about the film. He had given virtually no publicity interviews, and he had kept writers and photographers well away from the set. In the few public observations he allowed himself on *The Two Jakes*, he spoke of his hope that the film would carry an extremely human story that would contain an underlying comment about Californian and American society.

"I never thought we'd get the damn thing made," he said. "There were so many more twists and turns getting this on film than there were in the script. Tell you one thing: I want this to be better than *Chinatown*, and that was a damn classic." Then he disappeared into the cutting room at Paramount Studios in late September and did not surface again for months. Originally scheduled for a Christmas release, *The Two Jakes* was pushed back first to May 1990 and then to later in the year. Everyone concerned said that the delay merely reflected Nicholson's insistence on producing a final print that would do the movie justice.

During the latter stages of editing *The Two Jakes*, he was distracted by events outside the cutting room. In October 1989, it was revealed that Karen Mayo-Chandler had sold her story to *Playboy*. She would be appearing in the December issue. Then on October 26 came another bombshell: A gossip column printed a rumor that Rebecca Broussard was pregnant. Another rumor said that Jack was the father and that he had installed her in a house he had bought for $385,000 in Benedict Canyon. Neighbors had seen her jogging and had seen Nicholson arriving and leaving the address.

Anjelica was naturally outraged by this news and, given her own ambitions of motherhood, deeply hurt. "Anjelica found out that Rebecca was pregnant from a tabloid reporter who called her," said my informant. "Jack did not have the decency or the balls to tell her. I asked his friends why Rebecca didn't have an abortion, and they said Jack's own mother wanted to abort him so he was extremely antiabortion. I guess it was also an ego thing for a guy that age, that he could father a child. So Anjelica went nuts. She drove over to Paramount Studios where Jack was still working and went absolutely ballistic; it was not a pretty scene."

"Is it true?" she demanded. It was true. She slapped him across the face and screamed: "That's it. Finished." And she stormed out, leaving Nicholson speechless and apparently in shock.

Abe Somer, Nicholson's lawyer and a close friend of Richard Perry's, tried to intervene before any further damage could be done. "Abe hated Rebecca," said Susan Anspach. "He told me she was messing around with a lot of fellows. After she told Jack she was expecting his child, Jack described her to me as 'a blackmailing c-u-n-t.' Abe wanted Jack to get a blood test to settle the paternity issue, but he said no, and a short time later he declared that he was head over heels in love with Rebecca."

After seventeen years, the switch from Anjelica to a new partner had been accomplished in no time at all. Jack moved the mother-to-be up to his house at Aspen away from the hordes of press people who were trying to get her story and waited for the inevitable to happen.

THE DECEMBER issue of *Playboy* landed with a thud. Karen Mayo-Chandler, a lover scorned, was doing a Nora Ephron, though not with anything like the same style, panache, wit, or reason. But then, she did not have Nora's material to work with; she had no "life with Jack" to reveal, no betrayal by a scheming, two-timing husband. Hers was the classic hit-and-run, kiss-and-tell story, and *Playboy's* presentation of her in scant attire, telling her tale of sex and woe, seemed almost a parody of those once popular but long forgotten excursions into the bedrooms of the rich and famous when even Victor Lownes, head of the London Playboy empire, and Hugh Hefner were "victims."

Unlike *Playboy's* normal style, the story of Nicholson's passion for Karen used colorful, cliched, tabloid language under the headline HE WOULD HOLD ME DOWN, RIP OFF MY CLOTHES, AND MAKE INCREDIBLE, MAD, WILD, WONDERFUL LOVE TO ME. Of course, this made Mayo-Chandler an instant star and the required guest of talk show hosts across America. In England, the *News of the World* and the *Sunday Mirror* vied with each other for the story, and she stood to collect a pretty penny from her fifteen minutes of fame.

She painted a picture that only served to enhance the old image Jack had carried since *Carnal Knowledge.* "I don't mind admitting that I learned everything I know about life, love, and sex from Jack. I did things with him that I had never done with any other man," said the now twenty-eight-year-old star of *Strip to Kill II*. "I was trembling like a child when he first carried me up to his bedroom; but he was very gentle, very loving, very romantic. He kept right on kissing me deeply, undressing me all at the same time. We did not sleep a wink that first night. He has amazing stamina and self-control, and we just kept on making love. He's a guaranteed nonstop sex machine."

In Karen's account of her "nights of torrid passion," when Jack wasn't watching basketball or other sports on television, out came the implements of fun he kept in a black bag along with a Polaroid camera for some saucy snaps. Kinky sex games, naughty pictures; whatever next . . . spankings? Of course. Jack loved to dish out a good smack across the bottom, and sometimes, she said, lovemaking became painful. He, meantime, grunted, groaned, and moaned; he loved to give and receive vocal encouragement. He didn't have many bad points, except that he snored loudly and ate peanut butter and jelly sandwiches in bed.

Nicholson shuddered when he read it. It was supposed to be a fun story; the tenor of the piece made it that way, and it was presented as the epitome of a vigorous interlude in the much-discussed, well-publicized sexual adventures of Jack Nicholson, movie star. He must have known that sooner or later a woman would go to the media and tell all. Perhaps at any other time in his life he could have shrugged it off as a lighthearted addition to the reputation he had carefully nurtured over the years. But now it was a problem for Nicholson, and he was desolate.

Why did Karen do it? Money? Notoriety? Revenge? It was a mixture of all three, although she explained that primarily she was fed up with being tagged as Jack Nicholson's former floozie and "just wanted to put the record straight." Perhaps to assure him there was no malice involved, she telephoned Jack before allowing British journalist Kenelm Jenour to release the story to *Playboy* and British and European newspapers.

In the old days, when studios drew the protective cordons around their stars, she would have been given a new car with a glove compartment full of cash and told to drive off into the sunset, stay silent, and keep out of his life. Jack did not even attempt to buy Karen off. He told her bluntly: "You must do what you have to do," in the full knowledge that her story could be damaging, coming as it did with Rebecca now firmly in his life.

But he has always maintained this openness. Once a secret corner of his sex life has been exposed, he has seen no point in trying to hide it. His reputation as a womanizer came as much from his own mouth, with admissions during the publicity interviews he gave in the early days, as it did from the gossip columns that have endlessly charted his dates and one-night stands. He has never sought to deny his prowess with women. He has also been honest about his drug usage, to the point that it became a bore to him even to discuss it. Sometimes he has regretted his frankness.

Occasionally, if the moment required it—for publicity purposes, for instance—Jack helped the cause along a bit with a knowing wink here and a weighty cough there as he talked to his interviewers in all frankness about his past. It is surely no coincidence that these interviews were granted only at the very moment another of his films was about to be released. He did a good double act with his press agent, Paul Wasserman, and had become, in the latter part of his career, an expert manipulator of the media.

HAVING accepted that Karen Mayo-Chandler was going to have her say, Jack just stood back and let the fur fly as far as he himself was concerned. However, there was nothing he wanted less than to have Rebecca plastered all over the newspapers, and she did not want that kind of publicity, either. She was carrying his baby, whose birth he began to look forward to with enthusiasm after the initial shockwaves had subsided. Because she was with child, his child, he threw a protective arm around her and tried to shield her from some of the media glare that he knew would follow.

Rebecca was stunned by the media reaction worldwide. She was getting the kind of publicity normally reserved for Elizabeth Taylor, and all she had done was to become pregnant by a famous actor. Jack promised her that when the time came he would take the burden of publicity. Indeed, when their baby daughter was born on April 16, six days before his own fifty-third birthday, he behaved like British royalty, letting a photographer or two in to take pictures for worldwide distribution and hoping the media would then leave them alone.

He posed with Rebecca and the baby, whom they called Lorraine after his sister-aunt, and he spoke of his pride at being a father. Jack and Rebecca looked happy and said they were. He brushed aside obvious questions about marriage. Rebecca's divorce from Richard Perry had become final in May 1989, but even Jack's closest friends would not be prepared to place a bet on whether or not he would marry her, particularly because he had set up a two-house relationship that would give them both a good deal of space. The media camped as close as they could get to Mulholland Drive but found little to write about.

They were back again the following month to observe the continuing saga of life in the compound. This time, the focus was next door on the Brando household, scene of many domestic upheavals in the past. Police arrived to arrest Christian Brando following the fatal shooting of his half-sister Cheyenne's lover, Dag Drollet, on May 16, 1990. When Marlon Brando was desperately seeking to get his son released on bail, Nicholson came to his neighbor's aid by writing to the Los Angeles court to state that he had known Christian for fourteen years and could vouch for his good character. He omitted to mention that he had once caught Christian raiding his pot stash and had threatened to "break his fingers" if he ever did it again.

Anjelica kept well away. Mutual friends felt she deserved considerable sympathy for the way she ended up, without Nicholson and without a child. At Christmas, she said bitterly: "Jack Nicholson has given me the worst two Yuletide presents I have ever received in my life." She was finished with him in terms of their romantic relationship and sought company elsewhere. She still spoke of wanting to be a mother. "Personally, I'd love to have a child. I'd like to have a husband and a child," she said just before Jack's new daughter was born. "It is not something I have immediate plans for because there is simply no one on my horizon, but it is something that certainly has to be considered. And also, I'd like to feel calm and happy."

She had gained new strength from her career, and in April 1990, she was at the Academy Awards once again, nominated for Best Supporting Actress for her role as Dolores, the put-upon, pill-popping mistress in Woody Allen's *Crime and Misdemeanors*. She also won the Best Supporting Actress award from the U.S. National Society of Film Critics for that role and immediately signed to appear in what would be another excellent movie, Nicolas Roeg's *Witches*, based on the Roald Dahl story.

As far as Nicholson was concerned, she saw Karen Mayo-Chandler's tell-all, followed by the revelation of Rebecca's pregnancy, as her own "public humiliation" by him. She was undoubtedly furious, but she would not discuss it. She said: "It's been a long relationship, and it is between us. I don't feel that it is for public scrutiny. If you are dealing with two very volatile people, such as we are, you go through many changes every day. The relationship is a fact of my life, and there is not an aspect of my life that has not been touched by him.

"He is a soulmate, and I hate to think of a world without him. It would be dismal."

18

CONNAUGHT ASTRONAUT

THE TWO JAKES was released in the United States in August 1990 while Jack was in France and grossed just $9 million before closing. Some reviews complained that the film was slow and lacked the magic of *Chinatown*. "I killed myself trying to make the picture work," he said. "I still don't know why it doesn't come off right for audiences, because I thought all the pieces fit." Roman Polanski, whom Nicholson always visited on trips to Paris, opined: "I was quite pleasantly surprised because I was actually admiring the way that Jack put this thing together. It was very well directed, it was wonderfully acted, it had a great look about it. Unfortunately, it's quite impossible to follow."

Nicholson was a committed Francophile. He spoke the language with a faint New Jersey accent and often expressed his admiration for Napoleon, whom he described as "simply one of history's greatest men." At one point, he even considered moving to France because "it's a smaller system, not as much expected of each film, and it just seems more sane." There was nothing new about his fascination with Napoleon. Soon after seeing Jack in *Easy Rider*, Stanley Kubrick had called him out of the blue and said: "I want you to play Napoleon for me."

"Fine," said Jack. "When do I start?"

But Kubrick had never managed to get the deal together. Many years later, Nicholson had started a Napoleonic project of his own. In 1982, he bought the film rights to a book called *The Murder of Napoleon*, which claimed that the great man had been poisoned by Bourbon spies while in exile on St. Helena. However, like Kubrick, he had never managed to interest a studio in making it.

Nicholson elected to return to familiar territory for his next film and make *Man Trouble* with his *Five Easy Pieces* collaborators, director Bob Rafelson and writer Carole Eastman. Jack played Harry Bliss, a trainer of guard dogs. When one of his beasts is hired to protect a classical singer, played by Ellen Barkin, he finds himself caught up in a farce of French bedroom proportions with the diva's several ex-boyfriends.

The film crashed at the box office. Ellen Barkin said: "I was out of the country and called up Jack after the opening weekend to say, 'How did we do?' and he said, 'Well, my queen, the movie made less money than you did.' "

Nicholson's own $7 million paycheck helped him to shrug off any embarrassment he might personally have felt. Then, for another $5 million, he knocked off four scenes in *A Few Good Men,* playing Colonel Nathan Jessop, commander of a U.S. Marine base in Guantánamo Bay, Cuba, involved in a sensational court-martial. As the older man among a young cast including Tom Cruise, he was treated with reverence on the set. His blistering performance made the movie one of the hits of 1992, grossing $100 million after its December release. One reviewer commented that, as an actor, he was "in a league of his own."

Nicholson had directed Danny DeVito in *Goin' South,* and for around $10 million, he returned the compliment to his friend in *Hoffa,* playing the title role. The corrupt union boss James Riddle Hoffa, eventually president of the Teamsters Union, fraternized with the Mob, clashed memorably with Bobby Kennedy, and served time for attempted bribery of a federal jury before disappearing altogether in 1975—assassinated, according to David Mamet's screenplay. Still, DeVito was unstinting in his praise of the union leader: "If we had a guy like [Hoffa] running the country, I'd breathe easy," he said in one interview.

To get into his role, Nicholson walked around the set chanting, "That's right . . . that's right," in Hoffa's midwestern twang. When his fifty-fifth birthday rolled around, the crew gave him a cake decorated with the words THAT'S RIGHT, JACK. IT'S YOUR BIRTHDAY. But Nicholson's chumminess with DeVito and the crew did not prevent the director from clashing with Jack's longtime associate Harold Schneider, who was quietly replaced as the line producer because of a "personality conflict" with DeVito and others on the set.

Judging the movie a huge success, Stanley Kauffman wrote in *The New Republic* that Nicholson had captured "Hoffa's color, flash, egotism, bulldog brutality, bulldog tenacity . . . the guts, the crassness, the cleverness." Filmgoers didn't agree and stayed away in droves, leaving Jack to lament: "I can't do any better work than I did in *Hoffa*."

Nicholson's relationship with Rebecca was still fairly intense, even though they maintained separate households. "Jack never wanted to live with Rebecca," said my source. "He likes having his independence. He could see Rebecca whenever he wanted. A lot of people thought it was very clever of her to have gotten pregnant. It had to be intentional. It meant she would have eighteen years of some type of relationship with Jack. Then she decided to have another child so that she was doubly insured. She believed that Jack was going to marry her sooner or later. When Warren [Beatty] got engaged, she definitely thought that was going to be her trump card, that Jack would say, 'Well, if Warren can do it, so can I.' "

Rebecca became pregnant with their second child in the summer of 1991, and a son was born on February 20, 1992, just a few days before Beatty and Annette Bening tied the knot. Although Nicholson wanted to call the boy Landslide, sanity prevailed; he agreed with Rebecca that Raymond might be a better choice of names. He took Rebecca to Barcelona for the 1992 Olympics to see America's Dream Team in action, and they went to the south of France, where they were photographed frolicking in the Med. However, a few months later, while *Hoffa* was in the final stages of postproduction, Rebecca had decamped. Nicholson was left to survey the wreckage.

The seeds of the rift had been sown some time earlier, but Rebecca's means of escape hadn't emerged until she was making a movie called *Blue Champagne*, written and directed by Blaine Novak. Nicholson was one of the producers. This as-yet-unreleased film noir about love, jealousy, and revenge was shot in the summer of 1991 at Nicholson's house on Mulholland Drive and at the new mansion he had bought for Jennifer on Sixteenth Street in Santa Monica. Jennifer also had a part in the movie. "Jack put $6 million into the film," Bob Colbert told a friend.

Rebecca's costar was the hunky young actor Jonathan Silverman, whose film credits included the black comedy *Weekend at Bernie's*. She wasn't particularly looking around for a replacement for Jack at the time, but when whispers reached her ears that he had been out with twenty-two-year-old French actress Julie Delpy and that he regularly entertained former girlfriends up on Mulholland Drive, they quarreled and separated in September 1992. Jonathan was there to comfort her.

"Just a silly interlude" was the way Jack described the two-month separation after it was over. "I'm very moody and difficult to live with, and I'm eccentric and restless if I have the same scenery all the time. But Rebecca saw it another way, and when she left me for that other guy, I realized that by carrying on in my old ways, I was making her insecure. And that wasn't fair, because she's really a very wonderful woman."

"Jack had got her a much posher house in the San Fernando Valley just four minutes' drive from his home," said a Hollywood socialite, "but the ring was not forthcoming, and they had many, many fights about it. Rebecca gave him an ultimatum: She wanted to be married by the time she turned thirty, in January 1993. She refused to accept the fact that Jack didn't want to be married, that he enjoyed things the way they were; that he enjoyed spending time with her and the babies, but did not want a permanent, live-in relationship with her—or anybody. One New Year's Day, in Aspen, Rebecca was in one of his houses with the kids, and Jack was living in another one of his houses and watching football with the guys at the Jerome bar. So even in Aspen they weren't staying in the same place. He's got to have his privacy."

AMERICA was about to elect a member of the baby boom generation as president, and nothing could have been more pleasing to Nicholson. He had never played an active part in conventional politics, but when Bill Clinton swept to victory over the aging George Bush in November 1992, he was jubilant. His politics were naturally liberal to begin with, and he had supported George McGovern in the 1972 campaign. He was outspoken about the evils of Richard Nixon's reign, despaired at Gerald Ford, laid a few choice remarks at the door of Ronald Reagan, and eventually gave his backing to Gary Hart in 1986 only to see the chances of having a friend in the White House scuppered by the kind of scandal normally reserved for himself.

Clinton made up for that disappointment, and Jack got his wish to be on first-name terms with the president. He was in one of the best seats at Clinton's swearing-in the following January, and he was in the VIP section at the MTV inaugural ball in Washington that night with Warren Beatty, Annette Bening, Uma Thurman, and Kim Basinger.

WHILE making *Batman* at Pinewood Studios, in 1988, Jack had stayed at the Connaught Hotel on the corner of Carlos Place and Mount Street in Mayfair. Robert Evans had once spent five months at the Connaught during his globetrotting excursions for Paramount and had thoroughly recommended the experience. Brando was also an old Mayfair hand, having stayed in a rented flat in Mount Street while making *The Nightcomers*, in 1971.

With gilt mirrors dripping from oak-paneled walls, antique furniture in every nook and cranny, and a grand mahogany staircase, the Connaught prided itself on being classier and more intimate than its big sisters on Park Lane and Piccadilly. During the war, it had played host to the Free French, and none other than Charles de Gaulle had occupied one of its best suites. The hotel staff, immaculate in black morning dress, were noted not only for the impeccable service they provided but also for their ability to handle even the most eccentric of well-heeled guests.

Jack liked London.

On a jaunt there in November 1987 he had gone shopping in Chelsea on his own without creating a riot. A few people had stopped to stare at him in the street, and drivers had honked their horns when they recognized him, but he wasn't mobbed.

He had started his shopping spree in a shoe store near World's End, and as he left he slipped on the sidewalk and crashed to the ground. No one noticed except David Koppel, a paparazzo who happened to be having coffee in a restaurant across the street. As Jack set off again, Koppel gave chase with his camera. "He walked the entire length of King's Road to a hi-fi store near Sloane Square," he said. "The store was crowded, and he went unnoticed, so he had to wait to be served. He just stood there in line clutching his shopping bags and looking bewildered."

Nicholson was back in London in February 1993, a free agent with time on his hands. He checked into the Connaught and brought a touch of the Hollywood hellraiser to Mayfair, a role he would play intermittently over the next four years in collaboration with his friend Michael White.

White, a tall, slender, bespectacled theatrical producer—and, at fifty-eight, still a relentless *bon viveur*—knew Jack from New York and Los Angeles, where he scouted for shows to bring to the London stage, and from the Cannes Film Festival, where he was an active member of the jet set who partied at the Carlton and roamed the Croisette. In winter, he and Jack often skied together at Aspen. White was twice divorced; his partner for ten years had been Lyndall Hobbs, an Australian journalist, who later moved to New York and into the life of Al Pacino. After Lyndall, the black supermodel Naomi Campbell was to be found on his arm as he made his seemingly endless round of shows, parties, and nightclubs. As one of his shows, the musical *Crazy for You*, was playing to packed houses in the West End, he had plenty to celebrate.

In fact, it was White who set up many of Nicholson's dates. As the man who had introduced the actress Koo Stark to Prince Andrew, White left nothing to chance to maintain Jack's image as the world's most lethal ladykiller. Jack's most constant companion on this trip was Amanda de Cadenet, the Levi's Girl in the Ridley Scott advertisement and estranged wife of Duran Duran's bass guitarist, John Taylor. Jack knew Amanda by sight before he met her in person because her voluptuous figure had appeared naked in the April 1991 issue of *Playboy* when she was seventeen years old.

Blond, buxom, and beautiful, Amanda was Jack's kind of girl, a raver with the wide-eyed innocence of an ingenue. The daughter of French race car driver Alain de Cadenet, Amanda had been a "wild child" in eighties London, a leading exemplar of that group of barely pubescent girls who got drunk in nightclubs, danced on tables, and dated men old enough to be their fathers. At fifteen, she had been forcibly removed from a lover's bed and placed in foster care by social workers "for her own protection." Now twenty-one and mother of a one-year-old daughter by Taylor called Atlanta, she was a willing handmaiden at the court of Dr. Devil.

Jack had arrived in the British capital with Danny DeVito and Alan Finkelstein. When they embarked on a night out in the West End on February 18, David Koppel picked up their trail. "They went to the Prince of Wales Theater in Old Compton Street, where *Crazy for You* was playing," he said. "For some reason, they didn't stay to watch that. [The performance was, in fact, canceled because of "technical difficulties."] Instead, they had dinner at the Ivy with Amanda de Cadenet, Naomi Campbell, and Christy Turlington. The photographer David Bailey, Jack's old friend, was there, and they chatted for a while before Jack, Danny, and the girls went on to Tramp."

Danny DeVito stayed for only an hour or so. As he left the club, he placed a ten-pound note in the tin of a panhandler who was camped at the entrance on Jermyn Street. Nicholson didn't leave until after 3 A.M. and by that time the Connaught Astronaut had lift-off.

Colin Morris, his regular driver, drove him back to the Connaught, and because of the late hour, the front door on Carlos Place was locked. Jack had to ring the night bell. While he was waiting, he was photographed and the pictures show that he had white powder on his jacket and trousers and up his nose as well. Five minutes after he was let in by the night porter, another car turned up with Amanda de Cadenet and two other women, and they also went inside.

When Nicholson returned to the Connaught in the first week of July 1993, he was again accompanied by Alan Finkelstein. "Jack and Alan . . . almost like brothers would be a good way to put their relationship," said an Aspen acquaintance. "Alan is a nice guy. I know him; he's good company and very likable. They've had lots of sexual escapades with girls, and it helped Alan tremendously having Jack there as the drawing card."

Mount Street, with its pink terra cotta façades adorned by bas-relief carvings and elegant statuary, was one of the grandest examples of Victoriana in England. But Nicholson made no concessions to the surroundings. Dressed more for Malibu than Mayfair, he ambled down the street in a bright blue, purple, and yellow shirt worn outside white slacks and with a pair of white moccasins on his feet. He watched tennis at Wimbledon and shopped in the boutiques of South Molton Street. Wherever he went, Finkelstein tagged along beside him. Slimly built with hair down to his shoulders and a drooping moustache, he was the embodiment of an earlier age when Carnaby Street was the center of the world.

One evening, Jack went to Brown's nightclub with Amanda de Cadenet and Naomi Campbell, then returned to the Connaught. The Greek paparazzo Nikos Vinieratos was waiting to greet their limo. He promptly photographed Jack with a fatherly hand on Amanda's knee while she covered her face with her pocketbook to avoid the flash. Later, Amanda came out of the hotel to get some tapes from the car, where Nikos was still waiting. He said: "She asked me, 'Why do you follow Jack?' I said it was because we never saw him in London. She said, 'Well, I see him all the time.' "

Nicholson returned to L.A., where he made a monumental decision: Clearly believing that Rebecca's affair with Jonathan Silverman was a thing of the past, he decided it was time to marry the mother of his two youngest children.

"Jack proposed to Rebecca," said my source. "According to Jennifer, he was like a kid, very boyish. He was really looking forward to it, but he waited until Christmas 1993. He had bought the rings, and he hid them behind his back when he said to her, 'I want to ask you something.' Rebecca said, 'What?' He produced the rings and said, 'I want you to marry me.' She said, 'Oh my God, no! I'm in love with someone else.' "

There was no sign of Rebecca when Nicholson spent that Christmas at home on Mulholland Drive with four of his children, Jennifer, Caleb, Lorraine, and Raymond. It was a rare occasion, possibly the only time that four of his offspring had been gathered together at the same time. Rebecca confirmed to Nancy Collins in an interview a short time later that a thirty-one-year-old actor who sounded very much like Jonathan Silverman was "a very important person in my life."

When an earthquake measuring 6.8 on the Richter scale hit Los Angeles at 4:31 A.M. on January 17, 1994, Jack's house was quite badly damaged. There were also some casualties among his art collection, including a couple of valuable Chinese vases. But his first thought was for the safety of Rebecca and her two children. Ignoring the rubble on the highway, the wail of sirens, and the prevailing air of chaos, he dashed down to her house in the San Fernando Valley and was relieved to find that, although frightened, they were unharmed.

On January 29, Jack attended a party at the home of *An Officer and a Gentleman* actor David Keith off Sunset Plaza. Four models were present, serving drinks and gradually disrobing.

Nicholson indulged in a sex-and-drugs session with one of the girls, who, it was later claimed, was only sixteen at the time.

This might never have come up if Keith had not discovered that $1,000 was missing from his home after the party. He asked Frank Monte, who had opened a branch of his detective agency in Los Angeles, to investigate the theft. The private eye interviewed some of the models, who angrily denied taking the cash. "One of them started talking about Jack and said that the girl he had been with was only sixteen," said Monte. "She claimed he had contributed to the corruption of a minor." When Monte reported this information to Keith, the inquiry into the missing money was quietly dropped. So was any more talk about underage girls.

NICHOLSON'S next visit to the Connaught was during a trip to promote his new movie, *Wolf*, in July 1994. The screenplay of this updated werewolf myth was written by a friend, Michigan novelist Jim Harrison, and the film was directed by Mike Nichols in his fourth project with Nicholson. For a fee of $13 million, Jack played Will Randall, a mild-mannered literary editor at a publishing house that is threatened with a hostile takeover. When Randall is bitten by a wolf, his life takes off in two unexpected directions: he begins a romantic liaison with a billionaire's daughter (played by Michelle Pfeiffer) and becomes a man-eating monster.

"All these mythic characters like Wolfman, Jekyll and Hyde, and Dracula are about a man contacting the repressed sides of his nature, the darker sides," Nicholson told an interviewer. "People ask me about fantasies—do I have fantasies of bestiality and seraglios, and do I think other men do? Well, of course all men do, but so do women. We're less likely to hear the fantasy of women who just want that beast who will come wandering into their bedroom and defile them and besmirch them and stink and rot and all that kind of thing—that I know from experience is a common fantasy among women, but they won't say it these days. They're not as free to express that fantasy as a man would be."

Emma Freud of the BBC's Radio 1 was one of the fortunate ones to be chosen for a chat, perhaps because of her ancestral link with the great Sigmund. "He never does television interviews," she said. "When I asked him why he agreed to ours, he said, 'On radio I can lie.' " Asked if Nicholson had flirted with her, Freud replied: "He was actually more flirtatious with my producer. He was illustrating how he can create an atmosphere without the camera even knowing. He said, 'Say the camera is close on my face. You can't see my arms, but I could be doing this. . . .' My producer was wearing a sleeveless T-shirt, and Jack ran his hand down her arm, very slowly and very gently. They both blushed. Then the producer's assistant said, 'Should I leave now?' That was the only moment I wished it was television."

Interview over, Nicholson joined the Pimm's-and-strawberries set at Wimbledon to watch some tennis. When the sun went down, he was back in uniform as Dr. Devil. One balmy night, in *Wolf* baseball cap, sunglasses, navy blue yachting jacket, gray slacks, and blue-and-gray shoes, his hair longer, grayer and shaggier than usual, he swung through the hotel's revolving door. Grinning broadly with a cigarette clamped between his teeth, he stepped toward his limo with no fewer than three beauties in tow. "One woman at a time has never been enough for me," he once boasted. "I've always seen myself as a juggler. You know—having all my balls in the air at once and fearing the painful consequence of dropping one or more."

Confronted with one of his own fantasies come to life, Nikos put his camera on autodrive and recorded the scene. The juggler had come out to play, big time. Nikos recognized the first woman as the *L. A. Law* actress Amanda Donohoe. The second was Amanda de Cadenet, dressed like a South Seas maiden in a white blouse and a diaphanous blue-and-white skirt that showed her navel.

The third young woman in the party turned out to be Jennifer Nicholson, dressed in a silk harem suit that matched her flowing mane of lustrous red hair. She was enjoying a holiday with her father after appearing as the battered wife in a psychological thriller called *Inevitable Grace*, which had been released—and widely panned—in February. "I followed them, and they went to the Ivy restaurant, and then Jack went on to Tramp with three of them, but he came back to the hotel with Amanda de Cadenet, who was also staying there," Nikos reported.

"Another night, he went out with Naomi Campbell and (guess who?) Amanda de Cadenet. Same thing: They went to Tramp, then back to the hotel. When he came out of Tramp, the beggar Danny DeVito had given some money to in February was there. Jack said to us, 'Are you ready?' and he grabbed the guy and kissed him full on the lips while we took the picture."

On yet another occasion, Jack went out with Naomi Campbell, the waif-like model Kate Moss, and Michael White to a studio in the Ladbroke Grove area of Notting Hill. "They stayed there . . . well, Jack didn't come out," said Nikos. "Naomi left about four o'clock, and we waited until six A.M. and he was still in there. His car was out front, so we didn't miss him."

Naturally, Amanda de Cadenet was invited by the press to talk about all this nocturnal activity, especially as her husband had moved to Los Angeles and the couple were officially separated. "There's nothing going on between me and Jack Nicholson," she maintained. "I don't want to waste my time denying this sort of thing." Privately, however, Amanda admitted the affair in a letter she wrote to Taylor. The rock star promptly consigned her confession to a trashcan, whence it was retrieved by an eager member of the L.A. paparazzi.

"Power, sexuality, deviance, human gameplay excite me," Amanda said in an interview. "I know I appeal to men on a primal level. I have tits and an ass. Sometimes you play men as a kind of mental exercise, just to see if you can and because it's so easy."

However, another possible motive behind her involvement with Nicholson emerged when Amanda turned up in Hollywood a short time later. Always ambitious, she exploited her connection with him to the hilt. In no time at all, she was seen as the virgin goddess worshiped by Madonna in the Quentin Tarantino portmanteau movie *Four Rooms*. Small parts in *Grace of My Heart* and *Valley Girls* quickly followed; then, amazingly, she landed the leading role in the romantic comedy *Four*. "She found it remarkably easy to shed her old image, particularly with the help of her illustrious benefactor Nicholson," Tony Gallagher wrote in the *Daily Mail*. "The mere fact that she was 'a friend of Jack's' was enough to open the doors of Hollywood's biggest agents and talent scouts."

Meanwhile, Nicholson had headed south to team up with Rebecca and the children at the St. Tropez home of his friend, the photographer Willy Rizzo. Looking plump in swimming trunks, he was full of praise for Rebecca. For her part, judging from the way she climbed all over him, massaging his crotch with her bare foot, she was delighted to see him. "She has a wild side that I adore," Jack said, explaining the reconciliation. "You live side by side with a woman, you think you know everything about her, and the minute she slams the door in your face, you realize you don't know a thing. I wasn't ready for that loss. I asked myself a lot of questions. After a year and a half of reflection, I thought that Rebecca must have been asking herself them, too. This separation was necessary."

But their reunion lasted only a matter of weeks. Nicholson was alone again in Los Angeles when he said: "I thought I had finally found happiness with a woman who could share my life in ways that I never wanted to share it before. It's tough accepting that it turned to dust. Even with Rebecca, I told her I needed to maintain a separate house because I need that time to work there and to be myself, so I can think devilish thoughts. I was totally committed to a life as a full-time father, yet we weren't able to work things out between us. C'est la vie."

Rebecca was understanding, perhaps a little too much so. "I know I needed to leave Jack," she said. "Jack comes out with all this man's stuff. But . . . underneath he's a puppy like most of the men I've known. You can call him to heel and say, 'Roll over,' and over he goes."

For Christmas, Nicholson invariably flew to Aspen, which had long since become home to more than thirty millionaires, including Michael Douglas, Clint Eastwood, Charlton Heston, Don Johnson, Don Henley, and Peter Guber. But he still enjoyed solitude. One of his favorite places was an Italian restaurant called the Ajax Tavern at the four-star Little Nell Hotel. "Jack loves the place," said my source. "If you went to the Ajax Tavern at 2 o'clock on any given day, Jack was having lunch there, often alone."

When he socialized, Alan Finkelstein was rarely far from his side. "Alan has a house in Little Woody Creek, which is part of Aspen on a road that has access only to the homes of Don Johnson, Don Henley, Peter Guber, and so forth," said a regular visitor to Hollywood-in-the-Rockies. "It's kind of a ritzy neighborhood, to say the least. Aspen is a very small town, and it's a difficult place to keep a secret, almost impossible. It's a very strong gossip mill, and word soon gets around about what Jack and Alan are doing.

"And then, of course, there was their partnership in the Monkey Bar. These L.A.-Aspen connections never cease. There was a restaurant in Aspen called Gordon's. It was considered to be one of the best; you always had to have a dinner at Gordon's—that was just de rigueur if you were anyone. Gordon Naccaroto was the chef, and Jack loved the food there. When Gordon decided to close after five or six years, Jack made him a deal, and Gordon became the chef at the Monkey Bar when it opened in 1993. So all everybody had to hear was that Jack owned the Monkey Bar and Gordon was cooking. If you'd ever been to Aspen, you knew the food was going to be incredible, and you had to go there."

SPOTLIGHTS picked out the three wise monkeys—hear no evil, see no evil, speak no evil—painted on a pink stucco façade flanked by tall fir trees at 8225 Beverly Boulevard, West Hollywood. Apart from a rooftop terrace with creepers and vines growing over white latticework, the exterior was remarkable only for its anonymity. The entrance was under a green canopy around the corner on Harper Avenue beside a barred window—the only window in the place. One thing the management of the Monkey Bar guaranteed its clients was privacy.

On a fall evening in 1994, the maître d' escorted two new customers to a booth in the dining room. One of the diners nudged his companion and whispered: "He looks like Jack Nicholson."

"That's because he *is* Jack Nicholson," replied his friend.

Nicholson, of course, was just helping his staff out or having a bit of fun, but it showed how far he was prepared to go to make the place a success. This scene was enacted before the Monkey Bar lost its charm and the movers and shakers departed to move and to shake somewhere else. As the Monkey Bar declined during 1995, so did Jack's demeanor: "I was driving down Beverly Boulevard late at night," a Hollywood actor told me, "and I saw Jack Nicholson outside the Monkey Bar howling like a wolf at the moon." A West Hollywood resident remembers what happened outside the restaurant on New Year's Eve. "Jack was so shit-faced drunk he went outside and pissed on the lawn in Harper Avenue," she said.

In the beginning, the Monkey Bar had attracted a celebrity clientele that included Glenn Close, Nick Nolte, Mickey Rourke, and Shannen Doherty. "The first time I went there, there were only about eight people and three celebs—Robert Evans, Harvey Keitel, and one of the Eagles," said a British newspaper correspondent. "But very soon afterward, there were Mercs, Rollers, and Jags parked outside, and it was a real powerhouse. All the film execs went there plus the music people, the bimbos, the girls-about-town."

A Hollywood socialite said: "Immediately on opening it became like a private club; if you weren't on the list, you didn't get in the door. People were standing out there fifty deep. You'd walk in, and there was a bar and enough room for maybe thirty people to be packed in uncomfortably. There was one little part of the dining room beside the bar, and then you went into a bigger room, mostly booths except for a few tables; very clubby in feel, expensive. It was almost like Helena's, and although there was no dance floor, you knew it was going to have that kind of cachet. Alan Finkelstein's job was to run the Monkey Bar. He was there almost every night. He sublet his home in Aspen and lived in a house on Mulholland Drive about a mile from Jack's place."

One of the earliest devotees of the restaurant's chic ambience was Heidi Fleiss, who could often be seen tucking into Gordon's lobster tacos in one of the booths with some of her girls. Frank Monte knew the place well. "The Monkey Bar was really a game that Nicholson was playing to repeat Helena's nightclub, but without Helena around," he said. "He went into partnership with Alan Finkelstein. Finkelstein was one of the greatest FBI success stories in the seventies when they investigated him while he was running Studio 54 in New York. He calls himself a producer these days and he did get a credit on *The Two Jakes*, but he's nothing but a lackey, and he wasn't a success at the Monkey Bar.

"A bunch of Australian criminals were dealing a lot of drugs from there and having parties. That was their business, selling drugs at parties. They were getting everyone to meet at the Monkey Bar and from there going off to late-night parties. The place got a bad name because it was packed with molls by 11 o'clock waiting to find out where the party was so they could get themselves a job. Decent people stopped going, and there were crowds of men hanging around outside trying to get in because of all the women."

A wealthy L.A. businessman described the party scene that revolved around the drug-dealing entrepreneurs at the Monkey Bar: "One of [the drug dealers] was fairly nice to me for a while," he said. "He and his partners invited me and my girlfriend to parties, and because we weren't into drugs, we'd arrive late when they'd already done drugs and were out of it. [There were] ugly, blubbery bodies lying around everywhere, needles everywhere, reefers everywhere, coke everywhere. My girlfriend has got a very nice figure. They tried to get us into going naked in the swimming pool.

"Jack Nicholson was at a couple of those parties—Jack and Mick Jagger and Alan Finkelstein—right at the time of the Heidi Fleiss thing. [They] cut me out of the scene completely when they realized they just couldn't get me involved with drugs. I said, 'Look, boys, do what you like—shove your face down on a plateful of coke, and we'll just watch a movie.' So they felt very uncomfortable with me. I've never done drugs and I wasn't about to start, but if you weren't into that sort of thing, you weren't welcome at the parties."

Everyone knew Heidi Fleiss. She went clubbing with Billy Idol and fraternized with Robert Evans. After her father bought her Michael Douglas's house off Benedict Canyon Road for $1.6 million, she threw a birthday party for Mick Jagger. She shared the sprawling ranch-style house with Peter Sellers's drug-addicted daughter, Victoria.

However, the brazen behavior of "Heidi and the whores" at the Monkey Bar started to attract unwelcome attention. "One night Heidi made a big scene because another girl called her a madam," said my source. "Heidi said, 'Well, at least I make a lot of money at it—you give it away for free.' It got really nasty. They almost came to blows. Staff had to come over and pull them apart. The whole restaurant witnessed this scene. It was one of the Monkey Bar's last big moments. A woman with some clout in this town who'd known Heidi for years took her aside and said, 'You've got to chill out on what you're doing. You're too public about this. Everybody knows.' This woman was trying to do her a favor, but Heidi ignored her."

Heidigate burst upon Hollywood after Heidi was arrested on June 9, 1993, while she was taking out the trash at her home. She was charged with pandering, tax fraud, and money laundering, for which she was later sentenced to thirty-seven months' imprisonment. After her arrest, she was released on $100,000 bail. At the time of the scandal, the manager of the Monkey Bar, Ron Hardy, told the *New York Times*: "She's welcome here any time. She's a pretty cool girl."

The presence of hookers and dealers in the Monkey Bar wasn't surprising, given the management's predeliction toward Hollywood's sex-and-drug culture. Word about these hijinks got around, and a wild, younger set started turning up to enjoy the action. In the end, it was "just a sleazy drinking club," according to one British patron.

To improve its image, the Monkey Bar shut down for one night and hosted a fundraising dinner for a church charity. Some of the guests were nuns. "I wanted to show off the Monkey Bar because we don't get a lot of nuns in here," Gordon Naccaroto told the *Los Angeles Times*. "Since we've been connected with Heidi and her ilk, it was nice having the opposite end of the spectrum to maybe exorcise the demons." But the infamy lingered on.

The Hollywood socialite I spoke to saw the Monkey Bar's decline and fall as inevitable. "It started going downhill and lost its popularity," she said. "Gordon left and another chef came in. Like everything else in this town, things wane fast, and once the nobodies came in, the somebodies got turned off and went looking for somewhere else. As we say, when the Valley people start coming over the hill, you don't want to be there . . . that and the Eurotrash—we have a lot of them here in L.A. The last time I went to the Monkey Bar, it was dead as a doornail. They tried having some live music to change it, but it just didn't make it and that was that."

Frank Monte said: "Finally, it went real bad. It was a lot of trouble for them at the end, a lot of trouble. Finkelstein divested himself of his interest in the club for a very small amount of money, and Nicholson got out as well." The Monkey Bar shut down quietly and ingloriously in the spring of 1996.

"It closed because they didn't pay the rent," said an insider who was privy to the establishment's accounts.

ASKED why men patronized Heidi's girls, Nicholson told *Vanity Fair*: "I don't know why a guy goes to a hooker. I'm too Calvinist. Besides, I'm Big Jack. I don't have to pay for it." While this might be literally true, it was well known in Los Angeles that Nicholson accepted freebies from one of Heidi's girls.

The hooker in question, Tiffany (her real name is Alexandra Datig), said she met Nicholson for the first time at one of Heidi's parties. "We connected from twenty feet away," she gushed in the kiss-and-tell memoir *You'll Never Make Love in This Town Again*. "I felt a sexual tingle right to my toes. Heidi walked over to Jack, took him by the arm, and walked him toward me. 'Tiffany, I'd like you to meet Jack Nicholson,' Heidi smiled. My knees became weak.

"Jack whispered in my ear, 'Let's get out of here and go to my house.' We did."

19

CROSSING THE LINE

None of Jack Nicholson's relationships with women evoked the same degree of guilt and hopelessness as his bonding with Pamela Liddicoat. Pamela was June's daughter by her husband, Murray Hawley. Nicholson had known her as a little girl during vacations on Long Island and again in Neptune City after Murray's heavy drinking and womanizing had split up the family. Pamela was nine years younger than Nicholson, and she called him Uncle Jack until it was revealed in 1974 that they were actually half-brother and sister.

Nicholson had lived with June, Pamela, and her brother, Murray Jr., in an apartment in Inglewood when he first moved to California in 1954. He had no friends of his own and doted on Pamela, a chubby-faced young girl with freckles and bangs. Whereas Jack argued with June like brother and sister, Pamela gave him the kind of unconditional hero-worship that he needed in this uncertain period of his life. "June and I had so much in common; we both fought hard," Jack told *Rolling Stone*. "It didn't do her any good not to tell me [I was her son], but she didn't because you never know how I would have reacted when I was younger."

At sixteen, Pamela had lost her baby fat and developed into a younger version of her mother with the same pert, pretty features and showgirl's figure.

Pamela had turned sixteen in 1962; that same year, her father died of alcoholism in Canada, and Jack married Sandra Knight. In 1963, June was diagnosed with cancer. Her weight dropped from a hundred pounds to eighty in six months, and she was in excruciating pain. When word reached Jack that she was dying, he was due to fly to Mexico to film his scenes in *Ensign Pulver*. The night before he left, he visited her hospital bedside with Sandra, Ethel May, and his aunt Lorraine. "Sandra was pregnant with Jennifer, and June was in a terminal state," Jack said. "She looked me right in the eye and said, 'Shall I wait?' In other words, 'Shall I try and fight this through?' And I said no." According to Lorraine in an article in *Family Weekly*: "When the door of the elevator closed, Jack slumped to the floor, sobbing hysterically." June passed away on July 31, 1963, at the age of forty-four.

After he became famous, Jack began sending money to Pamela, at irregular intervals. "They fell out at one point when Pamela sold pictures of Jack and Sandra Knight to the tabloids," said my source. Pamela had moved to Georgetown, northeast of Sacramento in Northern California, where she used some of Jack's money to open a beauty parlor like the one her grandmother, Ethel May, had operated in Neptune City. She was married twice, first to Doug Mangino and then, in 1980, to Mansell "Mannie" Liddicoat. "Mrs. Liddicoat had a daughter, Kristi, from her first marriage, and Kristi also has a child," said a friend. "These are all blood kin to Mr. Nicholson. When Kristi was younger, she was introduced to Mr. Nicholson as his niece."

The Liddicoats' marriage started to crumble in 1993 after Pamela showed increasing signs of having inherited her father's alcoholism; her brother, a sailor in the merchant marine, had already died of the illness in the 1970s and been buried at sea. Jack's checks enabled Pamela to finance a self-destructive lifestyle. Tom Daly, editor of the local Georgetown newspaper and a friend of Pamela's for twenty years, said: "Pamela began to drink heavily to ease her pain. But deep down she was a good woman whose life fell apart."

Mannie Liddicoat's attorney, Freda Pechner, of Garden Valley near Georgetown, told me: "One thing that has always bothered my client is that Mr. Nicholson was sending Mrs. Liddicoat money and this facilitated her spiral down into what eventually happened to her—hanging out with the wrong sort of people with alcohol and drugs involved. He has felt some bitterness because he made contact with Mr. Nicholson and told him what was going on with her. He asked him to stop sending money.

"Lots of money came from Mr. Nicholson to Pamela, and she at one point gave him a deed of trust on some property, the duplex she was living in. She never paid any money back; he never asked for it, she never offered it. It was always money that he was giving to her.

"Mr. Nicholson had blocked her invitation to a big night that honored him [the American Film Institute's Life Achievement Award on March 3, 1994]. He invited all these other family people, but not her. Mrs. Liddicoat was turned down, and that was another reason why she was so upset. This wasn't a stranger—they were half blood; they spent many years of their lives together growing up.

"The last time he gave her money, $10,000, was four months before her death. He'd already gotten a call from my client saying, 'She needs rehab. Don't give her any money.' That was his [Nicholson's] response. It was the biggest amount of money he'd given her in a long time, and that was supposed to make her feel better because he wasn't letting her come to his lifetime honor party. That's what he was buying her off with."

Pamela's daughter, Kristi Scott, said: "Uncle Jack loved my mother, and he was desperately worried about her. He came to see her to plead with her to get professional help for her drinking. He tried to help her pull herself together by telling her how much he cared for her. One night when Uncle Jack put his arms around her and kissed her cheek, she told him, 'Jack, I'm trying. God knows, I'm trying.' "

Pamela had separated from Mannie Liddicoat five months earlier, and on February 27, 1994, she was out bar-hopping with an acquaintance, twenty-five-year-old Michelle Burns, in the logging town of Lotus. Tom Daly said: "They were at a tavern called the Coloma Club when they met David Fellows, thirty-three, a white-water rafting guide. All three were laughing, talking, and drinking shots. Just before last call at 2 A.M., they decided to go back to Fellows's home a mile away. Sometime between 3 and 3:30 A.M., neighbors heard gunshots, but it wasn't until 7:30 A.M. that Michelle made a 911 call to the El Dorado County Sheriff's Department. When police reached Fellows's house, he showed them Pamela's naked, lifeless body lying face down."

Pamela, who was forty-eight, had been shot three times in the head at close range. "There is a strong suspicion that this was a drunken orgy that got out of hand," said a source in Georgetown. "Both women ended up having sex with this one guy, and then [Michelle Burns] apparently is the one that pulled the trigger."

Police officers found a .22 caliber rifle in the house and arrested Fellows, who denied shooting Pamela but was charged with murder. A few days later, Michelle Burns was also charged with murder. Both were subsequently convicted of the crime and imprisoned.

Nicholson learned of Pamela's death in a phone call from her first husband, Doug Mangino, and he cried out: "Oh my God, not Pamela. Oh, no!" One of the people he turned to for comfort was Marlon Brando, whom he had supported through several tragedies, including the suicide of Brando's daughter, Cheyenne. "The murder helped to bring them closer together," confirmed one of Nicholson's girlfriends.

Mannie Liddicoat told the *National Enquirer*: "Jack loved Pamela very much. He's trying to put on the bravest front possible, but he's grieving to the very depths of his heart." But Liddicoat later told his attorney, Freda Pechner: "Look what he did. I told him not to give her money, and he kept sending her money, and I told him what was happening. She was really upset because she wanted to go to this family thing and he wouldn't let her go, and that's another reason she was hanging out with those people, and that is the behavior that ended up getting her killed."

Pechner was called in when Nicholson claimed that the money he had sent to Pamela starting in 1979 had, in fact, been repayable loans, subject to interest. "After her death," Pechner said, "Mr. Nicholson's lawyers put a claim into her probate, but there wasn't anything in her probate, so it just got denied and that was that. However, on July 2, 1996, I got a letter from John Hatherley of Mitchell, Silberberg and Knupp saying that Mr. Nicholson was demanding over $200,000 from Mr. Liddicoat, which includes a little over $100,000 that he gave his sister over the years plus $100,000 worth of interest; a total of $206,822.83, to be exact.

"Like he needs it. And let me tell you, the deed secures a little duplex that's just a dump up here in Georgetown. What's he going to do? Foreclose on it? Give me a break! But they're asking for the money. He's already missed his time to sue. There's a statute and he can't sue the estate; the estate is closed. But he still wants to go personally after my client because he has a deed of trust on the property, and I am sure his attorney believes the deed of trust is valid, even though the underlying debt is not. It is my position that since nothing was done to ask for or collect this debt for so many years, the majority of it, except perhaps money he gave her shortly before she died, was a gift. We're not going to pay it back and they can't make us pay it back, and it's going to have to go to litigation because his attorney doesn't have the same opinion. I'll let him come right up here to El Dorado County, the gold discovery county of California, and explain himself to a local jury. I'm sure they'll just be hanging on every word."

On July 30, Nicholson's attorney John Hatherley told Pechner that his client intended to proceed with a foreclosure on the property. "I was really surprised at his attitude," she said. "He said, 'We'll just foreclose.' my response was, 'I'll file a lawsuit and you won't foreclose. Look, you filed a claim in Mrs. Liddicoat's estate and it was rejected and you had four months to file a lawsuit and you didn't. You've got a problem here.' He said, 'What else?' I said, 'The money was a gift to his sister.' His response was, 'We're going to foreclose.' I have a printout from them of what they want. They're talking about money that was loaned in 1979 without a payment ever being made.

"My client is disabled, and he makes his living selling wood that he cuts. He's not a person in a high-income situation. Now Mr. Nicholson is looking at taking away the only thing that was giving him income, because he's rented out this duplex. Mr. Liddicoat is fighting a guy with all the money in the world. He has photographs going back over forty years of Mr. Nicholson as a young person, he has photographs of him as a teenager, he has photographs of him when he first started to act. He has letters, he has history going back to Grandma and Grandpa who Mr. Nicholson took his name from. We have copies of checks from Mr. Nicholson; we've got a wealth of information."

Mannie Liddicoat told me he had never met his brother-in-law and had only talked to him twice on the phone, "once when I was trying to get Pam put into the hospital for her alcohol abuse, and then he called me at the time of her funeral and told me I had plenty of money to bury her."

Jack did not attend the funeral, Liddicoat added tearfully, and did not send flowers.

Freda Pechner drafted her lawsuit in November 1996 and sent a copy to Nicholson's lawyers after they filed a notice of default against his client for failing to pay an initial demand for $31,000.

JUST weeks before Pamela's murder, Nicholson had been reunited with Anjelica Huston to make *The Crossing Guard*, written and directed by Sean Penn. Hollywood's enfant terrible had matured considerably since his directorial debut in 1991 with *The Indian Runner*, a self-indulgent two-hour drama about a small-town cop and his wayward brother.

Penn, the son of actress Eileen Ryan and actor-director Leo Penn, was naturally anxious to improve on that disappointing beginning and admitted that he would have shelved *The Crossing Guard* if Nicholson had turned it down. As the budget allowed him to offer Jack only the scale rate of $485 per week, money clearly wasn't going to be an incentive. Jack, however, put friendship first and accepted the role as a professional challenge, saying: "I've kept the license to pick and choose—that's why I wanted to support Sean. I play the father of a young girl who gets run over and killed by a drunken hit-and-run driver. I can't get it out of my head. Six years later, I try to exact vengeance on the perpetrator. It's a wonderful picture."

Penn had started writing *The Crossing Guard* in Ireland during the spring of 1993. Robin Wright was making a movie there, and he wanted to spend some time with her and their daughter, Dylan. The couple split up after they moved back to Penn's fifty-acre hilltop ranch in Malibu, and he continued to write in a rented apartment at the beach. When the ranch house burned down in a brush fire later that year, Robin decamped with her daughter to the safety of Santa Monica, and Penn moved into a silver Airstream trailer, which he hauled to the peak of his scorched property and set in concrete on the side of a hill. Living as a virtual recluse, with an occasional visit from Nicholson to drink some beer and cheer him up, Penn managed to complete his screenplay.

Apart from Nicholson as Freddy Gale, a Los Angeles jeweler who leads a rhinestone kind of life, he cast David Morse, who had played the lead in *The Indian Runner*, as John Booth, the drunken driver who must die to satisfy Freddy's self-loathing. Robin

Wright is JoJo, a wholesome young artist who manages to penetrate the shroud of guilt with which Booth has covered himself during his incarceration for manslaughter. Anjelica Huston was chosen as Freddy's ex-wife, Mary.

"When you look for an actress of the right age with the stuff to stand up to Nicholson, the list gets very short, and Anjelica Huston is on it," said Penn. "What you see on screen is two titanic actors using whatever they have to fill a scene with natural emotion."

Freddy Gale's reaction to the death of his seven-year-old daughter, Emily, has been to throw himself body, mind, and soul into a netherworld of booze, brawls, and broads, all the while planning the murder of Booth when he is released from prison. Mary has divorced Freddy because of his irrational behavior and remarried a stable, loving man to give a father to the two sons whom Freddy, in his misery, has abandoned.

As Jack and Anjelica had been married in all but name, and as Anjelica had later married the Los Angeles sculptor Robert Graham, the onscreen tension between them is one of the film's major emotional threads. Indeed, the opening scenes establish the schism between the two characters that was as real off screen as it is on film. Cinematographer Vilmos Zsigmond's first shot is a slow motion close-up of a stripper rubbing a flaming torch over her bare breasts, and there, getting off on the eroticism in the gloomy background, is Freddy Gale. Penn intercuts between the strip joint and a therapy group to which a weeping Mary takes her bereavement.

In one scene, when Freddy summons Mary to a diner late at night to discuss his mad scheme to murder Booth, the lines that Penn wrote for them have more than a faint echo of real life.

MARY: I've been so angry at you for so long. Too angry to see you or care about you.

FREDDY: We were pals, right? Best buddies?

Nicholson described the experience of working with his former lover to journalist Fred Schruers: "We're both tried-and-true professionals and certainly have had more than the average amount of complications in our lives. None of that comes up. You know, we're moviemakers."

The film, however, almost drowns in the self-pity of its two principal characters. Nicholson cries not once but twice, while Morse is guilt personified. After serving his time, Booth leaves prison and moves into a trailer, identical to Sean Penn's, next to his parents' house. Freddy, who has been counting the days to Booth's release—marking them off in thick black crayon on a calendar—bursts into the trailer, points a gun at Booth's head, and presses the trigger, only to find himself clicking on an empty chamber; he has forgotten to load the bullets. Disconcerted by Booth's fatalistic attitude toward his own death, Freddy announces that he will return in three days' time to finish the job.

Does Booth call the police? Tell his buddies? Run? No, he gets on with his life and waits to die. Penn, meanwhile, charts Freddy's continuing disintegration as he visits one dive after another. He brings a songwriting stripper called Mia home with him and guzzles bourbon from the bottle while she serenades him with one of her own compositions.

Drunk and disorderly, with his gun now fully loaded, Freddy sets off for Booth's trailer, but is stopped by a patrol car for erratic driving. He breaks free from the law and becomes a fugitive himself, breaking into a house and, symbolically, taking refuge in a little girl's bedroom to give a police search party the slip. Arriving at Booth's trailer, he prepares to carry out his death threat, only to find himself looking down the barrel of Booth's rifle.

But Booth is incapable of pulling the trigger and throws the rifle away. There follows a chase through Los Angeles, which enables Zsigmond to put a different face on the city, making its very ordinariness seem chilling. Penn also uses Zsigmond's artistry for the finale, in which Booth kneels beside Emily's grave and waits for the end: Instead of a gunshot, there is a moment of redemption as the camera pans the streaky crimson lights of dawn breaking over Glendale.

The Crossing Guard took eighteen months to edit and, according to *The New Yorker*, was "brooding, contemplative, and rather colorless. . . . All that melancholy stifles the characters."

Nicholson said: "I think Sean did a helluva job with it, and it's the kind of small character film that gets lost in today's movie market. It needs whatever help I can give it." Marlon Brando also appreciated what Penn had done and described the result as "the first time I ever saw poetry on film."

IT WAS during the filming of *The Crossing Guard* that Nicholson's own roadside behavior brought him into serious trouble with the law. At 11:50 A.M. on February 8, Robert S. Blank was waiting for a red light to change at an intersection in Toluca Lake when a black Mercedes pulled up beside him. Two men got out, and the driver, whom Blank recognized as Nicholson, told him: "You cut me off." Sensing danger, Blank locked the doors of his car.

Nicholson took a two-iron from the trunk of his car and repeatedly struck the roof of Blank's 1969 Mercedes before moving to the front of the vehicle and shattering the windshield with another blow while the thirty-eight-year-old salesman cowered in terror. "I use graphite clubs," Jack said later, "and I expected the club to break." The attack was weirdly reminiscent of the famous "Heeeeeeere's Johnny" scene in *The Shining*. Blank reported the attack to police and named Nicholson as the assailant.

When Detective Robert Searle tried to interview Nicholson, attorney Abe Somer informed him that his client would have no statement whatsoever to make to the police. However, the city attorney's office went ahead and filed misdemeanor counts of assault and vandalism against Jack. "This case went beyond property damage," said deputy city attorney Jeff Harkavy. "Mr. Nicholson assaulted the victim, who suffered some minor injuries."

As Blank had also filed a civil action for damages, Nicholson's criminal lawyer, Charles English, had the opportunity to negotiate a settlement with him. With the aid of his client's checkbook, English persuaded Blank to settle for an undisclosed sum believed to be around $500,000. English and Blank then trotted off to Van Nuys Municipal Court and asked Judge Martin Suits in chambers to drop the charges. His Honor did so. He ruled that an 1872 law permitted many misdemeanor charges, including assault and vandalism, to be dropped if the accused paid the victim.

English said Nicholson had "some extraordinary circumstances going on in his life on the morning this happened," citing the rigorous shooting schedule on *The Crossing Guard* and the death of one of his closest friends. Jack said later: "I was out of my mind. A good friend of mine, Harold Schneider, who produced all the movies I directed, had died that morning, and I was playing a maniac all night. It was a shameful incident on my behalf. I am very vociferously against violence."

What remained a secret from the press was that, on the day of Schneider's funeral, his widow received a demand for repayment of $125,000 that Nicholson had advanced to the producer for a movie project. "Several of Jack's old pals were astonished," said my source. "It seemed such a cold-blooded thing to do."

The city attorney's office wasn't happy with the outcome of the case of the People of the State of California vs. Jack Nicholson. Jeff Harkavy claimed that the prosecution should have gone ahead because Nicholson had swung the golf club toward Blank's face and Blank's nose had been cut by flying glass. "A crime of violence toward a person takes on a very different dimension than a crime against property," he said. "In this case, Mr. Nicholson, whether or not he intended it, placed Mr. Blank in danger of injuring his eyesight."

Susan Anspach said: "Jack is a typical example of the spoiled celebrity syndrome that makes gods of people who were not bred to it and who can't handle it. You can walk up and smash somebody's Mercedes and scare the driver to death and not even know what that means to that person. All you know is that you are a god and gods are supposed to have the lane that they want on the freeway.

"It didn't even occur to him what that man must have been feeling. To Jack, it was like a movie: 'The guy knows that after I bash his window, the scene ends. He doesn't have to worry about dying.' Everything is part of a script."

Jack's final word on *The Crossing Guard* struck a poignant note that had more to do with his own private life than with the movie. "I've had several friends who've had this experience, about which it says in the Bible that when a child dies before the parents even God weeps," he said. "Five or six people have said to me after *The Crossing Guard,* 'I'm going to go home and call my child.'

"When you have a child [the film] affects you differently."

20

"SPECIAL PEOPLE"

THE LOCATION IS HEAVEN, right by the Pearly Gates. Improbable though it seemed, Jack Nicholson was reading a scene in which God's girlfriend talks to a twelve-year-old boy who has just been run over and killed. God, however, did not weep; he was incommunicado. His girlfriend explains to the boy: "Ordinarily he'd be here himself; there'd be no problem, he'd let you in even though you're not really qualified. You never knew your father, so you were sort of robbed a bit. But he's so upset with his creations that he's absolutely refused to reveal his tenderness. He simply won't show his face. You can imagine how tough this is; I mean, living with him is the greatest, but he's so sick and tired that he just wants to abandon the whole thing. It's the father thing which is the problem here."

Fatherhood, illegitimacy, and mortality weighed so heavily upon Jack's mind that he had commissioned the screenplay, *Children's Heaven*, from Blaine Novak in 1983. Novak had been at Mulholland Drive when Jack opened a Christmas card from Caleb, who was then twelve, the same age as the recently deceased and unnamed boy in the story. Novak delivered the first draft of the eighty-nine-page script to Mulholland Drive in January 1984, the year that Caleb and Jack finally met.

Twelve years later, in August 1996, a copy of *Children's Heaven* arrived mysteriously at Susan Anspach's home on Sixteenth Street in Santa Monica. "I had heard whispers about *Children's Heaven* and was anxious to read it," she said. "All I knew was that it was about Jack, Caleb, and me. Then it turned up out of the blue in a package with a Colorado postmark, but there was no covering letter or anything to indicate who sent it." After she read the script, she said: "We sure know what that first speech was about. Not being able to show tenderness—it's justification for behavior. God just can't show affection and tenderness to boys who have imperfections, and this boy's imperfection is that he never had a father. That's what this is saying."

The central character in *Children's Heaven* is named Edward Towne (as in Robert Towne). Edward is a philandering entrepreneur who owns a basketball team and several office buildings. Other people in Jack's life are also represented: Alan Finkelstein thinly disguised as Lowenstein; Colbert and Somer as a couple of Irish sidekicks who protect their boss, often by paying off women to have abortions and to leave Edward Towne alone.

Susan said: "To get into Heaven, the kid has to come down to Earth and win his father's love. He has to audition for his father, so to speak. Luckily, the father likes the kid and really wants to be close to him, but he wonders how he's going to fit him into his life. He brings women into the hotel room, hides them, and makes the kid sleep on the couch while he has sex with them. However, the kid is going to die and go to Heaven unless Edward can find his [the boy's] mother. But he can't remember who the mother is, so he auditions all these women he was screwing at the time to see which one is the mother.

"If this is not a paean to sexism, I don't know what is. Mother—she doesn't get a name—is now trying to find the father, and she writes from hotel rooms the way I used to write letters to Jack. The woman who's running the show for God is called Girlfriend. She's eighteen or nineteen and gorgeous. God isn't seen for most of the movie—he's heard as a voice-over—but when he does appear, he's this middle-aged, frazzled man.

"A lot of it was right from our lives, incredibly close to home, and it was gross to read it. In one speech, Edward declares: 'Now look. We're big and every day we're getting bigger. But this ain't like a business in any way because I don't see business as a business either. To me business is a game, like a poker game, you're playing for chips but the most fun is the game. I may do a lot of foolish things, but I'm a deadly serious person in trying to accomplish things just for the satisfaction of accomplishing them.

Struggling hard to achieve something is the most fun I get. All my life is a game.'

"Edward Towne is the guy Jack would like to be. When Jack was discussing the collatoralization of loans in his deposition, you'd think he was Jupiter Morgan himself. . . . 'When I make a loan, I collateralize it; it's just good sense.' "

Mercifully, Jack slung *Children's Heaven* into a bottom drawer, and there it remained, although it is intriguing to note that when he made *Broadcast News* two years later, one of the foreign correspondents in the film was given a familiar name: Edward Towne.

Novak's character was out of sync with Nicholson in one important respect: Jack has never been in favor of abortion. "I think it would be comically incorrect for someone in my position to be for abortion," he said. "But I am pro-choice. People always say, 'How can you be pro-choice and against abortion?' Well, I tell them, this is one of the ways." One of the few people who seemed to understand what Jack was talking about was Sharon Stone, who claimed to be "moved by his vulnerability." "I've always loved men who seem to have a cavalier approach to life, but deep down are sensitive," she said.

Nicholson's "cavalier approach" came across in numerous interviews. "Good sex always has an element of recklessness to it," he declared. "The first time a man and woman begin ripping each other's clothes off is about as intense an experience as you can find. The way the world is today, we spend a lot of time trying to deny that we have sexual energy because we're afraid to admit the contradictions about sex and love. Sometimes you indulge in lust for lust's sake."

In Nicholson's case, one "element of recklessness" was apparently a refusal to use birth control. He was questioned about fatherhood during his 1996 deposition when Paul Hoffman asked him how many children he had at the time he learned about Caleb's birth. His lawyer Russ Frackman instructed him not to answer the question, stating that it had "some privacy implications." As Nicholson had let the world believe that Jennifer was his only child until the birth of Lorraine in 1990, this was an intriguing piece of information. Hoffman then asked:

Q At that point, you had Jennifer as a daughter, is that right?
A Yes.

Q Did you have any other sons at the time?

Frackman jumped in and instructed his client not to answer that question, either. In fact, there were in 1996 eight offspring from Nicholson's innumerable unions with women to prove that, when he slipped between the sheets, he let nature take its course. Referring to Lorraine and Raymond, he said: "I didn't plan the children. It's chance. It's life."

Apart from Jennifer, Caleb, Lorraine, and Raymond, there were two other children—a son and a daughter. Only very close friends knew anything about them because Nicholson's connection with each child's birth had been hushed up. Jack had taken care of these children financially, and they lived normal lives with their mothers well away from the glare of publicity. Nicholson's secret daughter stayed with him and Jennifer at the Connaught in 1994 and went on shopping expeditions with them. "She was about twelve at the time, and she looked very much like Jennifer," said my source. "When you saw them together, it was pretty obvious they were related."

The remarkable thing about Nicholson's sex life was that he had so far managed to avoid that occupational hazard of the famous male stud, the paternity suit. Asked about this by Nancy Collins in an interview in 1984, he had candidly admitted he was tempting fate, and he seemed to enjoy it.

Q You never insisted on birth control with your lovers?

A No.

Q But you're such a target for a woman who would want to press a paternity suit.

A That's right. But there you have it. I've had no paternity suits.

Like a self-fulfilling prophecy, the first paternity case duly rolled along. In April 1994, Jenine Gourin, a beautiful twenty-one-year-old cocktail waitress, announced via the tabloids that Jack was the father of her daughter and that she was suing him. Jack's lawyers dealt with Gourin's claim, and she retired quietly from the scene.

Case number two followed exactly two years later, in April 1996, when a girl called Denise made an identical claim, though without the headlines. This time, however, there was an added complication in the shape of a cuckolded boyfriend. The episode developed sinister overtones when Jack was secretly threatened with exposure. He asked Alan Finkelstein to act as a go-between in settling the matter, but according to my informant, Finkelstein "was warned off and couldn't do it." The man called in to replace Finkelstein in the negotiations told me: "I was paid $11,000 to do a one-day job for Jack acting as middleman in paying off Denise's boyfriend. Jack is the child's father, and that is why the girl had already been paid $800,000. My job was to drive to Pasadena and hand over $150,000 to shut the boyfriend up.

"I arrived in a hired car, and the guy's friends had a movie camera set up to film the payoff. That didn't bother me. I thought, 'So what? Some stranger drives up, identifies this guy, hands him some money, gets a receipt, and drives off. So what if that appears on TV? It doesn't prove anything.' I gave the guy his money and got a receipt; Jack's lawyers had insisted on that: no receipt, no money."

Whatever the merits of that case, the fact remains that seven of Nicholson's children were born illegitimate and are, therefore, susceptible to the same emotional pain and soul-searching that he has suffered since he found out the truth about his birth. Given his fame, it was quite likely that his own children would be made aware of their illegitimacy at far earlier ages.

Nicholson once referred to illegitimate children as "special people" and maintained that they had "special problems" to deal with in life. Even though his own illegitimacy wasn't a problem during childhood, it had turned into a major concern after he had learned the truth about his real mother in 1974. And it wounded him deeply. He speaks almost bitterly of having his "own downtrodden minority. The bastard. I tell myself I've got the blood of kings flowing through my veins." However, Nicholson's stated attitudes toward sex, birth control, and abortion were largely responsible for the "special problems" that each of his illegitimate children would face in life—and that was difficult to reconcile with his stance as an avowed humanitarian.

Caleb was the obvious case in point. The psychologist Hermine Harman, Susan Anspach's friend, said: "I personally feel very angry at Jack Nicholson over his lack of kindness and consideration toward Caleb. How can he hurt and humiliate his son like this? Caleb is a bright star, a child of light. He did really well at school and college, and he's done extremely well at CNN. He has never needed to live off Jack Nicholson—he just wanted a relationship with the man. Jack's quasi-acknowledgment of him is so abusive. Caleb is his progeny, and yet he wouldn't even take a blood test to prove it.

"He [Jack] has a lot of hostility toward his mother, his aunt, all women. This hostility is beyond male chauvinism; it's his misogynistic way of getting even for being abandoned as a child by his mother." Actress Sharron Shayne supported this view. "I don't think he ever worked out that basic rage at his own mother," she said. "It's all transferred to Susan. He's making Susan, a.k.a. his own mother, crawl and beg. He's punishing her."

Talking about *Wolf* in *Esquire* magazine, Nicholson could easily have been discussing his rage against Susan, and women in general, when he spoke of the dark side that "every man has . . . buried, hidden, or simmering just beneath the surface. You can never predict what will trigger the thing which we keep carefully locked up inside us." In his own psyche, the trigger was abandonment by his real mother and father.

Hermine Harman said: "Jack is a drugger, and that's why he's doing this to Susan and Caleb; it's the evil part of him, that dark side. If he's thinking, 'I made it on my own, so let him make it on his own,' then it's a very sick perception—but with a distorted mind it's easy to have a sick perception. Jack has a very powerful ego, and he's in touch with the dark side because heavy drugs put people in touch with the dark side. Some of his conversations with Susan were just crazy—going completely off the deep end, not remembering what she said, being abusive and maligning. He even told Caleb that Susan must be sleeping with her lawyer!"

Nicholson also remained resolute in ignoring the other claimant to a blood tie with him, Donald Furcillo, the man who claimed to be his natural father. At the age of eighty-six, even though Furcillo was partly paralyzed and almost blind from a stroke, he had not given up hope of meeting Jack. In June 1996, Furcillo appealed: "All I want to do is put my arms around him and tell him I always loved him from a distance. Financially, I am quite comfortable, so I don't need the money. It's just that time is running out, and I want to feel his face and touch his cheek before it's too late."

After marrying his present wife, Dorothy, Furcillo had a daughter named Donna, who would be Nicholson's half-sister if her father's claims are true. Speaking at the family home in Palm Beach, Florida, Donna said: "We're speaking of a last wish. If my father's time comes, I want him to go out thinking it was granted." However, Nicholson informed Furcillo through his lawyers that he did not wish to have any contact with him. "He doesn't want to know me," sighed the old man.

NICHOLSON needed some R&R with the boys. He flew into Inverness airport in the northeast of Scotland on Sunday, June 9, 1996, for a quiet, no-publicity golfing holiday in the Scottish highlands. He had once described golf as "zen archery," and he was looking forward to coming to grips with some of the famous Scottish courses. Accompanying him were Michael Douglas and the Hollywood producers Shep Gordon and Woody Johnson. Secrecy was the keynote.

Even the chauffeur of the vintage Daimler that met them at the plane wasn't informed of the group's identity in advance. However, as they set off along a winding highway across silver inlets and through yellow gorse-covered mountains to the great castle of Skibo on Dornoch Firth in Sutherland, a photographer was broadcasting news of their arrival. He had spotted them at the airport and snatched a picture, and their cover was blown before they reached their destination.

Formerly the property of the Scottish-American steel magnate and philanthropist Andrew Carnegie, the seven-thousand-acre walled estate had been opened as a private club by the British entrepreneur Peter de Savary. There was golf at the Carnegie Club's course, grouse and pheasant shooting, falconry, and fishing. For complete privacy, the Famous Four—as Jack and company were instantly code-named—were housed in two converted farmers' cottages set apart from the castle. Douglas, Gordon, and Johnson bunked down in the larger, two-storied Ivy Cottage, while Jack was in the Round House next door behind closed curtains and thick granite walls. At eight o'clock on Monday morning, a kilted piper aroused guests with some spirited bagpipe playing on the grounds, but Jack slept on. "He didn't wake up until noon, then drove himself over to the castle in one of the club's golf buggies," I was told by one of the staff. "He was too late for breakfast, and lunch is always served down at the golf clubhouse, so he went into the castle's kitchen, cooked himself bacon and eggs, and sat down and ate it there."

Every able-bodied man on the estate, including gardeners, had been pressed into service with the regular team of uniformed security guards to keep intruders at bay. "Gates leading onto the estate were locked except for the East Gate, where we checked every person arriving," one of the custodians told me. "The problem was that on Tuesday there was a press conference about an upcoming contest between Greg Norman and Corey Pavin on the Carnegie course, so the golf writers had to be allowed in. But the tabloid reporters tried to get in as well, posing as golf writers. They just wanted gossip, like were there any girls, but none of them got as far as the castle."

Nicholson and Douglas played the Carnegie links, then went over to Royal Dornoch, a historic course dating from 1616. Word of their presence in the neighborhood had spread, and a sizable crowd had gathered. "It got a bit tense," said one of the castle staff who accompanied them to Dornoch. "You could tell from their body language that they weren't comfortable with the attention." A golf professional rated Douglas as the better golfer of the two superstars. "Jack has some funny little loops in his swing, and he moves his backside around," he said. "He's a twelve or thirteen handicap player."

One blustery afternoon, Nicholson drove over to the castle on his own to take tea in the drawing room. A gifted pianist, seventeen-year-old Robert Ellis, was playing some of his own compositions. Jack went over and thanked Robert for his recital, but apart from that he was a man of very few words. He certainly wasn't giving interviews. A member of the castle's hierarchy commented: "They were all super guests and treated the place like a private club. They did mix with the other guests, but just enough to be sociable and no more."

On their final night, the Famous Four dined with de Savary in Carnegie's book-lined study. They drank 1975 Margaux and 1976 Californian Jordan; the menu was French onion soup with ginger (made by Shep Gordon from his own recipe), warm scallops, and roast venison. In the study was a copy of the magazine *Cigar Aficionado*, featuring a photograph of Nicholson on the cover with the headline JACK NICHOLSON: HOLLYWOOD ROGUE. Inside the magazine was an interview that Arthur Marx, son of Groucho, had conducted with him on Mulholland Drive the previous summer. Nicholson sighed and lit up a pre-Castro Ramon Allones cigar worth $300. Even behind granite walls five feet thick in a remote region of Scotland, Big Jack could not escape from his reputation.

At 5 P.M. the following evening, a red-and-white helicopter landed on the castle's front lawn, and I watched the Famous Four prepare to depart. Jack scrawled "Jack Nicholson, U.S.A." immediately underneath my name in the visitors' book in the castle's baronial hall. Then he and his companions flew off for some more golf at St. Andrew's, Gleneagles, and Turnbury.

A few days later, Nicholson and Douglas teamed up with Paul Newman, and the trio flew across the Irish Sea to Dublin on Friday, June 21. From Dublin airport, they took a stretch limo to the city's Temple Bar area and checked into the $1,500-a-night penthouse suite at the Clarence Hotel. Newman retired to bed, but after a bracing week in the Scottish glens Nicholson and Douglas were ready for some action. One of the hotel's owners was the Irish rocker Bono, of the group U2; Nicholson knew him from L.A., the south of France, and elsewhere. In true Irish style, Bono threw a party for the superstars at his mansion in Killiney. Hijinks were still going on around the pool at dawn. Nicholson and Douglas took the limo back to the city center and had breakfast at 9 A.M. before returning to the Clarence. Just two hours later, they were out of bed and preparing for an afternoon's golf at the exclusive K Club at Straffan in County Kildare.

With Paul Newman in attendance, they emerged from the hotel at noon to face a battery of press photographers. Nicholson was wearing an olive green sweater and tweed trousers; his long hair and sideburns protruded from beneath a red-and-green tartan golf cap. In Scotland he had grown a moustache, and with wraparound sunglasses covering his eyes, he was effectively in disguise. He showed no signs of wear and tear from the night before.

Nicholson flew across the Atlantic in time for the New York premiere of the summer's big movie release, the sci-fi blockbuster *Independence Day*. One reason Jack wanted to see *Independence Day* was that he was preparing himself to play two roles in another space oddity called *Mars Attacks!* for *Batman* director Tim Burton. Jack had been signed to appear as the president, James Dale, and as a Las Vegas real estate hustler, Art Land, in a comedy based on the sixties bubble gum trading card series about a Martian invasion of Earth. Neither part was destined to enhance his acting reputation. When the film was released in December 1996, Roger Ebert of the *Chicago Sun-Times* found the dual role "unsuccessful and unnecessary."

While in New York, Jack stayed at the Carlyle Hotel and visited a favorite restaurant, Marylou's, on West Ninth Street in the West Village. He was greeted by the restaurant's namesake, Marylou Baratta, a big personality in blue denim overalls and sneakers. Spotlights picked out show posters on the walls; candles flickered on peach tablecloths; a cool sax played over the sound system; the barman made big martinis, undecorated.

Nicholson loved the ambience of the place, which was described to me as "a downtown Elaine's full of wiseguys and showbiz types." The chef was Marylou's brother, Tommy Baratta. It was to Tommy that Nicholson had turned to lose fifty pounds for the filming of *Wolf*. The chef had devised a special low-fat diet for him, even traveling with him to make sure he stuck to a rigid calorie count. The dishes included barbecue chicken, steamed bass with lemon grass, and grilled swordfish with bean salsa.

Nicholson was so grateful to the Barattas that he allowed them to call a cookbook they published in 1996 *Cooking for Jack*.

21

LAST TANGO WITH DR. DEVIL

WHEN *The Crossing Guard* opened at the Curzon Cinema in London's West End on August 16, 1996, one British reviewer noted that "Nicholson is on really tremendous form here—his Freddy is a fascinating monster, stewing in vengeance and bourbon." Four days after the opening, Jack Nicholson turned up in London to live out Freddy Gale's fantasies in person. Rarely had he worked harder at living up to his Dr. Devil image.

For five Devil-may-care days, the most striking similarity between Jack and his celluloid alter ego was that neither seemed capable of functioning without a glass of bourbon at his lips or a phalanx of female bodies at his side. At the Curzon, filmgoers watched the demented jeweler join a Shirley Temple look-alike in a rendition of "The Good Ship Lollipop" on the stage of a Los Angeles strip joint, have sex with one of the strippers beneath the black satin sheets in his Early Pimp apartment, smooch with a dancing girl in a dive called Dreamland, drink Tennessee Wild Turkey from the bottle, and generally do his damnedest to destroy himself.

Not far away from the theater, the real Jack Nicholson was behaving in an almost identical fashion in nightclubs and hotel bedrooms, cuddling scantily clad showgirls in public, getting so drunk that he needed physical support, taking one young woman after another—one of them a self-admitted cocaine addict—to his bed, and all the while reveling in the day-by-day notoriety that this inevitably brought him.

This was *Last Tango in Mayfair*. The line between art and reality had disappeared altogether.

The tone of his whisky-soaked odyssey through the demimonde was encapsulated in one of the jokes he related to some of his buddies: "Guy goes into a bar and sees two gorgeous women sitting there. He tells the bartender, 'Give 'em a drink.' 'Won't do you any good,' says the bartender, 'they're a couple of lesbians.' The guy says, 'Give 'em a drink anyway.' The girls take the drinks and say nothing. So the guy buys 'em more drinks—five or six in all—and still they don't respond. The lesbians go out into the parking lot, get into a car, and start having sex. Then one of them comes back into the bar, walks up to the guy, and says, 'Wanna know what she's like?' " With that, Nicholson leaned over and exhaled heavily into the face of one of his listeners.

Coincidentally, it was the lipstick lesbian musical revue *Voyeurz*, produced by Michael White and directed by Bob Rafelson's son, Peter, and Michael Lewis, head of an L.A.-based record company, that was responsible for Nicholson breaking off a vacation in St. Tropez and flying to London. "Jack was staying at his friend Tony Moire's place in St. Tropez," said New York society columnist Norah Lawler. "I saw him in Rampoldi's in Monte Carlo on August 6 with another guy and two girls. He walked out of the restaurant totally smashed. Two days later he was at La Voile Rouge, a restaurant-disco on the beach in St. Tropez, with blond girls all over him."

Michael White phoned him at Moire's house and told him that *Voyeurz* was bombing and needed some publicity. "He asked if Jack would pop over to London, see the show, and get some headlines for him," said my informant.

Nicholson, whose appellation for White was "O Mighty Michael," dutifully obeyed the call and turned up at the Whitehall Theater with Alan Finkelstein. He posed for photographs before watching the cast romp through such numbers as "Cruel & Unusual," performed by a four-girl band called Fem 2 Fem. Nicholson was in his Freddy Gale role again, and the set was a nightclub called Voyeurz; the scene one of sadomasochism and satanism.

One member of Fem 2 Fem, Christine Salata, a twenty-four-year-old New York–based singer-dancer, caught Jack's eye. Baring her breasts and almost everything else, Christine simulated sexual intercourse with several girls, performed fellatio on a rubber penis, sucked on a lollipop, and assisted in the gang rape of a protesting virgin with an implement that she plucked from a first-aid kit. This was *Rocky Horror* without that memorable touch of Transylvanian humor, or, indeed, any other kind of humor. Clinically kinky it might be; erotic it was not. Nick Bromley, the company stage manager, told me: "Jack must have liked the show, because he went backstage afterward."

Grinning broadly, he posed for pictures with showgirls clad in chains, bustiers, and garter belts, as well as a variety of rubberware and PVC outfits that had been copied from a fetish catalogue. Another celebrity guest, the Simply Red singer Mick Hucknall, was also present, but he barely rated a second glance from the girls. Like the witches of Eastwick, they wanted only Dr. Devil. With Michael White playing Pied Piper, Nicholson, Hucknall, and Finkelstein traipsed off to San Lorenzo, the Knightsbridge restaurant run by Princess Diana's friend Mara Berni. The men had no fewer than fourteen showgirls on their arms, including Christine Salata, now almost demure in a simple black see-through minidress. By the time the party had adjourned to Tramp for after-dinner drinks and dancing, Nicholson had singled her out as his date for the night.

Hearing that Christine was the ex-girlfriend of club owner Peter Stringfellow, he whisked her off to Stringfellow's table-dancing establishment in the West End, where he settled down at a table in full view of the go-go dancers. After more drinks, he was out of his mind and on his feet, bumping and grinding along with the professionals to the heavy disco beat while an appreciative gaggle of drinkers shouted encouragement from the bar.

Peter Stringfellow said: "He was in great form. Jack knows how to have a good time. He loved the go-go dancers, and at one point I thought he was going to join them onstage."

But Jack stopped short of mimicking Freddy Gale to that extent; resuming his seat next to Christine, he gazed into her eyes and stroked her shoulder-length black hair. At 4 A.M., he found he was having trouble standing up, and it required two burly security men to help him from the club. "He was in a terrible state—very shaky on his feet," said one of the paparazzi who saw him climb slowly into his hired Mercedes. Colin Morris, who had been booked for more-or-less round-the-clock duty for the duration of Jack's stay, drove him and Christine back to the Connaught, where they disappeared into his third-floor suite.

Just after noon, I phoned the hotel and was put through to Jack:

JN (sleepily): Hello.
PT: Hello, Jack, this is Peter Thompson.
JN: I understand.
PT: I wonder if we could have a chat sometime.
JN: What would it be about, Peter?
PT: It would be about a book I'm writing about you.
JN: Oh no, I've never talked for any of those, er, books.
PT: I appreciate that, but I thought at some point I could run a couple of things past you.
JN: No, I just never do it. I made that decision as a very young man. I just don't want to be involved, and I don't think people should write biographies about (*throaty chuckle*) someone like me.
PT: You're on the front page of the *Evening Standard* today.
JN (suddenly waking up): What've we got today?
PT: Today you're down at *Voyeurz*.
JN (brightening up): Okay! Good, good!

The newspaper had published a photograph showing Jack in the midst of four brunettes, three blondes, and a redhead from the *Voyeurz* cast, so his mission had already produced the desired tabloid result. O Mighty Michael had got his pound of fleshy publicity.

Just before 5 P.M., Jack threw open one of the windows of his suite and peered out as though checking which city he was in. He had recently admitted that one of the things he didn't like about being almost sixty was "waking up feeling stiff and tired even if I didn't do anything before I went to bed." This time, however, there was no mystery about the aching muscles and pounding cerebellum. The most famous eyebrows in Hollywood since Groucho Marx's were unevenly arched, the eyes themselves mere slits cut into bags of swollen flesh; the hair stood crazily on end like the bristles of an old wire brush, and judging from the ripe, red marks tattooed across his naked torso, that selfsame brush had been used to give his body a thorough scouring.

Columnist Lowri Turner commented: "Staring out of that window, in Jack's case, is preferable to looking in the bathroom mirror at the grim truth—the pleated eyebags, pet Pekinese chin, sagging chest, receding hairline, expanding belly, and the realization that even if endless nymphets are happy to feel old age creeping over them, you just might not be up to it anymore."

Another press commentator, Cheryl Stonehouse, pulled no punches about the decline of the man she called Jack the Sad: "Lack of attention is a vacuum which must be filled at all costs for a child. For an adult, it should be a sign that behavior needs to be toned down rather than cranked up toward the outrageous. But Michael White and Jack Nicholson appear to some to be a hormone-driven sixteen, so when White's 'fun musical' *Voyeurz* failed to pull in the crowds despite its acres of naked, mainly female flesh, what did the pals do? They brought the flesh out onto the streets, got drunk, and threw in an aging film star whose private life makes most of us wince."

AT 5 P.M., Colin Morris was summoned to take Christine back to her home in Victoria. "There is no point denying we spent the night together, because I've only just got home and I'm still wearing the same dress," she gushed. "We had a fantastic night. We hit it off straightaway. I was very flattered that he was particularly interested in me. Jack didn't need a chat-up line. That voice is enough. Jack has one helluva reputation as a ladies' man, and I can confirm he thoroughly deserves it. He's charming, sexy, and great fun."

An hour after Christine's departure, Jack bounded out of the Connaught in a smart navy blue jacket and cream trousers like a man who had just finished a bracing workout with his personal trainer. His recuperative powers were remarkable to behold. I watched him sign autographs for fans and pose for photographs, working his patch of sidewalk with the quick, precise reflexes of a boxer in the ring.

Hangover? What hangover?

Asked about the secret of his success with women by a reporter from the *Daily Mirror*, he said: "My greatest asset is my candor. It's always nice to say to a lovely, slender, young woman that it's such a shame we hadn't met before she got pregnant. The only reason I'm the sexiest grandfather on the planet is because I've got the sexiest daughter on the planet—who gave me a beautiful grandchild. At the moment, I'm just kidding around."

Than he joined Michael White and Alan Finkelstein to see the Russian ballet star Mikhail Baryshnikov dance at the London Coliseum. After the performance, Jack signed more autographs in the foyer and posed for yet more photographs, some of which clearly showed white powder on the front of his navy jacket. Pushing through the crowd of well-wishers and the merely curious, Jack jumped into Colin's Merc with White, Finkelstein, and an unidentified young woman and took off at high speed through the London streets, heading west.

As they thundered past Kensington with the paparazzi in hot pursuit, Jack asked White: "Where the fuck are we going, man?" White had chosen the Belvedere, a restaurant in a stately mansion set in spacious, wooded grounds in leafy Holland Park. The restaurant's owner, Johnny Gold, greeted the new arrivals at the entrance and slammed the front door on the paparazzi.

Waiting beside his Merc in the parking lot, Colin Morris chuckled about the car chase. "Michael White was giving me directions, and I didn't have a clue where we were going," he told me. "Jack thought he was being taken out into the country." When I asked Colin about Jack's stamina, he said more seriously: "I don't know how he keeps going. I've been driving him every time he comes to London for the past eight years. I drove him for four months while he was making *Batman*, and he was out until 4 or 5 o'clock every morning. I live at Chobham, which isn't far from Pinewood Studios, but I had no chance of getting home. So I'd just pull around the corner from the Connaught and grab a couple of hours' sleep before picking him up again at 7 A.M. to drive him to Pinewood. Michael White and Alan Finkelstein call him Dr. Devil, but I worry about his health; I'm afraid he'll just drop dead one day from a heart attack."

For once, Jack did the sensible thing and returned to the Connaught at 1 A.M. Even then, he didn't sleep. My source said: "Colin was sent to pick up a girl who lived in Clapham and bring her back to the hotel for Jack."

Nicholson had told me that he was in London for "just a couple of days," but he extended his stay to dine at San Lorenzo with the upper-crust socialite Tara Palmer-Tomkinson and her sister, Santa. As close friends of the heir to the throne, Prince Charles, the Palmer-Tomkinson sisters were several rungs higher up the social ladder than the girls from *Voyeurz*, but that didn't inhibit Dr. Devil. According to an eavesdropping diner, "his conversation was mostly totally uninhibited requests for sexual favors. The girls seemed to think it was all absolutely hilarious." Then they trooped off to a private party at the home of Robert Hanson, heir to the transatlantic business entrepreneur Lord Hanson, in Cheyne Walk, Chelsea. Christine Salata was also there, and during the festivities, Jack invited her and a twenty-one-year-old cocaine addict, whom I'll call Marianne, to join him back at the Connaught for after-hours refreshment. Marianne, a beautiful Chelsea blonde with a colorful past, had been struggling to beat an addiction to alcohol and drugs for two years. Her encounter with Jack did nothing to help.

Nicholson left the party at 3 A.M. and drove back to his hotel. Within minutes, Marianne turned up in her own car. Shortly after she had dashed inside, Christine arrived and joined them in Jack's third-floor suite. "You can draw your own conclusion about the sleeping arrangements," said Ray, a photographer who waited outside the hotel all night. He was not disappointed. At 11:30 A.M., a topless Christine appeared at one of the windows of Jack's suite and briefly looked out. Five minutes later, Marianne also showed her face at the same window; shortly afterward, she left the hotel through a side entrance and headed for her car. When Ray took her picture, she slapped his face and said: "I'm married. You're going to ruin my life."

At lunchtime, Jack was back in San Lorenzo with Tara Palmer-Tomkinson for some more of Mara Berni's exquisite Italian cuisine. After the meal, he discovered that the restaurant didn't accept credit cards, so he popped outside and borrowed some cash from Colin. Tara might have rejected his advances, but she had chosen the briefest of ragged denim shorts to show off her long, shapely legs and, in a pair of platform-soled clogs, towered over her grinning companion. With mobile phone in one hand and copycat sunglasses hiding her eyes, she led Nicholson on a shopping expedition through Knightsbridge.

At midnight he was back at the Connaught, but at 1 A.M. he summoned Colin to drive him to Tramp for a nightcap. "He staggered out at 3 A.M.," one of the paparazzi told me. "He was too drunk to pose with his old friend, Mick the beggar."

The following day kicked off with pure slapstick when Jack went shopping in Jermyn Street off Piccadilly and spotted a girl with long blond hair looking at a window display. "He sidled up to her, put his face into hers, and grinned," said a paparazzo. "The girl squealed with delight when she recognized him. Jack stepped back, tripped over an ice cream seller's stand, and nearly fell on his face."

At dinnertime, he was at the Collection, a trendy new bar-restaurant in South Kensington. When he emerged at midnight, he was with four young women, including the Chelsea blonde, Marianne. As she latched onto Jack's arm, the folds of her leopardskin dress billowed around him, and she fluttered her eyelashes in his face. I saw his expression change in an instant to pure thunder; no one took these liberties with him in front of the paparazzi's cameras. Without a word, he executed a neat sidestep, disengaged from the embrace, and left her floundering on the walkway. Placing a cigarette in his mouth, he joined me at the restaurant's entrance.

But Marianne wasn't going to be brushed off as easily as that; among Chelsea girls, Jack Nicholson was a trophy worth fighting for. She tried to drag him away, but he slipped out of reach and, mumbling that he needed to buy some more cigarettes, moved toward the curb. "Is that shop across the street still open?" he asked me. It wasn't, so he jumped into his limo. The four girls piled in after him, and in a flurry of arms, legs, and leopardskin, Marianne managed to pop up beside her quarry. They went to Brown's nightclub in Great Queen Street, where Jack settled in for a long session, sitting in an armchair with a large drink in his hand while his youthful harem vied for his attention. At 3:15 A.M., Christine Salata arrived in a cab and dashed inside. As Jack's sex life was, like the weather, now subject to hourly updates, there was speculation that another threesome might be in the offing.

However, when he came out half an hour later, he was on his own. With a tumbler of bourbon and ice clutched in his right hand, he moved in slow motion across the wide expanse of Great Queen Street. He reached the Merc without mishap and waited inside, sipping his drink, until Marianne came stumbling out of the club on the arm of one of the staff and climbed in. We all raced back to the Connaught, Grand Prix style. When Jack got out, I inquired about the blonde in his car.

"Blonde? What blonde?" he asked me.

"The blonde in your car," I replied.

"I didn't see any blonde in my car," he said, aiming rubbery legs in the direction of the flower-decked portico. Much to the bemusement of the night porter, he was still clutching his bourbon on the rocks. And Marianne? After an unsuccessful attempt to smuggle her through the delivery entrance, which was shut, Colin had to escort her through the front door. It was 4:20 A.M.

Less than five hours later, I saw Jack appear naked from the waist up at his third-floor window. Once again, he looked as though he had survived an explosion in a boiler room. But when he emerged from the hotel at 10:20, he had undergone another miraculous transformation. Bathed, shaved, and neatly dressed, he bounced down the steps carrying a brown leather briefcase. As the rest of his luggage was loaded into the trunk of the Mercedes for the trip to Heathrow, he stood on the sidewalk handing out banknotes from a thick wad to the hotel staff. Even the sunglasses were pushed briefly back on his forehead to reveal bright, shining eyes. Of Marianne there was no further sign.

Nicholson flew out at noon, leaving behind the most hostile press he had ever received since his love affair with London had begun back in the seventies. A. A. Gill wrote in the *Sunday Times* that "a sad and salutory blow" had been struck at the testosterone sacs of all men. "Jack Nicholson did it in Stringfellow's and all over the tabloids," he said. "It was pathetic. Old Mr. Sly Smile, Old Mr. Balding and Plump but Still Ravenously Sexy. The nearly sixty with the naughtiest grin on the planet let the side down badly. We saw a legend die in an arthritic shuffle."

A London agent revealed in the *Sunday Express* that Jack's friends took practical measures to ensure that he never ran short of young women during his visits. "They ring the girls on the circuit—the ones whose principal occupation is looking good, shopping, lunching, and being seen with film stars," he said. "He's seen with them, they're seen with him; it's a bit of a joke with us. He flies in saying he'll be here two days. If it goes well, he 'misses his plane,' as he did for Tara, and he goes on missing his plane until the girls run out."

Columnist Jessica Davies commented in the *Mail on Sunday:* "If the trademark grin was still in place—which it was—that may be more to do with the fact that he remains a great and convincing actor."

One little detail went unreported. Jack slipped out of the Connaught one afternoon and spent several hours at the National Gallery perusing the paintings and drawings in a Degas exhibition. The antics of Dr. Devil were headline news; no one was interested in Jack Nicholson, art lover.

22

JACK ATTACKS!

IN HIS SIXTIETH YEAR, Jack the artist and Jack the man remain, as they have always been, one and the same. He still vacillates between gentleness and rage, magnanimity and stinginess, silence and volubility. The difference is that, these days, the pendulum swings in a wider arc.

"I'm almost Pollyanna in real life," he says. "I'm a very quiet man." Then, in the next breath, he adds: "I'm totally wild, but only when it's good for things."

And life should be good.

"He is more hip than any man I know," says Mark Canton, who helped to make Jack as rich as he is today by persuading him to play the Joker in *Batman*. "I've never known anyone who enjoys being himself more than Jack. He brings out the child in himself and everyone else."

George Miller, who has never forgotten the debt he owes to Jack for his loyalty during the making of *The Witches of Eastwick*, told me: "He's a great sage, and at the same time he's still got that child quality about him as well, so he's playful. He's the best of human beings in that he's got that combination. He's a two-thousand-year-old child."

His friend photographer David Bailey calls him one of "the new old—the old that are still young." And he *is* still hip in an age of grunge, rap and hip-hop: suits by Paul Smith and Armani, sunglasses by RayBan, sounds by the Eagles and the Eurythmics, cars by Mercedes-Benz.

In pure economic terms, there are few to match him anywhere except, perhaps, Arnold Schwarzenegger, who signed up to play Mr. Freeze in *Batman and Robin* for $25 million. Jack's nineties films alone have brought him conservatively around $100 million. The U.S. treasury took a good slice, yet he remained "exceedingly financially viable"—his words—to the degree that he could, if he so desired, retire from acting and concentrate on directing.

But there is no sign of him slowing down despite the speed bumps that periodically pop up in his private life. Brad Pitt, Keanu Reeves, and Matthew McConaughey might be the new Hollywood pinups, but there is only one Jack Nicholson, and he is still very much a player. "How many jobs can you really get better at after thirty-something years?" he asked. "You can in mine. I can guarantee I'm better now than I was in *Five Easy Pieces*."

He describes Proteus as "my corporation," and that is precisely what it is: a one-man enterprise with a bigger revenue than many companies quoted on the New York stock exchange. "I'm a very good businessman," he says, although his stock holdings normally remain a closely guarded secret. When it was deliberately leaked that he was an investor in Lynx, the golf equipment manufacturers, the plug for the firm's products was embarrassingly obvious.

Mulholland Drive is the epicenter of his world, where Annie Marshall needs the help of two other secretaries to cope with the demands of his schedule. In the driveway is a garageful of cars, ranging from a classic BMW to the latest Merc, and inside the house is his fabulous art collection. Although he's listed as America's sixth largest private collector, the absence of a Nicholson Gallery for public display suggests that many of his paintings are for investment purposes only.

In terms of property, he has the two houses on Mulholland Drive, at least three properties in Aspen—including a three-bedroom condo at Pomegranate Lodge on the golf course of the Maroon Bells Club—a ranch at Malibu, another house in Southampton, Massachusetts, and a half share in Jennifer's home in Santa Monica.

He hires drivers, accountants, gardeners, a chef, and more attorneys than any other star; at one point in 1996, he had six lawyers working on cases for him. As he says himself, "If I have a weakness, it's in the area of 'I don't want to know.' " In other words, he pays other people to read the fine print and to deal with the problems that inevitably accompany each project.

"When I'm working, I'm totally involved," he says. "I can't run a marriage at the same time. I can't run a stock portfolio. I can't do anything but act. I have to give my life to the job."

He has never been averse to speaking his mind. Asked what he thought about the not guilty verdict in the O. J. Simpson murder trial, he replied: "I've always liked Juicy. He's a sweet man when you're around him. I'm not a close friend of his, but he's always been very nice with me. I mean, if the world's worried about this, if they're worried that a guilty man has gotten away with something, they should stop and think what it's like to have to lie to your children for the rest of your life."

He is able to summon up an apt quote for any occasion. Talking about women, he quoted Schopenhauer: "It's a sin for a man to ask a woman to keep an oath." In other circumstances, three short words of his own will do:

"Now listen, pal. . . ."

The voice is threatening, and his choice of the word "pal" is not meant as a term of endearment. He uses it when he is angry or sarcastic; otherwise it's "babe." The eyebrows arch upward, and the lids over those eyes—likened by Candice Bergen to a cobra's—narrow to a slit; the gleaming white teeth flash through pursed lips. He shows his annoyance by using intimidating facial expressions, backed up by a sparse selection of adjectives invariably involving the *f* word. He is capable of rages as intense as those on-screen moments when he can scare the living daylights out of an audience.

Then the anger subsides as quickly as it flared. His speech goes back into a relaxed drawl, eyebrows half-cocked this time, and a mischievous glint makes the instigator of this flash of temper wonder whether he meant it in the first place. He did. He's talked enough about drugs. That's it. Why talk about it any more?

For a time, he stopped promoting his opinions on the revision of the marijuana laws, yet he told Lucy Kaylin in a 1996 interview for *GQ* magazine: "There is no dope business without illegality—that's what's causing it."

"I don't know one human being who feels he or she has coherent conversations with Jack," says a woman who has known him for twenty-five years. "Now, that isn't a putdown of Jack. Sometimes it's to do with drugs, but a lot of times that's just his intelligence. I've often chalked his sideways talk up to the fact that he's very brilliant and most of us can't keep up with him. I prefer to think positive things, but a lot of people just roll their eyes and figure it's drug talk because he's not coherent."

The drug-related deaths of John Belushi, River Phoenix, and, more recently, Don Simpson underscored the rising toll of fatalities and hospital admissions from cocaine-induced seizures, brain hemorrhages, and cardiac arrests. And Jack is certainly not immune. His drug-taking has adversely affected his health on at least one occasion.

When Luana Anders, one of Jack's oldest friends from his early days in Hollywood (they were messengers at MGM at the same time, and later she had roles in *The Trip* and *Easy Rider*) died of cancer in July 1996, he was unable to attend the funeral. "People were upset that he wasn't there, because he had helped with some of Luana's medical bills," said a friend. "He didn't make it because he had an allergic reaction to cocaine and blew up like a balloon. He's been smoking joints since then to chill out." When I asked my informant how she could possibly know this, she replied: "This information comes from his drug dealer."

Jack sometimes sits alone at L.A. parties saying nothing to anybody. Observing him in this isolated mode, Ali MacGraw remarked to a friend: "There's no one at home."

The scene switches to another party, stacked wall to wall with Hollywood big-time players. Nicholson is standing on the edge behind his black sunglasses, bored and looking at some of the guests with extreme derision over the top of his champagne glass and blowing smoke rings in their direction.

Jim Brooks comes over and leans his head toward Nicholson's as if he's going to impart some secret information. From the corner of his mouth, he says in an attempt at disdainful irony: "You got the feeling that somehow these people own you?"

"Own me? You've got to be joking." Jack thinks for an instant and chuckles, then his face goes serious. "I'm one of the few people alive—not just in this room, but alive—for whom that question isn't even hypothetical," he says. "I'm a pawn in nobody's game."

That is true, but it is also true that other people are pawns in the games Nicholson plays. As America's foremost character actor and biggest, hippest personality, he enjoys kudos wherever he goes. He has a warm personal relationship with President Bill Clinton, sometimes writing letters to him in his firm, bold handwriting.

So when his status—and the motion picture industry that gave it to him—is threatened, his friends in the media close ranks and treat him like a protected species. When I pitched an item about him to *Primetime Live*, a leading investigative TV show, an assistant told me: "My boss is a friend of Jack Nicholson's, and he won't want to make this program."

MORE by good management than good luck, he remains a virtual untouchable. Prospective interviewers are carefully screened, and successful candidates meet him in a suite in a five-star hotel or at a table discreetly booked at a favored restaurant. A few are allowed to go inside his home. *GQ* magazine rhapsodized: "Perched on a couch in a Hollywood hotel suite, wearing golf gear, he still radiates that movie-star sheen: the untouchability of an icon." The session is likely to begin over a plate of food and some French wine, followed by a good cigar. The result is invariably a "subject-friendly" interview. Rod Lurie, one of the most incisive interviewers in Los Angeles, commented: "When Jack Nicholson makes himself available to you, even if it's just for half an hour, you get in your car, go anywhere he desires, start asking questions and hope for the best."

While Jack considers his relationships with women to be "personal" and not a matter for newspaper talk, he has manipulated the media with tantalizing tidbits about them for years.

Example: One day when an interviewer is at his home, Jack is holding forth about his latest film. The door opens, and an aide calls in, "Jack, there's a girl on the phone. Says her name is so-and-so. Says you'll remember her."

Jack says, "I don't remember the name."

Aide says, "'She met you in Aspen, and you told her to give you a call when she got back into town."

Jack says, "I don't remember. I've met a lot of girls in Aspen. Take her name and number and tell her I'll call her back."

If there was a courtroom specially set aside for feminists to bring charges against men who have sinned against the rights and dignity of women, someone could make some charges stick against Jack Nicholson. He would put up a stout defense, of course, intelligently reasoned, eloquently argued, and resolutely denying anything other than a total fondness for them spiritually, sexually, and in terms of pure and simple friendship.

There is too much evidence against him: chasing stray "pussy" with anyone who would join him (self-admitted), "skunk-spotting" with Beatty (self-admitted), having a young model fly ten thousand miles for a weekend of sex (undisputed), smacking the bare bottom of a young actress during lovemaking (not challenged), screaming abuse at Susan Anspach (not denied), not to mention some classic putdowns.

He's at a party in Toronto to honor Beatty, and there's a blonde approaching. Beatty thinks he's got it made, but she turns to Jack. She's a reporter, and Jack knows it. She tilts forward slightly, revealing an ample cleavage, and brazenly says to Nicholson, "Hi, Jack, would you like to dance?"

He pauses before answering, eyes going up and down, mouth narrowing to a leering smile. "Wrong verb, honey. Wrong verb."

That's the image: womanizer. Is it true? Of course. Does he encourage it? Always. In the seventies, that image was important to him professionally; there was still the lurking doubt that anyone would call and offer him a great new role, an insecurity built on the fact that no one did call in the first fourteen years of his professional life. It was always the other way around. Then, when he found overnight fame, he clung to it with both hands and worried sometimes that it would go away again.

In later life, his ego still needs massaging from a chorus line of adoring young women who will decorate his arm, laugh at his jokes, go to bed with him, tell him he's wonderful—and then leave.

One of them, Los Angeles model and partygoer Janice Dickinson, said: "We'd make love on the terrace, on the lawn, in the pool, even in the backseat of his parked car. Jack got off on playing love games with me and two other women at the same time."

Nicholson uses a stock line to dismiss such exposés. "I don't care to acknowledge having slept with any particular woman," he says. "It's all hearsay, which I allow because it's good for business."

For him, success with women is gratifying and displays his ability to attract them by means other than looks. Unlike Beatty, who always had the advantage of being the living image of the Hollywood leading man with dark, mysterious eyes, classic features, and a huge mop of hair, Nicholson is an unlikely romantic hero, but then it was not his good looks that made him famous. When stardom struck, he was in his thirties, his hair showed signs of receding, and he was already having to watch his weight.

Although there are plenty of examples of his deep love of women, not merely for their sexual attraction but for their companionship, conversation, and intelligence, he can be struck by an infatuation for women he has never met. He invariably falls in love with his leading ladies, some of whom carry a torch for him long after the flame has gone out.

When I suggested to one such actress that Jack was "one of the most famous men in the world," she bridled. "Get it right," she corrected me. "*The* most famous."

More famous than Brando?

"Jack's seen at the Academy Awards every year by a billion people on television," she replied. "Billy Crystal had only to refer to 'Jack,' and everybody knew who was going to take the stage."

Nicholson himself, however, still regards Brando as number one and chooses to believe that, as Beatty put it, when Brando goes, everyone moves up a place. In his seventieth year, Brando surprised a lot of people by admitting that he was a shameless philanderer with other men's wives. Summing up, he wrote in *Songs My Mother Taught Me*: "I suppose the story of my life is a search for love, but more than that, I have been looking for a way to repair myself from the damages I suffered early on and to define my obligations, if I had any, to myself and my species."

Perhaps Brando's self-revelations prompted Nicholson to say: "All my life I've lived true to how I feel. I know I've caused pain to some of the women I've loved, but I won't defend myself, because I've never, never pretended to be something I'm not."

Many old lovers and quite a few male friends have drifted out of his life, including Bert Schneider and Robert Towne, but Alan Finkelstein, Michael White, Robert Evans, Harry Dean Stanton, and Roman Polanski are still there after twenty or more years. While some swear that Jack is generous to a fault, one female friend notes: "The minute you seem like you need something and he could be of help, he's scared you don't love him for himself."

After he and Rebecca had split up in 1994, Jack said: "Now that my family is no longer intact, I feel burned. I miss our time together—even more so because I was a cynical man before our relationship began and now I'm even more cynical about the notion of domestic tranquillity. I just wonder if the whole process is too rich for my blood."

However, he gave Susan Anspach a very different reason for his reluctance to become involved in family life: "They talk among themselves, they make things up, they lie; that's what I hate about families."

In the final analysis, it was Jack and only Jack who had nailed himself. When the night skies close over his fortress atop a rocky spur overlooking Beverly Hills and the pepper trees whisper in the wind, his mind starts to play tricks. "I have this fear of the dark," he admits. "Sometimes at night I get scared. I see things in the shadows."

WHEN he woke up around noon on Saturday, October 12, 1996, he had no need to ask his secretaries Annie, Gloria, and Diane, "What've we got today?" He already knew the answer himself; memories of the night before lurked in those same shadows like a bad dream. And the answer was: trouble. Big trouble.

Jack had arrived back in L.A. two days earlier after completing his latest film, *Old Friends*, for Jim Brooks in New York. Relaxing at home on Friday night, he decided he needed some high-heeled-blonde action. Maybe he'd had a little too much to drink; maybe he'd had a toot or two; maybe he was just lonesome. Whatever the reason, he rang Catherine Sheenan, a self-confessed prostitute, at 3 A.M. to invite her up to Mulholland Drive to have sex with him. He knew Catherine from previous assignations; I later learned that their lovemaking had physically injured her on at least one other occasion. "She was battered," a friend told me, "and she sought professional counseling about it from a shelter for abused women. But Jack can be very persuasive, very contrite, and she went back up there even though she had been warned that this type of behavior is often repeated."

This time, however, Catherine took the precaution of calling Nicholson back at 4 A.M. and asking if she could bring along a female friend. In a subsequent lawsuit resulting from the events of that night, it was alleged that he agreed that Catherine would bring the other woman, and asked them to wear "little black dresses and no stockings." The legal statement said: "Having donned the requested black dresses, [she] and her friend drove to the residence, calling Nicholson from the vehicle to inform him that they were on their way. When they arrived, [Catherine] and her friend were greeted at the door by Nicholson who, after offering them a drink, invited them upstairs to the bedroom. [Catherine] confirmed with Nicholson that both she and her friend would receive the sum of $1,000 each for the performance of sexual acts with him. He said he would "take care of it later."

The two prostitutes then allegedly performed sexual acts with Nicholson. At 7 A.M., Catherine, noting that Nicholson was "fatigued," asked for the money, but he "became loud and abusive, stating that he had never paid anyone for sex as he could get anyone he wanted as a sexual partner." Catherine claimed she told Nicholson that she knew he had paid others to perform sexual acts with him and attempted to call a mutual friend for help. Nicholson pushed her, attempted to grab her, raised his voice, and showed signs of becoming more and more violent. However, she did manage to make the call, and the friend advised her to leave the premises immediately. "Nicholson then demanded that [Catherine] empty her purse and she did so, allowing Nicholson to determine that she had not taken any of his possessions," the complaint alleged. As she attempted to leave, she implored Nicholson to remain calm, but he "forcefully grabbed her by the hair," before demanding that the other prostitute also empty her purse, which she did. [Catherine] asked her friend to get dressed so they could leave and Nicholson's response was to go after Catherine and, "yelling and screaming, again grabbed at her . . . and shoved her into a chair. Terrified for her physical safety, [she] reached for a telephone to call for help. When she tried to call the police, Nicholson threatened [her] with a raised arm and clenched fist. He was enraged and yelled that he would give [her] a reason to call the police. He further threatened to throw [her] over Mulholland Drive." When she pleaded with him to let her leave, he "took hold of [her] and violently threw her out of the residence." Then he dashed after her and "violently lifted [her] off the ground, stating that he would kill [her]," and flung her into a hedge on the property, causing further injuries. She eventually managed to lock herself in the car and call the police.

A squad car containing two officers arrived at the scene and, after speaking to Nicholson, they drove off without making an arrest. Catherine's friend took her to Cedars Sinai Medical Center, where she was treated for her injuries and advised to make a formal complaint. When I received a call about the attack from a

Los Angeles source less than forty-eight hours later, I was told that one of the silicon implants in Catherine's breasts had been ruptured.

My informant told me that Catherine feared for her safety and had hired bodyguards to protect her at her home in Brentwood. But it wasn't until the following week that she filed an official complaint at the West L.A. division of the LAPD.

There, police spokesman Eduardo Funes told me: "West L.A. area patrol responded to a battery investigation at the home of Jack Nicholson on October 12. Officers completed a preliminary report which listed Nicholson as a party to the crime. West L.A. detectives are conducting the investigation." The spokesman could not, however, confirm that there was damage to Catherine's breast implant; officers investigating the alleged attack had noted in their report that no injuries were visible.

Helena Kallianiotes told me: "I didn't hear anything, and I live in the next house." When I told her that police confirmed they had been called to the premises, she replied: "The police come up here constantly. I call them, Jack calls them, Marlon calls them. We get fans up here all the time, and they're a pain in the neck."

However, Ira Chester, a friend of Catherine's, said: "Police are investigating and will present their report to the district attorney and that, I hope, will lead to this man's arrest. Jack Nicholson beat a woman to within an inch of her life."

On November 8 in the Los Angeles Superior Court, Catherine's lawyer, Paul Kiesel, filed a civil action against Nicholson, claiming unspecified damages for his client for assault, battery, and emotional distress. Kiesel said in a statement: "Ms. Sheehan suffered numerous injuries as a result of this unprovoked assault and she is undergoing treatment for head trauma and other physical injuries." He said that his client had filed the civil action "because she lacks confidence that the California criminal justice system can work when the defendant is a wealthy and powerful member of the community. Her motivation is to seek justice for herself and to encourage women, and all citizens throughout the country, to have the courage to stop the cycle of violence against women."

Nicholson wasn't at home when I called him to discuss the allegations against him. His secretary Diane said: "I don't know anything about it. Jack is working, and I don't know when he'll be back."

So 1996 ended just as it had begun, with an explosive lawsuit that exposed Nicholson's private life to the glare of publicity. But neither the lurid tabloid headlines nor the items on TV news programs deterred the custodians of one of Hollywood's most popular tourist attractions. Three weeks before Christmas, a crowd of 1,500 gathered at the Hollywood Walk of Fame to watch the unveiling of a new terrazo-and-brass star dedicated to the man himself.

Acting as though nothing in his private life was amiss, Nicholson arrived for the ceremony with Rebecca and their children Lorraine and Raymond, and Jennifer Nicholson turned up with his grandson Sean, now ten months old. Flashing the most famous smile in the world, the guest of honor embraced his family while press and TV cameras recorded the scene.

Then he did something that only he would have dared to do. Striking his axe-wielding pose from *The Shining*, he shouted that most chilling of lines from all his movies: "Heeeeere's Johnny!"

The fans loved it.

But then, Jack knew they would.

SOURCES

I AM indebted to John Parker, author of *The Joker's Wild* (Anaya Publishers, 1991), for giving me total access to his research files and interviews about Jack Nicholson's life and films. He has also kindly allowed me to use extracts from his book.

I spoke to Jack Nicholson on three occasions during my inquiries, but he declined an interview, saying that he had decided many years ago not to cooperate with biographers who were writing books about his life. However, he did talk to me briefly "on the run" between his various social engagements in London in August 1996.

Fortunately, Jack has been interviewed literally hundreds of times over the years by a huge cross-section of the press, and these interviews cover not only his prodigious filmmaking career but also many aspects of his extraordinary private life. I refer in particular to the *Playboy* interviews, the work of Nancy Collins for *Rolling Stone* and *Vanity Fair*, Rod Lurie in *Empire*, Lucy Kaylin in *GQ*, and Arthur Marx in *Cigar Aficionado*, as well as articles in *Time*, *Newsweek*, *Esquire*, *US*, *Hello!* and the *National Enquirer*.

I also read well over two thousand articles about Jack published in the *Los Angeles Times*, the *New York Times*, and the *Times* and *Sunday Times of London* over the past five years.

I interviewed Susan Anspach in Santa Monica about her son Caleb and their relationship with Jack, and I attended several of the court hearings relating to her lawsuit against Jack, his business manager Bob Colbert, and his company Proteus Films, Inc. I am grateful to Susan's lawyer, Paul Hoffman, for his guidance on this case. I also met Caleb Goddard twice, although he declined a formal interview.

Jack's lawyer from Mitchell, Silberberg and Knupp and his agent, Sandy Bresler, maintained their client's line in declining to comment.

Many other people were more informative, including George Miller, Frank Monte, Freda Pechner, Bert Schneider, David Helsten, Helena Kallianiotes, Dr. Paul Fleiss, Hermine Harman, Sharron Shayne, Laura Levy, Carol Green, Kathleen Courtney and Bonnie Robinson. I met Arthur Penn in Los Angeles in July 1996 and am grateful for the time he gave me.

Several other people in the motion picture industry agreed to speak to me but asked specifically for anonymity, and I have respected those requests.

Certain members of the paparazzi were extremely helpful with information about Jack's extracurricular activities in London and supplied me with unpublished pictures of some of his nocturnal escapades.

The books I read included *Jack's Life* by Patrick McGilligan (HarperCollins, 1994); *The Kid Stays in the Picture* by Robert Evans (Hyperion, 1994); *Songs My Mother Taught Me* by Marlon Brando with Robert Lindsey (Random House, 1994) and *Hit and Run* by Nancy Griffin and Kim Masters (Simon & Schuster, 1996).

INDEX